Fashion in Focus

The study of fashion has exploded in recent decades, yet quite what this all means, quite where it might take us, is not clear. This new book helps to bring fashion into focus, with a comprehensive guide to the key theories, perspectives and developments in the field.

Tim Edwards includes coverage of all the major theories of fashion, including recent scholarship, alongside subcultural analysis and an in-depth look at production. Individual topics include:

- men's fashion, masculinity and the suit;
- women's fashion and the role of sexuality;
- children, the body and fashion;
- the role of celebrity and designer label culture;
- globalisation and the production of fashion.

Fashion in Focus is the ideal companion for students in the arts and social sciences, especially those studying issues such as fashion, gender, sexuality and consumer culture.

Tim Edwards is Senior Lecturer in Sociology at the University of Leicester. He has published and researched widely in the areas of masculinities, sexuality, fashion and consumer culture. He is the author of *Cultures of Masculinity* (2006).

Fashion in Focus

Concepts, practices and politics

Tim Edwards

Routledge
Taylor & Francis Group

LONDON AND NEW YORK

First published 2011
by Routledge
2 Park Square, Milton Park, Abingdon, Oxon, OX14 4RN

Simultaneously published in the USA and Canada
by Routledge
270 Madison Ave, New York, NY 10016

Routledge is an imprint of the Taylor & Francis Group, an informa business

Typeset in Sabon by Taylor & Francis Books
Printed and bound in Great Britain by TJ International Ltd, Padstow, Cornwall

British Library Cataloguing in Publication Data
A catalogue record for this book is available from the British Library

Library of Congress Cataloging-in-Publication Data
Edwards, Tim, 1963–
Fashion in focus : concepts, practices & politics / Tim Edwards.
p. cm.
1. Fashion--Social aspects. 2. Clothing and dress--Social aspects. I. Title.
GT525.E34 2010
391--dc22
2010022456

ISBN13: 978-0-415-44793-5 (hbk)
ISBN13: 978-0-415-44794-2 (pbk)
ISBN13: 978-0-203-83688-0 (ebk)

Dedicated to the Three Wise Women:

Veronica Moore
Janet Perry
Carla Willig

Contents

List of plates   viii
Acknowledgements   ix

1   Fashion foundations   1

2   The classical tradition: early perspectives on fashion   11

3   The clothes maketh the man: masculinity, the suit
    and men's fashion   41

4   The woman question: fashion, feminism and fetishism   67

5   Who are you kidding? Children, fashion and consumption   87

6   Express yourself: the politics of dressing up   103

7   From rags to riches: fashion production   120

8   Desiring subjects: the designer label and the cult of celebrity   137

    Conclusion: the fashion invasion   159
    Bibliography   162
    Index   175

Plates

The below images have been reproduced with kind permission. Whilst every effort has been made to trace copyright holders and obtain permission, this has not been possible in all cases. Any omissions brought to our attention will be remedied in future editions.

1	Three piece suit. Courtesy of the author	40
2	Stiletto shoe. © iStock Photo / Nadejda Reid	66
3	Children in contemporary clothing. © iStock Photo / Ekaterina Monakhova	86
4	Indian wedding dress. © iStock Photo / Evelyn Peyton	102
5	Street style. © iStock Photo / Joselito Briones	102
6	Designer handbag. © iStock Photo / Ilie Victor Oancea	136

Acknowledgements

Writing a book is a bit like building a house – ultimately you are on your own with it but you need structural support. I am particularly grateful then to Natalie Foster, Charlie Wood and Emily Laughton as well as others at Taylor & Francis for providing the foundations and tolerating a sometimes decidedly unreliable workman. Much brick carrying has been provided by friends past and present including Sam Ashenden who also provided some interesting insights, Espe Bielsa who occasionally repositioned the windows, and Stalø Phylactou who simply provided shelter once when the walls were falling down. Others of course just stand by the operation rather than do runners and they include Peter Handford, Simon Hardy, Philip Hoggar and Hüseyin Tapìnç. There are others, though, who quite literally get you through and they include Veronica Moore, Janet Perry and Carla Willig – I will remain indebted to these three very wise women forever for shining lights when the fuses had completely blown. For reasons he will never know, I also remain eternally grateful to Chris Stephenson for simply throwing me a line and giving me an escape route out of the house when needed. Lastly, but not least, Chris Marsh abandoned the house but did not abandon me while Casper sat, purred, and told me to remember my priorities – eat, sleep, and smile …

Chapter 1

Fashion foundations

Fashion is perhaps the proverbial Pandora's box. In opening it up to scutiny, its colours, fabrics and enchantments fly out along with all their magical, seductive and even nerve jangling meanings that – try as one might – one can never contain again. That is its fascination and indeed its difficulty – its lack of parameters, lines or even limits. The study of fashion has similarly exploded in recent decades – art histories, anthropologies, psychologies and exhibitions – and all on an increasingly global scale. Yet quite what all this *means*, quite where it might take us, is not clear, fuzzy, out of focus. So this text is primarily a synthesis, an attempt to bring fashion into focus, though hardly exhaustive. The vehicle and indeed lens for this is sociology. Interestingly some of the first – and most powerful and influential – analyses of fashion were sociological, particularly in the work of Veblen who more or less coined the term "conspicuous consumption" and Simmel who perhaps inadvertently set up a paper chase all of his own for the study of fashion (Simmel, 1904; Veblen, 1934). In addition, almost all theories of fashion, past and present, have as their central point awareness of dress, style and adornment as signifying rather than functional phenomena, a point that in itself is perhaps primarily sociological. Yet, despite the influence of feminist and postmodern analysis of fashion, little as it were *core* theory has truly developed here since the early nineteenth century. With the rise of celebrity, designer labels and global levels of exploitation and production this is perhaps surprising and considered in later chapters.

Part of the difficulty is that sociologists, like the population as a whole, tend not to take fashion that seriously. Worse, fashion is also often the object of ridicule and seen as frippery by so-called serious intellectuals and the politically correct, morally suspect or even downright narcissistic by the conservative or the religious, or deviant and just not "the done thing" for half the population, namely men. The problem here is primarily a moral one – people object to fashion on the basis of mores and value judgements around other people "knowing their place" or "being responsible". Some of this centres on money – spending one's disposable income on housing improvements and one's family's future is often seen as more appropriate, more mature and more acceptable than blowing it on yet another pair of hopelessly impractical shoes – and some of it is centred on sex, as a concern with one's appearance is frequently seen as flaunting it or showing off and of course what is "shown off" is precisely oneself and one's sexuality. Not surprisingly, it is one of the primary intentions of this text to take fashion seriously and to demonstrate its importance. This similarly rests on its more sociological significance, for fashion is the most profoundly social yet individual phenomenon, an act of will and yet totally controlled, hyper capitalist and yet not explained by the industrial revolution, consumerist yet reliant on archaic modes of production, violently oppositional yet deeply conservative, a matter of standing out and fitting in. And the fabric that underpins these jostling contradictions is identity – a similarly contradictory phenomenon – for fashion is that most personal of things, our second skin, and it is the thing that binds us to our society, how we make sense of who we are and who everyone else is too. This is not only a communicative or signifying function, rather a set of feelings as fundamental as the senses which it also invokes – sight, sound, touch, smell even – and not so many miles from our very survival: keeping us warm, protecting us and telling us who is friend and who is foe, who is ruler and who is ruled, and who we can mate with. Fashion may be like language, and there is some parallel with nonverbal communication, but actually that comes later – if a Martian dropped onto the planet Earth tomorrow we would primarily make sense of him or her though how they looked and how they presented themselves or, in short, their fashion.

Fashion meaning

One of the primary problems that besets us in studying fashion is being clear about what it is and what it is not – style, design, clothing, adornment, change and taste are all elements of it yet not the same. Importantly, then, in this section, I wish to unpack some of these distinctions, though of course they interconnect or overlap in practice and in the collective conscience of what constitutes fashion.

In the first instance, we must separate fashion as the study of dress, adornment and clothing from the analysis of fashion as a wider phenomenon of social change. Jewellery, hair styles, shoes and accessories all constitute part of fashion alongside clothing, yet the second – if connected – factor is they also change in their design, production and more significantly in relation to matters of taste. The matter of taste – the sense in which the same item can be *de rigueur* one year or even one day and *abominable* the next – affects far more than clothing or any other form of self-presentation, a point made forcibly by the famous sociologist Bourdieu in his study of the Parisian middle classes (Bourdieu, 1984). Interior design, for example, is caught up in similar oscillating processes along with various technologies – particularly the more personal ones such as mobile phones and mini music players – and even cars, culinary tastes, music itself, the arts and architecture. A key factor here is the role of design *per se* and the expansion of an increasingly media driven visual and consumerist culture that turns almost anything into far more than its function. More "postmodern" analyses have considered this development in some detail arguing that symbolic meanings – or signifiers – have become increasingly commodified, caught up within wider processes of consumer capitalism, and indeed separated from the objects that they originally repre- sented referring more to each other (Baudrillard, 1998). Thus a BMW becomes understood more as an aspirational object choice rather than an actual car for which it relies upon separating itself from its competitors so "Audi" does not mean "BMW". Branding is obviously key here and studied in more detail in Chapter 8. Our point here is that fashion as a *phenomenon* involves far more than fashion as *dress*.

Dress similarly means more than just dresses yet does not have the scope of fashion. Its primary emphasis is upon clothing yet it may well include the total look of a person or their complete outfit. Ceremonial or uniform dress for example involves not only clothing but footwear, hair styles, accessories and often symbolic object attachments such as swords or crowns. What is inter- esting here also is the sense in which dress remains relatively static compared with the high motion oscillations of fashion. In relation to our ceremonial example many of these outfits have remained unchanged for centuries whilst many uniforms are set up in some kind of implicit or explicit opposition to fashion. Similarly, we understand the distinction of formal from informal or casual dress with considerably more stability than we maintain the distinction between what is in or out of fashion. This sense of opposition between fashion and dress is significant, for what often motivates a mode of dress as opposed to a fashion is precisely its symbolic importance as something that does *not* change rather than something that does. Thus, interestingly, how we adorn ourselves may not only signify flux but also stasis.

Adornment is a rather under-used term that tends to refer more to the "how" rather than the "what" of fashion. More significantly, it also invokes the centrality of the body. More anthropologically, bodies may be adorned with symbolic objects such as neck rings or paintings, without involving much in the way of clothing at all. In more western terms it also creates more focus upon makeup, hair styling, accessorising and indeed the wearing of clothes rather than the clothes themselves. The most fundamental point here is the linking of personal display to status, communication and the choices – or constraints – made by or placed upon the individual. Unlike fashion that can become abstracted from the body that wears it or buys it, adornment constantly connects matters of appearance back to the individual and the bodily.

It is perhaps this tension between seeing fashion as an individual phenom- enon or as a more collective one that informs questions and understandings of the most complex term of all, style. Style may simultaneously refer to the "what" and the "way" of fashion – its design and how it is worn. This is at once collective, for what we understand as stylish is clearly culturally learned, and individual, as some people are simply perceived as having more style than others. Style, if taken away from its conflation with design, is for the most part a judgement call. It is indeed the most *moral* aspect of fashion. As any cursory glance at any glossy magazine will tell you there is a relentless attempt to divide "good" from "bad" style, fashion statements from fashion *faux pas*, what is to be aspired to from what is to be abhorred. When the abhorred is on the backs of celebrities and the famous, those people become the subject of mockery, scandal or somehow morally suspect. The connection with taste here is fundamental along with the role of choice. Step out on the red carpet in the wrong dress and the consequences are to say the least negative. That negativity centres on seeing the individual as making the wrong decision – "what possessed her to wear *that*", "how *could* she", "*I* wouldn't be seen dead in it". The assumption of voluntarism is essential here and also underpins its opposite, the valorising of those who are seen to "have" style. Having style is somehow seen as an innate quality when clearly it is more strongly related to making the "correct" decisions, knowing what suits one's figure, what colours coordinate and so on – a form of cultural capital although an extremely idiosyncratic and personal one. The rise of style experts, makeover shows, personal shopping services etc. almost *ad infinitum* highlight the degree of individual – and cultural – anxiety that is often invoked here given the consequences of "getting it wrong". When Sinatra sang about style in the 1960s, asserting people either had – or had not – "got it", he could have had little clue quite what he was starting.

Fashion method

As already stated, fashion is a multifaceted phenomenon studied in a multitude of ways. The variation in the ways fashion is studied also reflects the diversity of meanings used and invoked. A casual glance at a bookstore's or library's shelves on fashion also reveals a variety of differing perspectives. Nevertheless, there is some sense in which these can be focused into roughly five sorts. First, and foremost, there are costume histories. These are, as it were, the mainstay of the study of fashion, reflecting the fact that, for the most part, fashion is catalogued under the auspices of art and design rather than social sciences. Costume histories attempt to document, often in considerable detail, who wore what when. At their simplest, they quite literally list in chronological order the details of dress and adornment according to different time scales and sometimes places. Interestingly, the element of place is often the one that is given most cursory attention. Part of this is a reflection of the globalisation of fashion that happened through processes of mercantile trade as much as any more contemporary emphasis upon technology. Thus, the styles of Elizabethan England were influenced by those in Spain and so on. Nevertheless, the relative neglect of non-European cultures has tended to remain evident until more recently. A second and key limitation of many costume histories is their emphasis upon more aristocratic, middle class or higher status dress. Working or lower class dress in many ways may not be seen to exist or simply to operate outside of fashion until the nineteenth century. This is primarily a reflection of a wider issue of methodology. Costume histories rely mostly on artworks, letters, journals, photographic plates and sometimes literature itself for their documentation. Those sources in themselves tend to focus more on higher status groups so there are generally more paintings of kings and queens, a greater number of letters exchanged amongst the middle classes given the slow development of literacy, and more photographs of affluent groups until more recently. As an overall rule, the further one steps away from European aristocratic and middle class circles and the farther one extends into the depths of time, the more spurious and specious the sources of information become. A more fundamental and indeed sociological point here is that no amount of documentation can account for the *meanings* of fashion. Given the enormities of on-going archival efforts into the study of fashion we may well know with some, if not total, accuracy who wore what where and when, yet we have far less understanding of what it *meant*. Other than in letters, diaries and other forms of journal keeping that were again more limited to wealthier or higher status groups we have little record of how particular forms of dress were necessarily understood or regarded. More recent costume histories, such as Riello and McNeil's collection on shoes, grapple with this question as does the work of Chris Breward or a variety of more contemporary and classical scholars, yet the sense of tension remains (Breward, 1999; Riello and McNeil, 2006). Documenting who wore what and when is one thing, trying to work out what it means is another.

A second approach underpins the study of fashion within colleges and universities leading to qualifications in art, design, merchandising and so on. These as it were "fashion manuals" focus on the how-to of fashion – whether that may relate to cutting and sewing or wider processes of merchandising and selling. Whilst this necessarily invokes more archival work and questioning the very foundations of fashion it is again less concerned with its meanings than with its mechanisms. Underpinning this is the tension outlined at the start of this chapter that centres on seeing *fashion as dress*, or quite literally clothing or accessories and how they are made and worn, with *fashion as a phenomenon* of social change that is centred more on an analysis of meanings, tastes and styles. The two clearly connect yet tend to pull in opposite directions when it comes to investing in their study. Consequently, fashion practitioners – designers, retailers and so on – tend to roll their eyes when confronted with wider theorising and academia whilst costume historians complain that social scientists do not spend enough time detailing what they are supposedly studying, i.e. the clothes. Conversely, the problem for any social scientist, and that includes sociologists, in encountering fashion is the interminable descriptiveness of much of its study and the lack of attention to the question of its analysis and its meanings or, to put it more bluntly, the "so what?" of fashion.

This problem also underpins the third perspective that focuses on case studies of particular designers. These often lavish books effectively celebrate the work of a particular designer, detailing and documenting what she, or more often he, did, yet say little of why any of it should matter. More particularly, this was a problem which beset me on attempting to study the rise of designer label culture in the last chapter – there simply weren't any analyses of designer brands at all that weren't an almost slavish adoration of this that or the other designer as celebrity. Rather like former UK prime minister Margaret Thatcher's infamous assertion that there was no such thing as society, only individuals, it seemed there was no such thing as a designer label culture, just designers and their adorers. The exceptions – various blistering polemics against "branding", most famously including Naomi Klein's *No Logo* – still left a wider analysis of what was happening wide open (Klein, 2000).

A fourth and most contemporary standpoint considers fashion and style more widely yet rather uncritically. These studies focus on seeing dress as a matter of self-presentation, providing "guides to style" and "getting it right" often alongside wider commercial initiatives and companies offering image consultancies. The most famous example here is the work of J. T. Molloy whose *Dress for Success* manuals, one for men and one for women, were runaway bestsellers in the US in the 1970s (Molloy, 1988; 1996). These works were essentially style guides for the corporate world giving advice on the correct suits, shoes and overall looks to present to get ahead at work. More particularly, Molloy is sometimes credited as coining the term "power dressing" and as having a significant impact on the equivalent "power look" of the 1980s. That look centred heavily on the suit for men and women, the now infamous involvement of shoulder pads, and an often confused cocktail of overt sexualisation, most notoriously in advocating the wearing of heels for women, and conservatism, in avoiding overly loud colours or flashy ties for men. Work dress is considered in more detail in Chapter 6.

Certain points are however worthy of note more immediately here. First, although many style consultants will deny it, the emphasis is primarily upon the corporate and commercial world of the office. Though applicable in principle, schools, hospitals and trips to the pub are less what this perspective is about in practice. Second, there is also an implicit though strong North American emphasis. This is hardly surprising given North American culture's often anxious concerns with fitting in, dressing the part and personal success. At the risk of invoking further stereotypes, legacies of Parisian snobbery and Italian style are not irrelevant, yet the emphasis here is more upon conservatism and commerce that have a stronger connection with the United States. A third – more critical – factor here is that these guides form an example *par excellence* of the role of cultural intermediaries, a term coined by

Bourdieu to describe "experts" in the world of style and taste including editors, advertisers and a whole host of increasingly image obsessed industries (Bourdieu, 1984). Their key and defining feature is that they act as arbiters of taste and they tell you what to do. Of course this is a phenomenon that has expanded almost exponentially in recent decades to include a wider and wider variety of arenas and forms. These include personal shopping services, now offered by many mid- as well as upmarket stores, and a plethora of television programmes and makeover shows that tell their participants and their audience how to "get the look". There are a variety of factors at work here including the rise of so-called "reality" television, cultures of celebrity and – arguably – disgust given the strong emphasis upon shock, awe and horror at how "awful" people look to start with, and the rather insidious use of a certain kind of pop psychology to justify the process. Susan Bordo's work on the body has been influential here (Bordo, 1993, 1999).

Thus "Trinny and Susannah" as a pair of upper class "experts" ran a highly successful series of shows entitled *What Not To Wear* in the UK where they generally took lower class women, turned them into objects of the gaze – quite literally in a three way mirror with a camera – raided their closets and their lives, and then transformed them into "new women", full of confidence and esteem with the aid of a makeover. The formula was then developed more commercially in the show *Undress The Nation* shown on ITV, the launch of various clothing lines in association with the Littlewoods mail order group, and taking the concept on a worldwide tour to Australia and the United States. Consequently what this plays upon repeatedly is the connection of personality with appearance – look good, feel good – and the sense in which dress expresses *oneself*. This theme and psychological perspectives on fashion are considered in detail in Chapter 2.

All of these four perspectives effectively define themselves and are defined by the final viewpoint that is most accurately entitled social scientific. To call it academic would rather discredit the scholarship and work often involved in many of the other viewpoints. However, social scientific work on fashion is markedly different due to its primary emphasis upon *theory*. Whether anthropology, sociology, psychology or history – and regardless of their often extensive use of empiricism – these studies are motivated to understand the wider mechanisms and meanings of fashion as a *phenomenon*. Thus, much to the annoyance of many art historians or practitioners alike, the emphasis shifts away from clothing and accessories themselves and more towards cultures, styles and practices. In essence we return to the distinction outlined at the start of this chapter that separates fashion as dress from fashion as a mechanism of social change. Social scientific investigation into fashion, as we shall see in Chapter 2, has a long pedigree extending well back into the nineteenth century in the work of Carlyle and Spencer, developing rapidly in the early twentieth century in the ideas of Veblen and Simmel, and further again with the theories of Laver, Flügel and Barthes (see Chapter 2). It has also taken on something of a renaissance more recently with the significant expansion of Berg's list of fashion titles and the launch of the journal *Fashion Theory* with the same publisher. Whether studying some obscure tribal ritual, trying to establish an overriding law of dress, or analysing the signifying processes of magazines, all of these studies attempt in some way to analyse fashion as a social phenomenon that represents wider issues of change, economics or the relationship of the individual to society. Whilst they may well overlap with and indeed utilise costume histories, they are not merely attempts to document who wore what where and when; rather they are more studies of how and why. As outlined at the outset of this chapter, this text is primarily sociological and therefore falls mostly – if not exclusively – into this fifth category.

Fashion *mode et mots*

The mode of analysis here, as already indicated, is primarily sociological and this forms the main means through which differing subjects are studied. It also informs, it should be said, the content and scope of the work which covers the social aspects of fashion rather than the science of cloths and dyes, a guide to cutting and sewing, a consideration of buying and merchandising, or an in-depth costume history. Consequently, following this introductory chapter, Chapter 2 provides coverage and critique of most, if not necessarily all, of what one might call the classical – or historically most influential – sociological, psychological and economic theories of fashion. Chapter 3 focuses extensively on the neglect of men's dress and the shifting meanings of masculinity in relation to fashion and, more particularly, pays significant attention to the suit. In conjunction with this, Chapter 4 focuses on the more contemporary construction of fashion around the feminine and the importance of female sexuality and fetishism within this. Having considered gender and sexuality, Chapter 5 looks at age in relation to fashion and more specifically focuses on children's clothing. This chapter also draws on a recent empirical study into the fashion industry and retail sector in relation to rising concerns with the so-called "sexualisation" or "adultification" of children's fashion. Comparisons are also made with fashion for the elderly. The role of identity in relation to fashion is considered extensively in Chapter 6 which looks at identity politics and dress, particularly in relation to the rise of new social movements such as feminism and civil rights as well as the established analysis of subcultural style. This incorporates a focus on gay male dress and, interestingly, a concluding section on the role of dress at work. This consideration of the politics of consumption is then juxtaposed with a consideration of the politics of fashion production in Chapter 7. Rather than forming an exposé, this chapter explores the peculiarities and idiosyncrasies of the history of the fashion industry in attempting to explain its more exploitative practices. This more political dimension also informs the most contemporary and last chapter, Chapter 8, which focuses on the rise of designer label and celebrity culture in relation to western fashion in particular. There is also some connection here with Chapter 4 given the tendency of celebrity culture to construct particular notions of femininity. As a final case study, the similarities and differences in the cultural significance of David and Victoria Beckham are considered along-side the formation of a new form of subjectivity in relation to fashion. The Conclusion also extends this argument on subjectivity more widely.

The following section outlines some commonly used words and terms – or *mots* – in relation to the study of fashion, particularly more sociologically, and as they are used in the rest of this work:

Aestheticisation Refers to the increasing emphasis upon the visual. This relates not only to the expansion of the mass media but also to the role of design and to the importance of how things look rather than what they do. Apple devices such as iPods and iPhones are examples of this process of attaching increasing importance to how things appear and their design.

Commodification Refers to the process of making everyday objects or practices part of a process of "buy and sell". Thus spiritual beliefs may be "commodified" by the marketing and selling of health clubs or retreats and spas.

Constructionism (also called **constructivism** and **social constructionism**) This term relates to the idea that identities, practices and preferences – or even ideas – are socially shaped and vary from time to time and place to place rather than having some fixed origin or meaning. Thus, homosexuality for example is seen as a modern western identity rather than as a transcultural or biological form of being and contemporary gay culture is radically different from Greco-Roman same sex practices.

Cultural capital A term formulated and developed by Pierre Bourdieu. It refers to the various ways in which those from middle or upper classes, or more affluent groups, may have resources or "capital" that are not purely monetary such as know-how, etiquette and skills that they may use to maintain their position whether in matters of appearance, presentation, dining, interacting with others, or networking.

Cultural intermediaries A linked term again used in the work of Bourdieu to refer to advertisers, editors, advisors and an array of "experts" who guide and dictate to others in matters of style and taste. They also form a new petite bourgeoisie and develop their own class and status position as a result.

Discourse A term widely associated with the work of Michel Foucault. Whilst it may be used more specifically it is used here to indicate a preferred meaning or interpretation of events. Thus an emphasis upon slimness is often part of a discourse of health that says being slimmer is "better" which is partially, but not wholly, substantiated by evidence. Discourse also often relates to power relationships – thus here the power of the medical profession and the media to define "health" and "sickness".

Essentialism The opposite of constructionism and implies there is some kind of fixed essence or meaning to ideas or things whether that is biological ("women's hormones") or some form of drive ("a maternal instinct") or even genetic ("a gay gene").

Ethnicity A more social and cultural term that relates to shared practices such as religion or language or nationality. Again the tendency is to blur this into matters of "race" and fixed categories.

Functionalism A term and branch of sociological theory derived and developed in the work of Emile Durkheim and later Talcott Parsons. Broadly speaking, it states that society is made up of interdependent parts that "function together" to create a whole. This not only relates to the individual and their relationship to society, but rather to institutions such as the family and education. More controversially, crime and deviance are seen to "function" as moral guidance for the rest of society. The perspective is critiqued not only for its lack of attention to conflict (which is why it is also sometimes called the consensus approach), but rather for its tendency to explain causes through effects, i.e. things are as they are because (the cause) they have a certain outcome or function (the effect). It is also a problem that besets some studies of fashion (see Chapter 2).

Gender Masculinity and femininity and those attributes associated with them. The emphasis is upon constructionism and seeing such attributes as learned rather than innate. Thus women may be masculine and men may have feminine attributes or characteristics.

Race The classification of the human population into distinct groups or "races" on the basis of certain biological or physical differences such as skin colour, face or body shape. There has been an increasing emphasis upon the construction of these differences given the enormity of variations that exist within and across so-called "races" such as "black" or "Asian".

Sex When not referring to sexual activity, this term refers to the biological difference between male and female.

Sexuality Relates to sexual identity, sexual desire and sexual preference including sexual orientation. Again this is not seen as determined by sex though often relates to gender in defining gay men as effeminate for example.

Chapter 2

The classical tradition
Early perspectives on fashion

Fashion is often seen as a slightly silly and certainly superficial interest or practice that people tend to associate with youth and dizzy individuals, rather than art, design or society, and consequently tend to dismiss as of only minor importance. The slippery relationship of the high-flown world of specialist haute couture to the more mundane and widespread use of the high street in particular has also created more coals for the funeral fires of fashion. These factors in turn start to have consequences for the politics of fashion which I consider in Chapter 6, where I also analyse more contemporary and often more politically motivated perspectives on the development of fashion, such as those derived from subcultural studies. It is my intention here, therefore, to consider those perspectives which either preceded or laid their roots prior to these later developments.

In the first instance, though, it is worth explaining and unpacking the foundations of the study of fashion that were first developed a hundred years or so ago and are still in place today. The study of fashion, like fashion itself, has its foundations in art and design, or at least in the history of art and design. Indeed, the study of fashion today is still primarily located in the confines of arts departments rather than the social sciences. It is this factor which accounts for much of the apparent and immediate distortion in the study of fashion, or the modern, western and haute couture focus that simultaneously locates and yet often omits consideration of the social context of dress. More importantly, as mentioned in Chapter 1, the earliest analyses of fashion were essentially costume histories, graphic accounts of dress through the centuries that were often painstakingly researched and skilfully compiled, yet which often opened up a complete omission, in fact a void, of theory. These texts, which are still in production today and used frequently as source books for courses in art and design, act as excellent reference texts, yet are at their weakest, with some exceptions, in explaining how and why fashion has come to claim its contemporary importance, its politics, or simply its fascination (Chenoune, 1993; Gibbings, 1990; Martin and Koda, 1989). This situation started to change in the 1970s and 1980s with the advent of cultural studies, the rise of more sociological and anthropological analyses of fashion and second wave feminism. However, it is worthwhile considering their early forerunners in the study of fashion for, as we shall see, these still form many of the mainstays of the contemporary analyses of fashion: in short, they constitute a classical tradition.

From here to modernity: perspectives on the development of fashion

Over the past hundred years, several perspectives have developed to explain the apparently increasing importance of fashion in western society. These perspectives are grouped relatively easily according to the emphasis they place upon economics, psychology or symbolic interactionism. It is important to point out that there are far more numerous variations on a theme here, yet the emphasis upon one of these elements still tends to remain. In addition, at the end of this section, I include a wider discussion of more contemporary developments and postmodernity in relation to the study of fashion.

Certain points are interesting to note prior to developing a discussion of these perspectives individually. First, all of these perspectives tend to see fashion as a predominantly western phenomenon of developed societies. With the exception of some more anthropological analyses and the evolutionary emphasis of some other studies, they also tend to exclude consideration of eastern dress or fashion design and use in the developing world. This is an increasingly serious neglect as western designers regularly plunder the rest of the world for ideas whilst the rise of globalised production methods exploits textiles and skills developed and practised there already, raising further, more political, issues covered in Chapter 7.

Second, all of these perspectives see fashion as a primarily modern phenomenon that is tied up with the development of industrial or consumer capitalism and mercantile trade. This is a point open to dispute due to the prevalence of complex designs in dress prior to capitalist development and the universality of styling in dress according to social values, tastes and systems across time and space.

Third, they also tend to place a heavy emphasis, whether explicit or implicit, upon fashion as haute couture or more middle class fashion. The clear difficulty here is the sense of distance from wider society, and indeed the high street, that this often invokes, creating a notion of fashion as "up there", "out there" and "somewhere" more or less separate from reality and society. Perhaps most fundamentally of all there is an almost constant skew towards the consideration of women's fashion over men's. Men's dress repeatedly ends up as a chapter, a point of comparison or a footnote and rarely studied in its own right. Given the fact that approximately half of the human population is male this is problematic and a point I explore more fully in Chapter 3.

The economic perspective (fashion as consumption)

> Within capitalism, therefore, it becomes possible for both fashion and clothing to
> be used to construct, signal and reproduce the desire for social mobility between
> classes as well as class identity itself.
>
> (Barnard, 1996: 105)

The economic perspective on the development of fashion states most
fundamentally that it is the advancement of western capitalism, particularly
consumer capitalism, which motors the creation, perpetuation and expansion of
the fashion industry. Fashion is indeed seen centrally as an *industry* reliant on
mass production to succeed and, in addition, a primary indicator of the
development of surplus production or excess in western advanced society.

It is interesting to note that orthodox Marxism, perhaps the most pervasive
of all economic perspectives, has had little to say on consumption, let alone
fashion. The Frankfurt School, in the work of Theodor Adorno and
Max Horkheimer particularly, has provided one of the most damning indict-
ments of the entire "culture industry", seen as the new opiate of the masses,
as "it perpetually cheats its consumers of what it perpetually promises" in
inducing "obedience to the social hierarchy" (Adorno and Horkheimer,
1973: 38). Critics of the concept of this perspective assert that the "culture
industry" is often an undifferentiated and ill-defined concept that renders the
individual a mere automaton, if not victim, of society (Du Gay, 1997). Fashion
per se is not considered directly here, yet the clear implication of such a perspective would be to see fashion as an industry not dissimilar to any other that
is motivated by the desire to make profit and stimulate demand. The fundamental distinction within Marxism between use value – or the functional
purpose of any commodity – from its exchange value – or monetary worth
in a system of trade – is of primary importance here. Thus fashion's only
use value is as clothes, and fashion *per se* is, or even epitomises, exchange
value. Given the fashion industry's notorious reputation for exploitation this
remains an important and sensitive point, yet it is fashion's more symbolic
significance that causes Marxist perspectives headaches. Dress and adornment
act universally as indicators of status, rank and as wider communicators
of identity in society, including societies that are not capitalist, and these
meanings are not straightforwardly reduced to a mere profit motive. However,
Marxist theory is equally not so easily discarded and the economic perspective
on fashion is in many ways a reworking of Marxist ideas of consumption as
we shall see.

Arguably the earliest attempt to at least begin to theorise this more social
significance of dress comes in the work of Thomas Carlyle, the famous
Victorian essayist and critic. His work *Sartor Resartus* roughly translated as
"the tailor re-tailored" forms the foundation for his analysis of dress (Carlyle,
1869). As Michael Carter argues:

The book steadfastly refuses a simple and open proclamation of its message, preferring instead to adopt a number of oblique approaches such as satire, caricature and irony.

(Carter, 2003: 2)

The reason for this is the work's own cross-pollination of genres – neither truly fiction nor fact and neither really satire nor serious, it tells the story of an unnamed editor who attempts to understand, compile and present the work of the famous philosopher of clothes, Teufelsdröckh, who is in fact entirely fictional. As is clear, the immediate difficulty is that neither Teufelsdröckh nor the editor are necessarily expressing the perspective of Carlyle himself whose opinions one ends up trying to deduce from the various differences in view-point. The importance of *Sartor Resartus* thus rests almost entirely upon an interpretation of the text in question. Its significance is perhaps summarised in two points: first, it remains the first serious attempt to theorise clothing and dress, however one interprets Carlyle's meaning or intention; and second, it repeatedly alludes to and perhaps even demonstrates the social significance of clothing:

The first purpose of Clothes, as our Professor imagines, was not warmth or decency, but ornament.

(Carlyle, 1869: 30)

It is this second factor which perhaps accounts for Keenan's overly grandiose claim that *Sartor Resartus* provides the foundation for nearly all studies of dress since, and that somehow "we are all 'Carlyleans' now" (Keenan 2001: 14). I would assert that it is also Carlyle's implicit setting up of the fundamentals of much functionalist analysis of fashion, whether intended or not, that gives it its importance. I will return to this theme of functionalism and fashion in the final section of this chapter. In particular, perhaps unwittingly, Carlyle also sets up the rather unholy trinity of seeing dress as first a matter of modesty, second as performing the function of protection and thirdly as a form of display and decoration. This triangulated view of fashion, as we shall see shortly, drives nearly every early analysis of dress from the work of Veblen and Simmel through most obviously to the work of Flügel and Laver. However, given the difficulties of interpreting Carlyle's perspective, it is difficult to see how the work progresses much beyond stating the obvious, namely that fashion performs a social and symbolic function. The one exception to this, his chapter critiquing upper class dandyism and working class drudgism also remains more important as part of his lifetime critique of spiritual decline under capitalism than a true analysis of fashion. Keenan's 40 plus page near sermon like declaration of Carlyle's significance does surprisingly little to articulate or explicate his ideas other than to state, over and over again, that Carlyle is the "true founder of dress studies" (Keenan, 2001: 28). As Carter in his more considered analysis of *Sartor Resartus* notes, Carlyle actually has little to say concerning fashion (Carter, 2003).

The analysis of the social, and indeed economic, significance of fashion perhaps more accurately starts with the work of Thorstein Veblen. Veblen has often been heralded, perhaps somewhat notoriously, as a pioneer of the sociological study of fashion and consumption. His primary work in relation to consumerism, *The Theory of the Leisure Class*, was partly a critique of late nineteenth century North American middle class society and partly a development of economic history (Veblen, 1934). It is worth noting that Veblen was never truly allied to any tradition of social science or social theory and was, in essence, a fairly prolific social critic. His comments on the middle classes have nonetheless since come under very serious scrutiny not least of all due to his development of the term conspicuous consumption which has, of course, long since passed into common parlance.

The perspective he developed put simply states that as society increases in affluence, through the advance of such factors as technology and mass production, there develops a middle or leisure class defined and maintained according to its consumerist as opposed to, or as well as, its productive practices. Interestingly, it is the concept of *leisure*, and its connections to consumption practices, which is at the crux of his analysis. As western society increases its wealth due to capitalist expansion and mass production, he asserts, so leisure itself comes to form a signifier of pecuniary status. What also comes under scrutiny here, and is also sometimes the cause of some confusion, is the strong association of consumption with wastefulness and idleness which clearly has a somewhat pejorative slant to it that is equally easily overestimated. At the same time, his analysis does also quite strongly invoke the sense in which consumption practices are, on occasions, strongly linked to questions of extravagance or perceived as having high status for no reason other than they are a waste of time and/or money. The enormous cost of haute couture is perhaps a prime example.

More importantly, at the centre of his analysis of the values of consumption are leisure or middle-class *women* who, in their roles as wives, are seen to perform primarily a status maintaining function. Interestingly, Veblen is sensitive to the sense in which women are themselves owned and commodified through their own consumption practices, which they are seen to perform in maintenance of the status of their male counterparts. At the same time, however, he is scathing of their activities in themselves. Moreover, his association of what he calls "new woman", broadly equated with first wave feminism, with some kind of earlier "barbaric" culture is, to say the least, a little unfortunate. However, given his ambivalence, this does not entirely add up to the sexism that Elizabeth Wilson accuses him of in her own work on fashion (Wilson, 1985).

The focus of his work is primarily upon North American society at the turn of the twentieth century and, as a consequence of their desire for status through consumption practices, "it is especially the rule of the conspicuous waste of goods that finds expression in dress" (Veblen, 1934: 167). In other words, dress, and especially haute couture or fashion, is seen as the epitome of superficiality and unnecessary luxury, of primary significance to the new middle classes of North America.

There is a certain common sense truth in this which may account for the popularity of the work. We quite clearly do not dress according to function or need alone and, in fact, the consumption of clothes increasingly serves no other purpose than to fulfil or express psychological or social, rather than practical, needs. The difficulty is that whilst it is true that we have widely exceeded the practical utility of dress alone, utility still remains and motivates many of the less fashion-conscious groups and individuals that make up society, let alone those who cannot afford to dress for fashion. This raises two further points: first, that Veblen's analysis is overly dependent upon attention to a single class or group; and second, that individual variation is undermined in what is an essentially structural perspective.

A second, and interlinked, element to the perspective is the notion that dress acts as a particularly visual display of an individual or group's status. He asserts: "expenditure on dress has this advantage over other methods that our apparel is always in evidence and affords an indication of our pecuniary standing to all observers at first glance" (Veblen, 1934: 167). As pointed out in the previous chapter, there is some evidence to support the notion that dress acts as a code or performs a signifying function, particularly prior to the twentieth century and in many non-western societies. The difficulty is that as society and dress increase in their complexity of components and populations, the interpretation of dress is ever more uncertain and, in particular, is increasingly contextually dependent. A suit at the opera is an appropriate example of middle-class consumption or attire; a suit on the sports field often simply looks silly or misplaced.

A more complex aspect of Veblen's analysis is the idea that, with the advance of industrial capitalism, men's dress develops along increasingly utilitarian lines so much so that women's dress alone represents conspicuous consumption whilst men's dress is indicative of the production that affords the consumption. Or, to put it more simply, men use their wives rather than themselves for the conspicuous display of their affluence. Evidence of this hypothesis centres on the intentionally impractical design of middle-class women's clothing in hampering movement and making many tasks difficult, particularly servile ones. The irony of this is that many servant costumes tended to mimic their middle-class counterparts in design and were therefore not particularly practical, with their trailing skirts and confining corsets conceding only coarseness of cloth and lack of decoration due to cost as much as practicality. As pointed out in Chapter 3, it is also a mistake to see men's dress, even at the height of the Victorian era, as merely a utilitarian uniform, as variations in men's dress and its associated meanings were more complex.

However, what is also at stake here is the adequacy of Veblen's theorising itself often amounting to little more than a simple form of structural functionalism. The analysis does start with some stronger foundations in a fairly unilinear form of economic history, yet, following an interesting analysis of fashion and some insights into pecuniary questions of taste, drifts off into a scattered collection of articles on various throwbacks to "barbarism" in modern life from gambling and feminism to, more convincingly, the predatory nature of commerce. As a consequence, any strong sense of direction or conclusion is sadly lacking. Most significantly, it is focused exclusively on the US, whose cultural history of consumption is unique in its early expansion and development on a mass scale, and of course on a single class.

The German philosopher Georg Simmel is most famous for his work in developing a more phenomenological approach to the social world and sociology in the early twentieth century. Put simply, this means that for Simmel the world, and our understanding of it, is as subjective as it is objective and that human psychology drives more social developments and *vice versa*. Thus Simmel's theorising of fashion is essentially an analysis of social and psychological struggle between the two opposing forces of individuation and sociality, or put crudely, the desire to fit in and the desire to stand out (Simmel, 1904). At the centre of this are the two key concepts of the processes of "imitation" and "differentiation" where imitation acts as a form of social adaptation or conforming, whilst differentiation acts as a form of individual separation or distinction. This tension is then mapped onto the question of social class as the lower or working classes are seen as trying to imitate the higher or middle classes who in turn try to differentiate themselves from the lower or working classes, setting up an endless paper chase. Sometimes also known as the "trickle-down" theory, it also starts to set up the parameters for much succeeding discussion of style and fashion.

At the centre of criticisms of this perspective is the very clear point that styles may equally trickle up as well as down and that lower or working class groups may in particular seek to react against rather than dumbly follow dominant patterns, primarily via more subcultural styles and consumption practices. One parallel in particular is the work of Pierre Bourdieu in *Distinction* (Bourdieu, 1984). The other, and I think more major, criticism to be made here is that Simmel's analysis is fundamentally essentialist, implying that fashion is reducible to "deeper human motives" – a point reinforced through his analysis of primitive cultures where fashion is less prevalent as the "socializing impulse is much more powerfully developed than the differentiating impulse" – and gender, where women are seen to be more involved in fashion due simply to their greater desire for individuation in the face of oppression. Third, there is a constant sense in which Simmel reifies fashion into a system semi-autonomous, or at least separate, from the rest of society and operating according to a set of internal logics of its own. Given the sense in which fashion is clearly strongly related to developments in the economy such as rising affluence and discretionary income, particularly in advanced western capitalist societies, wider social processes of individualism across the world, as well as shifts in technology in facilitating both its production and consumption *en masse*, this is arguably rather short-sighted. It is also understandable given the time and context in which it was written. Much of our contemporary understanding of fashion did not arise until the twentieth century and there remains a sense in which fashion is a fundamentally modern, or even contemporary, phenomenon.

An interesting example of the more contemporary applications of Simmel's ideas on fashion is also given in Grant McCracken's *Culture and Consumption* (McCracken, 1988). McCracken criticises the simplicity of Simmel's analysis and, in particular, asserts that the processes of imitation and differentiation apply to more groups across more factors of stratification including gender. In considering the style cultures of the 1980s, he sees women's executive dress, as exemplified in the heavily shoulder-padded suit, as imitating that of men's more traditional work attire; whilst men's own increasingly "heroic look" of double-breasted power suits, braces and pinstripes is perceived to form an attempt at differentiation. The conservative if not reactionary sexual politics of such an analysis are clear and this is a point I contest in Chapter 6. However, Simmel's analysis has still seemingly influenced many later studies of the interaction of subcultures and dominant culture (see, for example, Hebdige, 1979; McRobbie, 1989; Polhemus, 1994). Moreover, Simmel's attention to the more conspicuously style-driven aspects of consumption also, somewhat indirectly, informs one of the most famous early studies of consumer society. In addition, he argues:

> This understanding allows us to predict not only that men will seek a new style of clothing but also that they will seek a style in which power and authority are re-established. As a superordinate group, men will seek to accomplish an act of differentiation that will do more than recreate an exclusive male clothing style. They will also seek to recreate an exclusive look of authority.
>
> (McCracken, 1988: 48)

This taps into some of the second-wave feminist points arising around the theme of the New Man considered in more detail in Chapter 3, though it also opens up a further question concerning class.

Whilst, in a sense, aspirational dressing for success is a key motivation in many working-class groups' consumption of fashion, this hardly explains either the equally striking countercultural impulses in fashion consumption or the trickle up of many street styles into haute couture (McCracken, 1988). The "trickle-up" theory, in particular, has developed some credence recently as the likes of Zandra Rhodes and Vivienne Westwood have put punk on the catwalk, whilst Katharine Hamnett made ripped jeans a designer accessory, and Paul

Smith is constantly reinventing the mod look. However, it is worth noting the heavy UK emphases here derived from strong traditions in street style (Polhemus, 1994). Wilson also highlights the technological determinism often implicit in such analyses, as the invention of the Singer sewing machine in 1851, for example, is often seen to herald a design revolution and mass production which, in fact, did not really happen for at least another 50 years, and design itself is perhaps semi-autonomous of technological invention, at least in terms of the intricacies of colour and detail (Wilson, 1985).

Perhaps the most sophisticated, and certainly the most influential, analysis of class and fashion is provided by the French social theorist Pierre Bourdieu. In his study of *Distinction: a Social Critique of the Judgement of Taste* (1984). Bourdieu's detailed observation of the habits and lifestyles of the French, paying particular attention to factors such as dress, haircuts and dining out, provides an excellent example of the more social importance of fashion in forming and maintaining personal or group status or identity as "taste classifies, and it classifies the classifier" (Bourdieu, 1984: 6). The difficulty is that this often leads to a reinvention of models of class and stratification rather than a more radical analysis of the complexities of culture, gender and identity. Interestingly, his conceptualization of the paper-chase of social position echoes Simmel's earlier analysis of imitation and differentiation cited previously, although he stresses differently the importance of what he calls "cultural intermediaries" in sustaining the process. Cultural intermediaries are often self-appointed arbiters of taste – editors, advertisers and similar media workers who make and promote their own judgements concerning what is "good" or "bad", "in" or "out", in terms of taste, style and fashion. They also form a new petite bourgeoisie, gaining wealth, prestige and status on the basis of networking and such "expertise" rather than through education, achievement or inheritance. The application of such concepts and ideas to the current world of designer fashion and celebrity culture is clear to see and studied more fully in the last chapter. Bourdieu's views on fashion, however, can be summarised thus:

> Fashion is the latest fashion, the latest difference. An emblem of class (in all senses) withers once it loses its distinctive power. When the miniskirt reaches the mining village of northern France, it's time to start again.
>
> (Bourdieu, 1993: 135)

The economic perspective on the development of fashion, then, emphasises the importance of fashion as a signifier of status and rank in society. Its near relentless emphasis upon social class is often overly simplistic, determinist and one-dimensional as an analysis of more complex phenomena, particularly in terms of the meanings of fashion goods and more individual variations – regarding something as "a bit of old tat" is about far more than class or economics, and exposes the often seemingly inexplicable forces of fashion to render something as *de rigueur* one day and *abominable* the next. It does, however, crucially highlight the significance of fashion as a symbolic phenomenon or, more widely, as a marker of individuality and difference particularly in modern western societies.

The psychological perspective (fashion as communication)

The psychological perspective on the development of fashion starts with an acceptance of this premise that dress is not merely a matter of utility or practicality. It is, more importantly, seen as a psychological code or device for displaying individual identity or personality. There is, in similarity to economic theory, some commonsense to this as there is little explanation, other than individual idiosyncrasy and personality, as to why we like or dislike certain styles, colours or designs and choose to don one costume rather than another when there are several appropriate to the occasion. In addition, though, the psychological perspective also often involves a form of functionalism exemplified in the forerunning work of Charles Flügel who, in *The Psychology of Clothes* (1930), developed an analysis of what he saw as the three of the most primary functions of fashion or dress: protection, modesty and display.

Flügel's key work simply entitled *The Psychology of Clothes* is an attempt to document the psychological – and often social – importance of dress and adornment (Flügel, 1930). Written in the late 1920s it inevitably feels rather dated but given its emphasis upon universal fundamentals of fashion and dress its relevance is more timeless. Flügel is very much concerned to establish a kind of "bottom line" of fashion, often reducing it to a series of lists and functions that add up to something approaching the universal laws of dress and adornment. It is perhaps this attempt at universality which accounts for its on-going significance. At the core of this are the three main "functions" of fashion: decoration, modesty and protection. Decoration most simply relates to clothing as display or what one might call the signifying or symbolic dimension of fashion. Modesty roughly equates with the near universal prohibition of bodily nakedness such as exposure of the genitals, although how this works in practice varies considerably from culture to culture and from one time period to another. The third function of protection relates to the ways in which clothing protects the body and or skin from pain or harm. The three elements are then unpacked at length and in detail according to his attempt to document a set of universal principles that are in turn dependent upon his dissemination of the prevailing anthropological and psychological literatures at the time. Of these the simplest is protection – clothing and other forms of adornment often perform the function of keeping people warm or cool, protecting the skin, or providing a more specific use such as prevention of harm through armour or specialist uniforms. Flügel however rather confuses this with far more complex issues to do with the more symbolic nature of fashion and dress, such as the attempt to ward off evil spirits or to avoid provocation of desire. He also tends to construct chapters around inordinate lists and categories, some of which are clearer and more useful than others. His listing of the "purposive aspects" or rather functions of decoration is typical − he usefully elucidates the importance of clothing as a signifier of sexuality and status whilst at the same time confusing this with other levels of functionality such as carrying essential items. The emphasis upon *display* here whether in relation to sexuality − genital or fetishised − or status of whatever kind − national, occupational or monetary − is clearly key to any analysis of fashion and dress. Conversely, his attempt to document the variable dimensions of modesty seems both clumsy and confused, juxtaposing questions of subjective motivation, or psychological reasons why such prohibitions may exist, with observation of the wider social and or sexual variations in how it is practised.

Arguably, Flügel's supposed "psychology" of clothing is also something of a misnomer for a more functionalist theory of dress. His analysis of fashion as a phenomenon of social change and taste in particular is peculiarly sparse. This is for the most part limited to what he calls the "evolution" of fashion which clearly implies a linearity and progression often rejected in many other analyses including Simmel's outlined earlier. Conversely, his documentation of the purposes of dress, whether individual or social, is immense and detailed. In addition, later chapters on what he calls the "ethics" of dress tend to collapse into more personal judgements on what is appropriate in dress. Key within this is his use of Freudian psychoanalytic theory, particularly that relating to Freud's concepts of the pleasure principle and the reality principle, to make wider more social points. Freud did not study dress but postulated the theory that people unconsciously avoid that which feels painful or invokes suffering whilst seeking to gratify their more basic needs − the pleasure principle expressed through the id − whilst also feeling a need to control and regulate such desires − the ego or reality principle. Flügel's adoption, or even adaptation, of this idea to dress comes through his recognition of clothing's more sensory importance or the sense in which it may feel nice, or nasty, to wear and arouses desire, or not, in the wearer or observer. Given the heavy emphasis often placed upon the visual dimensions of fashion, for Flügel in the significance of decoration this more sensory importance is often lost in many analyses of fashion past and present, and it is unfortunate that it has not been developed further in more contemporary work with some exceptions (Johnson and Foster, 2007). Another almost wisp-like factor raised by Flügel is the future of fashion where, at the very end of his analysis, he postulates: "the possibility that dress is, after all, destined to be but an episode in the history of humanity", hinting that society may evolve beyond the need for fashion at all (Flügel, 1930: 238). This is an intriguing idea rarely considered elsewhere despite the immense and rapid changes in dress and fashion during the twentieth century. Later theorists have since criticised the simplicity of Flügel's analysis and also the implicit ethnocentrism and sexism in his interpretations (Barnard, 1996; Barnes and Eicher, 1992; Eicher, 1995). The internal contradictions of such interpretations were also exposed through the work of another classical theorist of fashion, James Laver.

It is debatable as to whether James Laver can truly be called a theorist of fashion. He is, however, one of most renowned of twentieth-century costume historians in the UK, particularly following his extensive work with the Victoria and Albert Museum in London starting in 1922, where he worked as a keeper until his retirement in 1959. During that time, he published many articles and books but his writings on fashion did not really begin until the 1930s. Despite his prolific output, little of his work, whilst often constituting significant, interesting and detailed costume history, can be said to construct a theory of fashion. One of his most popular works *Costume and Fashion* forms a primary example of his approach – a simple chronology of what people wear and have worn across time and space from Ancient Egypt to Edwardian England, and covering the rise and fall of Spanish and French fashion along the way, drawing on sources as diverse as fashion plates, art, carvings, letters, journals and fiction (Laver, 1982). Whilst often entertaining and wryly observed, the primary emphasis is descriptive rather than analytical and there is almost no attempt to problematise the reliability or validity of the sources used.

His more theoretically informed work on fashion, simply entitled *Taste and Fashion*, is more focused, narrowing its canvas to mostly northern European if not English fashion during the 150 year period from 1789 to 1939, originally published in 1937 and revised in 1945. His analysis still slides rather uneasily between addressing key themes such as romanticism and nature or aestheticism, and women's independence and case studies of particular garments or aspects of dress such as crinolines, the bustle or sportswear. He constantly remarks on the tensions between functionality and decoration or the differences between women's dress and men's but it is not until his concluding chapter that any wider theory really emerges. Here he asserts:

> Every age has enjoyed what luxury it could, and the degree of its luxury has been, almost always, the measure of its civilization.
>
> (Laver, 1945: 196)

He then proceeds to analyse the contradictory nature of fashion given its tendency to both protect and assert the individual self and to consistently act as "the mirror of the soul" whilst constantly changing (Laver, 1945: 198). His sense of both the endless mutations of fashion and its importance as decoration leads him into an analysis of taste that in some ways foreruns the work of Bourdieu many years later. In particular, through what has sometimes come to be called "Laver's Law" he documents how the same costume is perceived in different ways through time, seeing it as:

Indecent	ten years before its time
Shameless	five years before its time
Daring	one year before its time
Smart	now
Dowdy	one year after its time
Hideous	ten years after its time
Ridiculous	20 years after its time
Amusing	30 years after its time
Quaint	50 years after its time
Charming	70 years after its time
Romantic	100 years after its time
Beautiful	150 years after its time

Whilst most people would recognise the tendency of various fashions to change meaning through time and to gradually gain a more nostalgic appeal from a distance, the variation in perceptions of different items – for example, women's skirts which now vary so enormously as to rarely be wholly acceptable or unacceptable at any one time, or men's suits which conversely only lose dignity when taken to particular extremes (overly shiny, overly tight, overly bright, etc.) – let alone differences according to context, rank, status, gender or race are rather missed. At the same time his comparison with interior design is more than apt and his recognition that fashion is "in short, the very spearhead of taste" is paradoxically well ahead of its own time (Laver, 1945: 211). However, Laver still struggles to grasp the essential nettles of his subject to develop a stronger argument concluding, rather glibly, that fashion seems to be a reflection of life itself.

The same rather contradictory tendency is present in the last of his more major works on fashion entitled *Dress: How and Why Fashions in Men's and Women's Clothes Have Changed During the Past Two Hundred Years* (Laver, 1950). Here he takes Flügel's tripartite model of analysis considering dress in terms of modesty, protection and display and attempts to turn this into something approaching a fundamental law rather than its original significance as a loose adaptation of Freudian psychoanalysis. He returns also to the theory of shifting erogenous zones, first mentioned in his work on taste, welding it to three further principles of seduction, hierarchy and utility in relation to dress. Laver's concept of the shifting erogenous zone is one of his most famous but least developed theories. In essence, he argues that fashion, in its connection with sexuality whether through modesty or decoration, also tends to reveal or conceal, hide or display, a particular part of the body such as the neck, ankle, bosom or buttocks, an emphasis that also "shifts" as fashions themselves change. Thus more romantic fashions in the early nineteenth century tended to bare, and therefore emphasise, women's necks whilst in later Victorian times the tendency to cover up completely lent an eroticism to the display of merely an ankle. Similarly, in the late twentieth century, the ubiquitous emphasis on tight fitting jeans for both sexes tends to emphasize the buttocks. Laver extends this idea further to assert that there are three principles of clothing – the seduction or attraction principle where clothing is designed to attract the opposite sex (seen as the primary mechanism in women's dress), the hierarchical or status-related principle where clothing is used to signify rank or standing (see as the primary mechanism in men's dress), and the self-explanatory utility or practicality principle that he hardly considers at all. These principles are seen to relate to the need of the human race to reproduce itself and there is much echo of the evolutionary angles on fashion advanced by many early theorists of fashion, seeing it as at once a throwback to, and advancement from, primitive or savage cultures. Apart from any accusation of xenophobia or racism, the more fundamental problem here is the assertion of a completely unproven set of human needs. This rather essentialist emphasis is particularly problematic in relation to any analysis of fashion. Fashion, in its emphasis on artifice, acting out and dressing up and in its ever changing, mutating cultural relativity is perhaps one of the most socially constructed of phenomena one could consider, and is not easily reduced to fundamental needs of any kind. This tendency to reduce fashion to a series of untested foundations in early theories on fashion has much to do with the legacy of both Darwinian theory and the exponential rise of psychoanalysis, the former asserting a biological imperative and the latter a psychological one. Carter's careful consideration of fashion theories of the late nineteenth and early twentieth centuries tends to highlight this both more generally and in relation to the work of Laver where he asserts: "It is this 'rear-view' perspective on the tradition that is, in part, responsible for the inability of Laver's thought to develop" (Carter, 2003: 136). Much the same could be said of many early theories of fashion as they are products of their time rendered increasingly anachronistic by the enormity and pace of many developments in the twentieth century.

Given the clear limitations of these perspectives, it is perhaps surprising that so much mileage is still made out of such psychological theories of fashion. The reason for this lies in the secondary invocation, and constant reinvention, of an unconscious self in relation to fashion. Thus, a more controversial question concerns the notion of an *unknown* expression through dress, a thesis invoked in Alison Lurie's study of *The Language of Clothes* (1981). She starts:

> Long before I am near enough to talk to you on the street, in a meeting, or at a party, you announce your sex, age and class to me through what you are wearing – and very possibly give me important information

(or misinformation) as to your occupation, origin, personality, opinions, tastes, sexual desires and current mood.

(Lurie, 1981: 3)

This statement then sets up the framework for the whole of the analysis that follows, an assumption that "the clothes maketh the person" and must signify something, if not everything, that constitutes them. Whilst there is some evidence for the notion that we dress to display ourselves and our personalities, there is also a constant sense of slithering into essentialism that undermines this argument – the idea that a piece of clothing or adornment must necessarily and intrinsically *mean* something or, more insidiously, *reveal* something of our *true* selves. This sense of lurking unconscious drives that we cannot necessarily control ourselves, or even know, yet which give off signals to outsiders, is never very far away in Lurie's detailed discussion of how fashion reflects youth, age, time, space, opinion, personality and sexuality. She even analyses, using physiological evidence, the significance and effects of colour. It is also often a seductive analysis as she writes fluently and perceptively. For example, she highlights how many more casual styles of contemporary culture rely on physical perfection with effects that undermine more traditional notions of masculinity:

The unathletic white-collar male who affects such styles, however, is taking a risk: presently, he may find himself looking remarkably feeble and podgy in his tight designer jeans and sport shirt while he (and if he is really unlucky, his girl-friend) wait for some trim, well-built auto-mechanic to diagnose his engine trouble.

(Lurie, 1981: 142)

Her ability to bulldoze the pretence of fashion and expose the strong sense of unease that underlies it is unquestionable, but it remains a problematic analysis on two primary counts. In the first instance, the emphasis on essentialist notions of dress, whilst not intrinsically disastrous, leads to an undermining of the contradiction, play and complicity that make up the interpretation of dress; and second, the stress on individual personality exposes a seriously asocial level to her analysis that underestimates the importance of wider economic or political implications. Her approach to punk, whilst novel, is a primary example. She writes: "At the same time, other aspects of the Punk Look appealed not only for attention, but for the love and care that we give to very small children, especially injured ones" (Lurie, 1981: 163). Safety pins and tufts of hair are a particular target here, whilst the far wider aspects of punk, if contentious, are left out completely. Wilson (1985) has called this intense attention to personality a kind of "psycho-functionalism" as it ultimately asserts that clothes perform functions of fulfilling psychological and intrinsic needs.

The tendency of many more psychological studies of fashion to impute an essential self is explicated most directly, and indeed has some of its origins in, Edward Sapir's short essay on fashion published in the *Encyclopaedia of the Social Sciences* in the early 1930s (Sapir, 1931). In a somewhat bad tempered and polemical piece, Sapir asserts that there are "fundamental drives" (140) or what he later calls "psychological laws" (143) of fashion. In modern society he argues the strongest of these is boredom "powerfully reinforced by a ceaseless desire to add to the attractiveness of the self and all other objects of love and friendship" (140). A second factor here, strongly linked to Simmel's analysis outlined earlier, is "the more vulgar desire for prestige or notoriety" (130). He then goes on to locate rather wider historical factors in the formation of modern fashion, setting up a tension between more essentialist, or driven and unconscious, and more constructed, or culturally relative and dynamic, elements in his analysis. However, this tension is clearly of little concern to him, at least when discussing the tendency to equate fashion with women and femininity rather than men and masculinity as in some preceding periods, arguing "Whether biology or history is primarily responsible for this need not be decided" (142). Such dismissals tend to perpetuate the strong sense of contradiction of such analyses with another common, or even primary, conception of fashion, namely that it is dressing up, acting out (a masquerade), playing at something not real at all, fooling or even tricking the onlooker. Such an approach implies that fashion, far from revealing truths, manipulates or even conceals them, whether consciously or unconsciously it makes little difference. What unites these apparently opposed perspectives, however, is the invocation of an essential self, whether revealed or concealed and with or without conscious intention. The stronger contrast here is with the concept of performance – the idea that fashion is always somehow play-acting, that it cannot tell truths – dressing is *de facto* dressing up. Such ideas often inform more postmodern theories that we will consider shortly.

Another key dimension of much psychological work on fashion is that it sees clothing, dress and adornment as forms of communication. For example, Alison Lurie states "we can lie in the language of dress, or try to tell the truth; but unless we are naked and bad it is impossible to be silent" (Lurie, 1981: 261).

Whilst such an analysis can easily lead to crude invocations of essentialism it can also form the foundation for a more semiotic analysis of dress. The analysis of the semiotics of dress and appearance is what inspires Roland Barthes's famous study of *The Fashion System* (1985). The fashion system is not, as one might assume, an economic or social system, rather "fashion is entirely a system of signs" (Barthes, 1985: 244). Barthes' path-breaking analysis contrasts "written clothing", or fashion as linguistic text, with the convention of "image clothing", or fashion as visual representation, neither of which is "real" clothing in the sense of the clothes we actually wear. Within this there is a series of "shifters' or linguistic devices that cause a transfer of meaning from one fashion system to another. This is an important set of insights that have had much influence over the analysis of fashion since. In particular, Barthes' work sets up many of the parameters for studies of fashion and dress within cultural studies that have developed since. However, it also tends to define its limits and pitfalls, as what ensues is an intense and serious analysis of the semiotics of fashion, so complex it is difficult for many to decipher and so conceptually advanced it removes fashion almost entirely from its more economic or political, if not more sociolinguistic, context. Ultimately *The Fashion System* can be said to constitute a study of semiotic methodology rather than an analysis of the full complexity of the production and consumption of fashion.

Joanne Finkelstein in *The Fashioned Self* has produced what is at once a more complete psychologically driven analysis of fashion, and its most severe critique (Finkelstein, 1991). Her central concern is with the conflation of reality and appearance through fashion leading on to the perpetuation of a myth that appearances "mean something" and are constitutive of character or personality. She focuses on the increasing concern with physique, fashion and appearance in the twentieth century, saying:

> This suggests that the perpetual conspiracy which allows the artificial complexion and body shape to be seen as a natural representation of character, and the fashioned styles of beauty to be accepted as expression of human sensibility, remains as convincing as ever.
>
> (Finkelstein, 1991: 3)

In so doing, she runs contrary to Lurie's analysis of visual linguistics in asserting forcefully that "the self has become a mass-produced, market product; buy this in order to be that" (Finkelstein, 1991: 172). The book is structured into three parts: the first considering the relationship of physiognomy and psychology within historical and more contemporary frameworks, the second conducting an analysis through case studies such as the face lift or the neck tie, and the third analysing the overall relationship between fashion, society and the self. Underlying this is a severe critique of fashion as communication thesis, not simply because that communication breaks down but because we assume, wrongly in her opinion, that fashion communicates at all and in particular that it communicates the self. Consequently she argues:

> Fashion has become a major source of personal identification; in effect, this has meant that we have learned to value the image of how we appear to be, how we are styled. This is fashioned self.
>
> (Finkelstein, 1991: 146)

She repeatedly returns to the role of the fashion industry, the media and the market in reproducing and reinforcing this sense of appearance as identity and clearly implicates the rise of visual cultures more widely as profoundly nefarious in constructing what is essentially a false notion of self:

> The sign, the fashion, the new, the well-presented, have become so distracting, so successfully deflecting of curiosity and the capacity for critique, that we accept the surface of it as if it were all there was.
>
> (Finkelstein, 1991: 193)

What Finkelstein's work fails to resolve is that if the commercially produced self is somehow false then what is real or true? We are returned once again to the tensions of essentialism and constructionism in understanding the relationship between fashion and the self. Does fashion communicate, mask or reveal the self or merely construct it as a passing artifice? This is a question Finkelstein never quite answers, given her indictment of contemporary consumer culture:

> It is the argument of this book that as long as we continue to value physical appearances, and sustain the enormous industries which trade on this value, namely, the consumer-oriented cosmetic, fashion and therapeutic industries, we authenticate a narrative of human character which is spurious.
>
> (Finkelstein, 1991: 12)

What exactly is spurious here and why? It is perhaps more accurate to see fashion as a contradictory phenomenon that express both artifice *and* essence, surface *and* depth, appearance *and* reality, not one or the other. Finkelstein's work is uneasily and, on occasions, contradictorily located into a social and psychological framework that incorporates some of the ideas of Elias, as the formation of modern men's tailoring, in particular, is seen as an example of the "civilizing process". Whilst such analysis produces insights into the gendered use of dress and shape (for example in the case of shoulder pads, which in the 1940s were used to heighten a man's stature and yet emphasise a woman's waistline, therefore differentiating genders with the same product), there is, in common with similar semi-functionalist accounts of fashion, a tendency to over-simplify the complexities of the relationship between the production and consumption of fashion.

Malcolm Barnard also attempts to re-evaluate the psycho-linguistic aspects of dress in *Fashion as Communication* (Barnard, 1996). In what is part textbook and part critique, he traces the etymology of fashion and analyses the various theories used to explain its importance, including more functionalist and semiotic approaches. He draws some inspiration from more postmodern approaches in explaining the often dual, if not contradictory, nature of fashion. In particular, he adopts Derrida's notion of undecidability in showing how dress constantly creates and destroys meaning, making it simultaneously meaningful and meaningless and infinitely dynamic. A clear difficulty he recognises here, though, is the slippage from dress as function to fashion, as contested meaning and interpretation, although he disputes the ease of the distinction. Underpinning all of this is an equally dualist focus: first, his assertion that fashion remains an important and worthy topic for analysis and second, his contention that most of the more famous attempts to explain that importance, from Flügel to Simmel and from Barthes to Baudrillard, are too simplistic. Consequently, fashion remains quite resolutely un-categoric in any sense and entirely context-dependent, for its meaning is constantly shifting from display to concealment, from modesty to seduction and from individuality to sociality, with the one polarity perpetually dependent upon the other. It is perhaps arguable however that Barnard, in nonetheless asserting that fashion must communicate something, is still wrestling with the essentialism that underpins that assumption. To put it more simply, the truer undecidability of fashion is not between it meaning this or that but between it meaning something and not meaning anything at all. It is this problem of meaning that also underpins the symbolic interactionist perspective on fashion.

The symbolic interactionist perspective (fashion as ambivalence)

What might be called the symbolic interactionist perspective on fashion develops, at least in the first instance, as a response to Simmel's famous essay on fashion outlined earlier. Of central importance within this is the work of Herbert Blumer who, following his participation in the Chicago school of sociology became a forerunning proponent of symbolic interactionist theory more widely. Whilst it is well beyond the scope of this book, let alone this chapter, to explicate the theory fully, symbolic interactionism broadly states that society evolves out of the interactions of individuals and groups and how such processes then start to constitute an on-going consensus and mode of living. As such it embraces both a grounded approach to social analysis and a rejection of the imposition of abstract structures and systems, whether from above or below (tendencies it argues that are demonstrated in both the functionalist and Marxist theory that preceded it). It also places an emphasis upon the changeability and interpretation rather than fixity of meaning. As such it is easy to see its application to the ever changing and apparently rather diffuse world of fashion. Blumer's article *Fashion: From Class Differentiation to Collective Selection* is, in the first instance "an invitation to sociologists to take seriously the topic of fashion" (Blumer, 1969: 275). Blumer criticises what he sees as the tendency of sociology to restrict its analysis of fashion to studies of dress and adornment, to see it as socially inconsequential, and to somehow see fashion behaviour as aberrant and irrational, claims which he rejects in their entirety. His other key source of opposition is to Simmel's work, and in particular Simmel's assertion concerning fashion's inextricable connection to questions of social class, status and prestige. He argues conversely that fashion is more about what he calls "collective selection" or the construction of a consensus around taste that then determines what is in or out of fashion. In this sense, his work foreruns with some significance that of Bourdieu but, unlike Bourdieu, Blumer resists any tendency to return questions of fashion to questions of class:

> The fashion mechanism appears not in response to a need of class differentiation and class emulation but in response to a wish to be in fashion, to be abreast of what has good standing, to express new tastes which are emerging in a changing world.
>
> (Blumer, 1969: 282)

In the final, and more contorted, section, he also outlines what he sees as the conditions of fashion and further explores the connection of fashion with modernity:

> These conditions – the pressure to change, the open doors to innovation, the inadequacy of decisive tests of the merit of proposed models, the effort of prestigeful figures to gain or maintain standing in the face of developments to which they must respond, and the groping of people for a satisfactory expression of new and vague tastes – entrench fashion as a basic and widespread process in modern life.
>
> (Blumer, 1969: 288)

As such, Blumer attempts to lay the foundations for the sociological significance of fashion whilst simultaneously setting out the main tenets of a more symbolic interactionist approach to it. What is more lacking is a thorough-going investigation of its applications to the worlds of dress and adornment or indeed any other clearly defined area.

Of some significance in this regard is the work of Susan Kaiser. Her ideas, along with those of her various colleagues are most fully explicated in a three part series of articles published in the *Clothing and Textiles Research Journal* in the mid 1990s and then spelt out in a more basic form in Kaiser's textbook on the social psychology of fashion (Kaiser, 1997). Kaiser, Nagasawa and Hutton's starting point is the question of fashion's relationship to social change:

> Fashion is a dynamic phenomenon that inextricably links aesthetics, culture, economics, and everyday social life. By its very nature and through its own impetus, fashion signifies change.
>
> (Kaiser, Nagasawa and Hutton, 1995: 172)

The thrust of their analysis is twofold: first, to provide an explanation of how and why fashions change; and second, to plug the perceived gap between more macro and micro perspectives on fashion. Here they draw the work of Blumer on collective selection, Davis on identity and ambivalence, and Stone on appearance and symbolic ambiguity to construct a series of fundamentals or principles that form the basis for a symbolic interactionist theory of fashion. These five principle are as follows: first the principle of human ambivalence or the assertion that human experience expresses a fundamental series of ambivalences and anxieties concerning a series of binary tensions, such as masculinity and femininity, youth and age; second the principle of appearance-modifying commodities in the capitalist marketplace or the development and perpetuation of a series of markets for goods that modify appearance, from clothes and jewellery through to creams and hair stylers, which express this ambivalence; third, the principle of symbolic ambiguity whereby the appearance modifications adopted by consumers express both their own personal and wider social patterns of ambivalence; fourth the principle of meaning negotiation and style adoption whereby patterns of ambivalence are collectively negotiated through group interaction; and fifth the principle of an ongoing dialectic whereby unresolved ambivalences fuel wider processes of social and stylistic change or fashions *per se*. It is arguable that these principles constitute foundation enough for building a wider symbolic interactionist theory of fashion. However, Kaiser and her colleagues then proceed to map these processes onto a wider question of social contexts or, more particularly, the rise of postmodernity. Here the five principles are reworked slightly according to the fairly clear assumption that postmodernity, as explicated in the work of Featherstone, Friedman and Kellner, to all intents and purposes intensifies, exacerbates or simply speeds up the principles in question. For reasons unknown, in the second part of the series, this then leads not to a working through of examples but to an attempt to extrapolate a wider theoretical synthesis and formalisation of the ideas employed in order to establish some kind of underlying logic to the theory proposed. This tendency to try and produce a formalised *model* of fashion change is then recapitulated in the final part of the series which directly attempts to apply the model of scientific inquiry to the theory proposed in part one.

The Kaiser, Nagasawa and Hutton model raises a number of concerns both internal and external to the theory. In the first instance, the attempt to form a symbolic interactionist model of fashion makes some sense given the primarily symbolic and dynamic aspects of dress and style. This does start to unravel however given the interdisciplinary focus of the analysis that draws on diverse strands of theory from symbolic interaction, scientific models, cognitive psychology, sociology and postmodern theory that do not necessarily fit well together when analysed fully. In particular the phenomenological emphasis of most symbolic interactionist theory that stresses the importance of fluidity of meaning and interpretation does not sit well with the more fixed positivist emphasis of either cognitive behaviourism or scientific method. A broader point is that the model is also almost entirely focused on fashion as a phenomenon of style and change rather than on the specifics of dress and adornment. As stated in Chapter 1, any theory that tends to overemphasise the importance of either aspect runs the risk of being one-sided or incomplete, particularly when accounting for the more psychological aspects of fashion which the model attempts to address. The tendency to try to provide a formalisation of the theory rather than an empirical demonstration is also problematic – the two very brief case studies of adolescent dress, particularly teenage girls' tendency to experiment, and men's business suits, are underworked in the extreme and used to demonstrate little more than an expression of ambivalence in the first case and repressing it in the second.

In addition, two responses in the *Clothing and Textiles Research Journal* highlight further concerns. Rita Kean makes the important point that fashion change is as much as anything else motivated both by producers in order to stimulate demand and also by shifts and developments in technology (Kean, 1997). Furthermore, the expansion of globalisation has highlighted the importance of power. Power and inequality are factors traditionally poorly explained in symbolic interactionist theory. Put crudely meanings are sometimes imposed by powerful groups on others – in this case multinational fashion companies and retailers increasingly driven by economies of scale and facilitated by technological developments can forcibly resolve consumer ambivalence through advertising and similar strategies. Kean also develops a schematic model of how this may apply to the fashion industry where buyers and retail consortiums are often powerful players and the individual consumer is often powerless and left with little more than a desire to assert their individuality in whatever way they can.

Pannabecker (1997) in an article on fashion theory more generally asserts that the Kaiser, Nagasawa and Hutton model underplays the importance of history and sees fashion changes at the expense of fashion continuities. She is also critical of their formalist stance when a more interpretive or narrative approach to fashion would be more appropriate. These are telling commentaries that reveal much weakness not so much in interactionist approaches to fashion but the overly simplistic welding of such a tradition of theory to formalised cognitive behaviour models. To put it more simply, much of the importance, and appeal, of fashion is that it is *not* rational and does *not* accord with any formalised logic of social change but is messy, subjective and constantly contradicting itself. It is perhaps this sense of the complexity and contradictions of fashion that underpins the development of more overtly sociological perspectives and their use of the wider concept of modernity.

Sociology and modernity (fashion as contradiction)

Fashion is modernist irony.

(Wilson, 1985: 15)

The most sociological of perspectives on the development of fashion seeks to undermine the determinism implicit equally in economic and psychological perspectives via the more open concepts of modernity and postmodernity. There is an immediate difficulty in defining these terms. At its most concrete, the sociology of fashion opens up to scrutiny and relevance a whole series of social and political, as well as economic, developments that characterise the twentieth century. These include: consumerism, individualism and the development of lifestyles around sport and leisure, as well as mass production, the media and the city, as central in creating openings for the fashion industry. As a result, it is argued that: "the word 'modernity' attempts to capture the essence of both the cultural and subjective experience of capitalist society and all its contradictions" (Wilson, 1985: 63).

In what remains one of the best, if albeit slightly dated, books on fashion entitled *Adorned in Dreams: Fashion and Modernity*, Elizabeth Wilson interrogates the significance of modernity in relation to fashion (Wilson, 1985). She sees fashion as embracing "a triple ambiguity" inherent within modernity: first, in its relationship to capitalism as the maker of dreams and nightmares, wealth and squalor, creativity and waste; second, in its connection with the contradictions of identity, the self and society expressing simultaneously individuality and sociality, the natural and the constructed, the magical and the mechanical; and third, through its interrelationship with art and artistic development where under modernism the very purpose of art comes into question (Wilson, 1985: 14). The clear danger here lies in the reification of the concept of modernity itself, in reality merely a shorthand term for a series of mammoth developments including industrialisation and capitalism, urbanisation and city life, the Enlightenment and secularisation, individualism and identity, and popular and consumer cultures. Modernity itself becomes an object reality that has the capacity to explain the importance of fashion when it truly only relates to a series of complex developments far less simply.

However, it is pointed out more concretely that many of the stylistic developments in fashion have accompanied similar developments in the world of art itself in making shape, colour and design into new constructions. In this sense, the society-level notion of moder*nity* is very much interconnected with the stylistic development of moder*nism*, and fashion as a phenomenon of style and design and as communicator of social change clearly relates to each equally. Anne Hollander in *Seeing Through Clothes,* for example, argues that fashion has followed traditions in figurative art in terms of form and design; whilst Wilson makes similar claims in *Adorned in Dreams* that modern fashion has echoed the forms of modern art (Hollander, 1988; Wilson, 1985).

The primary importance of the concept of modernity, though, is its capacity to capture the contradictory and dynamic nature of the fashion phenomenon: the restless and dissatisfied desire for something new that permeates and underpins many forms of modern industrial capitalism. Wilson writes:

> Yet the word "modernity" attempts to capture the essence of both the cultural and the subjective experience of capitalist society and all its contradictions. It encapsulates the way in which economic development opens up, yet simultaneously undercuts the possibility both of individual, self development and of social cooperation. "Modernity" does also seem useful as a way of indicating the restless desire for change characteristic of cultural life in industrial capitalism, the desire for the new that fashion expresses so well.
>
> (Wilson, 1985: 63)

Thus, in one sense, the concept of modernity is far more accurate as a *description* of the practice of fashion and yet this is precisely its weakness, its lack of more *explanatory* power. The concept of modernity expresses much, yet explains very little. And rather like fashion itself, one needs the twin elements of the social and the artistic, modernity and modernism, to make much purchase on what Wilson calls "the enigma of its Mona Lisa smile" (Wilson, 1985: 247).

One variation on the theme of fashion and modernity comes in the work of Entwistle (Entwistle, 2000). In what is part monograph and part review, Entwistle is deeply critical of much of the prevailing literature on fashion at a more theoretical level. Her book *The Fashioned Body* makes the obvious but important point that fashion and dress are, in many ways, about the body:

> Fashion is about bodies: it is produced, promoted and worn by bodies. It is the body that fashion speaks to and it is the body that must be dressed in almost all social encounters.
>
> (Entwistle, 2000: 1)

The critical point here, to paraphrase Chris Shilling, is that if the body constitutes an "absent presence" within sociology it becomes near ghost-like within the study of fashion – a point rather poetically put by Elizabeth Wilson in her observation of mannequins in museums of costume – what she calls the "dusty silence" that besets the living observer moving through cabinets and stands of dummies dressed in clothes that once rushed through streets or danced through halls on living bodies (Shilling, 1993; Wilson, 1985: 1). Indeed, clothing and jewellery are often some of the most touching – and painful – reminders of those we have lost, not easily discarded when someone dies or departs. Similarly, clothing in particular is often rather meaningless when hanging on rails and piled on shelves in shops. Despite the very clear seduction of advertising and branding it is the imagining of what something is like to *wear* that really gets the pulse racing. It is this touchy, feely, experiential and subjective dimension of dressing that is often so grossly neglected within more sociological accounts of fashion in particular. As Entwistle notes there is strong tendency to render fashion an "abstract system" in need of explanation for its "mysterious movements' (Entwistle, 2000: 3). As she also aptly perceives, this has much to do with the distinction between fashion and dress; and social scientists, with the exception of those conducting empirical case studies under the auspices of anthropology, hardly ever discuss dress at all. Indeed much of the work surveyed in this chapter so far says nothing about clothes whilst discussing fashion, as a phenomenon of style and social change, *ad nauseam*. Entwistle's proposed solution to this problem or conundrum is to attempt to amalgamate a sociology of embodiment, as developed through the work of Foucault, Bourdieu and Merleau-Ponty with an analysis of fashion. Thus Foucault's ideas of knowledge, power and inscription on the body become transcribed into "discourses of dress", increasingly perpetuated and reinforced in more contemporary society by Bourdieu's concept of cultural intermediaries such as designers and magazine editors, and then absorbed into Merleau-Ponty's analysis of space and perception and adopted to varying degrees by real people who adorn and dress their bodies in all sorts of ways. This she calls "situated bodily practice" or the process by which fashion, the abstract entity dreamed up and promoted by designers, manufacturers and retailers becomes dress or the clothes and accessories worn by regular men and women. The problem here is twofold: first, Entwistle's work is more critique and prescript for future research rather than an explication of how such connections work either theoretically or empirically; and second, her attempt to simply pool together the discursive (Foucault) with the socio-structural (Bourdieu) with the phenomenological (Merleau-Ponty) is underdeveloped and she tends to end up muddying the waters rather than clearing them. It's tempting to await a sequel.

In addition, the concept of postmodernity has rapidly overtaken that of modernity as a descriptive, and perhaps also more explanatory, tool in analysing the system of fashion, a question to which I now turn. There is no one theory of postmodernity and it is not my intention to provide a definitive account of its importance. Nonetheless, there is a sense in which the concept and theories applied to it have increased in their significance for the study of fashion and society more widely. The immediate difficulty lies in the definition of the term and it is first of all necessary to separate the notion of postmodernism, as a series of artistic and stylistic developments in the arts, literature and architecture, from postmodernity, or the more social, economic and sometimes political terms used to understand and/or explain developments in society during the twentieth century and particularly since the Second World War.

However, additional difficulties are encountered in relation to the question of whether the theory of postmodernity is necessarily also tied up with either postindustrial theory, primarily an economic perspective emphasising the importance of multinational corporatism and the separation of ownership and control, or poststructural theory, which seeks to implode the division of action and structure often through the concept and practice of discourse. It is my concern here, therefore, to consider the theory of postmodernity primarily in relation to the study of fashion and not in relation to wider questions of social theory.

There is, as yet, no single full-length study of the significance of fashion and postmodernity and, similarly no theory of the importance of postmodernity to the study of fashion. However, numerous contemporary theorists have used fashion as an example to highlight specific aspects of their theories, and it is easy to extrapolate the importance of central concepts to the study of fashion. The primary application of postmodernity theory to the study of fashion comes through its analysis of the concept and practice of consumer society. Postmodernity theory primarily assumes that consumerism, as concept and practice, acquires increased significance under conditions of what is sometimes called "late" or "high" capitalism. It is asserted that, in particular, people spend increasing degrees of time consuming as opposed to producing, and that these activities therefore come to gain added significance in the formation of their individual and group identities. As dress constitutes a significant and visual factor in the formation of individual and group identities, there is a clear conflation of fashion and consumption that is potentially self-perpetuating in its importance. This accounts partly for the primacy of fashion as an example of the excesses of consumer society under conditions of postmodernity. At a more commonsense level, the high cost, high turnover world of haute couture also illustrates the nature of postmodernity itself, in its heightening of the importance of representation and appearance to the construction of personal identity (see, for example, Faurschou, 1988).

There are similar applications of the concepts of commodification and signification to the study of fashion. Commodification refers to the increasing involvement of goods, services and indeed everyday life in processes of advertising, promotion and monetary exchange. The privatisation of health, education and transport are examples of this process, as are many leisure activities and the explosion of financial services for every real, and imagined, need and anxiety. Signification refers to the process of increasing importance of social, symbolic and representational value applied to commodities and indeed all aspects of everyday life. The logos and design cultures of the 1980s are key here as well as advertising and the sometimes ludicrous status values attached to goods – Levi's "original" 501 jeans, "it's a Sony" stereos and BMW's "ultimate driving machine" exemplify this process.

Similarly, for Jean Baudrillard, dress and fashion form primary examples of the "commodity sign", as an axiom of where the processes of commodification and signification come together (Baudrillard, 1983). His secondary argument, that the sign value is increasingly autonomous of the commodity value, is also highlighted in the ludicrous costs of haute couture, as is the desire for authenticity in the construction of "classics" and individual designer styles differentiated from their imitators. More importantly, this also ties up with wider societal processes of "reproduction", "simulation" and their implied impacts of uncertainty and confusion of social values as the significance of fashion and dress is seen as increasingly out of control and anarchic. The processes of reproduction and simulation refer, in particular, to the importance of the media and similar visual cultures in representing goods so effectively that their simulations, or visual representations, gain greater significance or status than the goods or services themselves. Moreover, this is then seen to lead to increasing confusion and uncertainty concerning what is real or authentic, in turn rocking the foundations of tradition and social values; a vision which, in its most extreme form, is almost apocalyptic.

For Fredric Jameson, there are similarly applications of postmodernity theory to the study of fashion in terms of the concept of "depthless culture", for the fascination of fashion is often the fascination of surfaces, of reflections, of packaging and of seduction (Jameson, 1984). In addition, for some feminists, these processes have had more positive consequences and led to the disruption of gendered traditions in fashion as "the dichotomy whereby fashion is identified with women and oppositional style with masculine subcultures was erased in postmodern fashion" (Evans and Thornton, 1989: 74). These are, however, questions to which I wish to give additional consideration in Chapter 4.

The ultimate application of the theory of postmodernity to the study of fashion comes in the work of the Krokers, whose analysis of everything from Eurythmics videos to Calvin Klein advertising teeters on self-parody:

> Indeed, if fashion cycles now appear to oscillate with greater and greater speed, frenzy and intensity of circulation of all the signs, that is because fashion, in an era when the body is the inscribed surface of events, is like Brownian motion in physics: the greater the velocity and circulation of its surface features, the greater the internal movement towards stasis, immobility, and inertia.
>
> (Kroker and Kroker, 1988: 45)

The implicit nihilism of this statement brings us neatly back in full postmodern circle to Baudrillard, but the irony of all these studies is that none actually ranks as a serious and detailed consideration of fashion itself – which returns us, once again, to the more classical tradition of fashion analysis.

Conclusions: the classical tradition

During this chapter, I have attempted to document and unpack the formation of what I have called a "classical tradition" concerning the study of fashion, that locates the analysis of dress within the context of the arts, haute couture or, most widely, modernity. The theory of postmodernity has done much to disrupt this perspective on fashion and yet provides a very fragmented set of insights into its more contemporary significance.

The concentration on men's dress or menswear in all of the aforementioned analyses of fashion is often thin. In particular, the economic perspective, whilst paying some attention to matters of gender, makes a series of serious assumptions concerning gender identity – most particularly that women are decorative and men are not – which are easily criticised and produce an essentially sexist history of *her* fashion (see also Chapter 1). The psychological perspective appears at first more fruitful, as issues of sexual identity are readily included in the psychology of fashion; yet what is not on the whole included is a consideration of the connection of gendered psychology to the wider economic or political (if not social) context. The sociological emphasis upon modernity is simultaneously the most all-encompassing and yet the least explanatory. Meanwhile, all these analyses tend to neglect the significance of dress or fashion for the *wearer* as opposed to the onlooker (Corrigan, 1993; Davis, 1992). This leads to an additional difficulty of resolving the significance of fashion for the individual with its wider social, economic or political importance. This issue is as yet unresolved, partly as a result of the lack of empirical or ethnographic – as opposed to theoretical or interpretive – study of dress and fashion.

It is arguable that all theories of fashion, early or late, are an attempt to grapple with the complexity of its meanings. I have repeatedly asserted here, as have some others, that fashion is contradictory, often oscillating between extremes on many levels: from moral censure to comedic silliness, from sociality to individuality, from modesty to seduction, from protection to display, and from the meaningful to the meaningless. Underpinning this in many ways is the very distinction between fashion and dress. Whilst dress has some kind of functional reality, however crude and simplistic that may be, fashion exists primarily as a phenomenon of social change. Early economic theories usefully highlight fashion's importance in both these senses – dress as symbol of status or rank and fashion as the mechanism that drives that along – yet become mired in over-simplifying the meanings of either as status related. Psychological perspectives attempt to find some space between the economics of fashion and the wider complexities of its meaning yet end up trapped in an essentialism of seeing fashion as the mirror of self. Symbolic interactionism attempts to break with this essentialism yet somehow ends up not really considering dress at all. Modernity as a concept and as shorthand for a series of more contemporary western empirical developments grapples most successfully with the contradictory and indeed contemporary nature of fashion yet rather loses its sense of dress in the analysis. As a way forward, then, we will consider an example of dress – the suit – and *add*ress the issue of gender in the next chapter on men's fashion.

Chapter 3

The clothes maketh the man
Masculinity, the suit and men's fashion

Fashion, it is commonly assumed, is a feminine phenomenon. It is therefore necessary to reiterate the increasingly frustrated assertion that the study of men's fashion remains secondary and indeed marginal to the analysis of women's fashion and dress. Despite the recent resurgence of interest in men's fashion, and attendant studies of it, its significance remains severely underestimated. This is mostly due, as Jennifer Craik has noted, to an historical equation of masculinity with Puritanism and restraint that reached its pinnacle of near masochistic self-control in the late nineteenth century, resulting in almost an entire disassociation of men and men's dress from the world of fashion, itself defined increasingly in primarily feminine terms (Craik, 1994). The potential impact of the near revolution in fashion in the 1980s – when "menswear" mutated into "men's fashion", and was put on display for the first time in designer catwalk collections, or hung on the shoulders of handsome young models and splashed endlessly across the pages of the new crop of style magazines for men – is easily overstated and not without precedent, yet remains significant.

The study and understanding of men's fashion across the population and academia alike is haunted by the ghost of Flügel who asserted with some aggression that men had "renounced" fashion in the early nineteenth century (Flügel, 1930). On the face of it there is some commonsense truth to this. Whilst Jane Austen's heroes such as Mr Darcy were decked out in plush velvet tail coats of many colours, silk waistcoats with frills, and figure hugging pantaloons, they became entrapped within the dull, dour and grey uniforms of the industrial revolution in a matter of decades. It is this sense of the decorous descending into dullness that has dominated understandings of men's dress for over a century, yet the evidence itself, let alone its meaning and interpretation, confounds this notion at every turn. Decorous masculinity was only truly demonstrated within a minority, namely the aristocracy, and the dull grey suit of the late nineteenth century was accompanied by city pinstripes, dashing evening dress and candy-coloured leisure wear. However, the evolution of men's dress was not uniform in any sense or any direction and it is the purpose of this chapter to capture the sense in which men's fashion did, and did not, accord to Flügel's interpretation and, if not "renounced", then shifted in its terrain of form and meaning. Central in this, even axiomatic, is the suit as the template for men's dress more widely, and the emblem of all that is loved or loathed about men's clothes. Consequently, this chapter has three sections: first, a consideration of the marginalisation of men's fashion *per se*; second, its reconsideration in the light of the increased attention to men's fashion since the 1980s; and third, a fundamental and detailed case study of the suit that in itself forms the core of this chapter and the analysis of men's dress alike.

The marginalization of men's fashion

> Women are fashionable but men are not ... Accordingly, the rhetoric of men's fashion takes the form of a set of denials that include the following propositions: that there is no men's fashion; that men dress for fit and comfort, rather than for style; that women dress men and buy clothes for men; that men who dress up are peculiar (one way or another); that men do not notice clothes; and that most men have not been duped into the endless pursuit of seasonal fads.
>
> (Craik, 1994: 176)

The study of men's fashion remains marginal, historically, to the comparative investigation of women's fashion and dress, with some exceptions (Byrde, 1979; Chenoune, 1993; Hollander, 1994; Laver, 1968, 1982; Martin and Koda, 1989). Some of this is explained as the result of a historical focus on haute couture which did not include men's dress or appearance until comparatively recently; or via the development of the women's movement and feminist analyses focused more on the importance of women's dress (Ash and Wilson, 1992; Ash and Wright, 1988; Craik, 1994; Evans and Thornton, 1989; Wilson, 1985). However, the greater explanation for this academic neglect of men's dress lies in the gendered development of fashion itself. Fashion for the past 150 years at least was, and often still is, seen as "feminine" or "not masculine" and therefore not connected to men. Ultimately, this has meant that men themselves are simply not "in fashion", in any sense, and men's dress is seen to lie outside of fashion itself. There is a strong sense in which this is *nonsense*, for men's clothes are produced and consumed in similar ways to women's; men, as approximately 50 per cent of the population, constitute a major, if not majority, sector of the fashion and dress industries. Thus, the primary difference here is the greater sense of frivolity attached to women's fashion; yet even that is perhaps misplaced when considering men's dandyism.

Nevertheless, fashion for men is rarely taken as seriously as fashion for women, and menswear is seen primarily in terms of utility – a perspective which cannot account for the specific forms and meanings of menswear. The main example of the utility of menswear, namely the suit, is arguably as much a symbol of masculine sexuality in terms of broadening shoulders and chest as it is a practical, if sometimes uncomfortable, uniform of respectability. The predictable plethora of papers following the development and expansion of "menswear", and the phenomenon of the New Man in the 1980s in particular, served to prove the point further in showing up the lack of previous attention to men's fashion and the inadequacies of many feminist and non-feminist analyses alike. These included the crude equation of sexual objectification with women alone and a historic lack of attention to detail and nuance in men's dress (Chapman and Rutherford, 1988; Edwards, 1997; Mort, 1996). It is a central intention of this chapter, then, to "redress" this situation in providing a thorough-going investigation into the nature, consequences and causes of men's fashion, the production and consumption of men's dress, and an assessment of the impact of more contemporary developments in menswear upon men themselves and upon society as a whole.

One of the strongest assertions of the following investigation, then, is that men's fashion is indeed something to take seriously in itself, and as a microcosm of the macrocosm of men, masculinity and society. The point, put most simply, is that it is perhaps not appropriately "masculine" to take a serious interest in men's fashion. Consequently, what the study of men's fashion represents, *par excellence,* is the persistence of gendered attitudes, gendered relations and gendered stereotypes concerning men, masculinity and their place in society. Interestingly, an interest in women's fashion is seen as slightly more appropriate, given women's stereotypical role in fashion's function as display and attraction (see also Chapter 2). As a result, the constant slithering of the "not masculine" into the "effeminate" and therefore the "homosexual" is particularly apparent. The equation of fashion with the feminine, with the not masculine, with the effeminate, as well as with the homosexual, remains a chain of socially constructed and perpetuated links that are decidedly difficult to overcome.

Studies of men's dress, like most studies of fashion, have historically tended to locate themselves within the confines of design or art history. These have taken two forms: first, lavish illustrated histories of men's dress of which Farid Chenoune's *A History of Men's Fashion* is a prime example; and second, guides to style and "looking the part" of which Alan Flusser's somewhat Anglo-American oriented yet nevertheless lovingly luxurious *Dressing The Man* is a recent illustration (Chenoune, 1993; Flusser, 2002). Whilst these studies have provided excellent sources of reference for academics, lay audiences and the fashion industry alike, there are two particular difficulties: first, the lack of a more social, economic or political focus to the work has left the study of dress in an often free-floating state devoid of theory or explanation for its significance; and second, the haute couture or up-market focus of many of these works has led to an elitist stance and a neglect of high street styles and cultures.

It is perhaps, then, important to try to discern to delineate some of the most important points concerning the development of men's fashion and dress and indeed what marks men's clothing as precisely *men's* dress and not women's. These fall roughly into five areas of concern.

> There has been an affinity between the fashions of the sexes but at no time since the development of tailoring in the fourteenth century have their clothes been completely identical or interchangeable; sex has almost always been clearly differentiated by clothing.
>
> (Byrde, 1979: 11)

First, at least in developed cultures, men's dress is and always was different to women's. This may well seem a statement of commonsense, yet it makes the vitally important point that fashion and dress have performed a more or less universal function of reinforcing gender difference. Whilst the form, content and meaning of costume have varied enormously, its overt sexing of the species has not. It is particularly important to note that as the complexities of dress and tailoring have increased and advanced, so the gendered differences in dress have often inversely increased in rigidity (Craik, 1994; Finkelstein, 1991; Hollander, 1994). For example, the suit in female form becomes nipped in at the waist to highlight the bust and cut shorter in length emphasising the curve of the hips – let alone when worn with a skirt rather than trousers – whilst its male variant rarely departs from the tendency to widen shoulders, broaden the chest and to set up a phallic "now you see it, now you don't" relationship with the hips, crotch and buttocks. In pre-mercantile times, in developing societies and in some non-western societies today, the gendered differences in dress are often far less pronounced: for example, in some African and Asian cultures as well as some ethnic groups, in Greco-Roman culture and, on top of this, in prehistoric times when simple tunics, cloaks or skins were worn (Barnes and Eicher, 1992; Eicher, 1995).

The role of dress in defining the genders is most evident, then, in modern western society and particularly in the case of children who are assigned to differing genders through their dress very early on and are "dressed for sex" almost *ab ovo:* blue for a boy, pink for a girl; trousers for boys and skirts for girls. This progresses further into adulthood when dress is often used to heighten anatomical maleness in widening shoulders and chests, or to emphasise gender difference in defining legs, thighs or crotch areas. The contemporary development of the apparently gender neutral pair of jeans is an excellent example of how even the same item of clothing is used to add to gender difference through its fit alone. Consequently, the cut of jeans almost uniformly highlights the shape of the thighs and buttocks, and sometimes the genitals, thereby heightening gendered difference.

Second, changes and developments in men's costume and dress are traditionally and historically slower and fewer than those related to women. This is an important point, but one that is easily over-stressed. Whilst it is true that fashion cycles and changes in overall form were, and to a lesser extent still are, faster for women than for men, the more muted changes in decoration, detail and nuance are far more similar for each of the sexes. It is also worth pointing out that the overall form of dress since the rise of mercantile capitalism and trade has altered little for either sex, at least until the twentieth century. Western men have for centuries worn some variation on a coat or jacket, with or without a waistcoat, covering some sort of shirt and worn with hose, breeches or trousers. They have worn, and some still do, tunics or robes, but have never worn dresses or skirts apart from ceremonial dress or perhaps the kilt, which remains a national tradition rather than a fashion. High fashion's recent flirtations with the men-in-skirts theme – for example, Gaultier's designs in 1984 and Westwood's collections in the early 1990s – have remained minority concerns that have never, as yet, hit the high street. Similarly women, in western society at least, have always worn some variation on the skirt and dress theme with some form of coat for further warmth. Women in trousers, at least without tunics that cover the top, did not appear until the twentieth century very much spurred on through their roles in "men's work". Quite why this is so is uncertain, but the significance of women's roles in reproduction and child rearing and men's roles in production and work would seem to have something to do with it, as skirts have traditionally facilitated sexual and reproductive access and trousers have tended to develop as part of more active lifestyles. What is more, in this sense, dress for women has actually changed, in the longest historical view, *less* than it has for men. Most of the major changes in men's dress such as the development of the modern suit were often technologically driven, via advances in tailoring methods and the invention of the sewing machine, which Singer patented in 1851. Zakim's study of shifts in production methods for tailoring in the United States documents this importance in more detail, highlighting the rise of more standardising techniques in making men's suits (Zakim, 2009). This does not account though, as we shall see in the final section, for the specific form or meaning that men's dress takes, and less still for the variety of decoration, detail and nuance that has always added to its complexity.

Third, and more controversially, there is a certain oscillation or tension in men's dress over the centuries, which I shall call "playboy" and "puritan" tendencies and that I will explore more later. These tendencies have coexisted in the past and continue to do so in the present, yet there is an added tendency for one or the other to gain ascendancy at a specific time or place. The fancy and decorous dress of the aristocracy in the early seventeenth century under the influence of France and Louis XIV is a clear case of more narcissistic and playboy-like influences, in turn echoing the grandiose extravagance of the Renaissance, and repeated in the romanticism of the turn of the nineteenth century and the dandyism of Beau Brummell; whilst the dour and industrially driven suits of the late nineteenth century echo prior medieval and Puritan factors that carry through to commerce in contemporary society, though often coupled with a more colourful and playful approach. It is important to add that the original Puritan dress of the seventeenth century developed as an opposition to the perceived extravagance of styles from Spain and France earlier on and has coexisted with this ever since. It is also interesting to note potential ways in which such changes intersect with the nature and position of men and masculinities. It is, perhaps, no coincidence that the rise of more formal or work-related dress in the 1980s occurred under the auspices of aspirationalism, recession and unemployment. These are very complex questions, though, to which I shall return later.

Fourth, men's dress has a strong history of association with status or rank in society. This not only applies to specialist, professional or spiritual roles and uniforms, but to the overall significance of class and work in men's lives. The lavish costumes of royalty in the fifteenth, sixteenth and seventeenth centuries were transferred into complex hierarchies of tailoring from the eighteenth century onwards. This still exists now in the minutiae of detail that accompanies formal dress, which can demonstrate status through the level of expense involved, and is often intricately tied to work roles where the rules of the right suit, knot in the tie and design of the collar are often more rigid than the tightest corset. This sense of constraint is not as strong in modern western women's dress where a wider toleration of variations – even in the choice of skirts versus trousers – is easily evidenced. Heavy restrictions upon female dress are often more strongly related to religious proscriptions as in Islamic cultures. Much of this is explained, once again, not in relation to fashion *per se* but gender roles and the confinement of femininity to the private sphere and the dependence of successful masculinity upon the performing of more public functions – work, politics, sports and so on. This has often led to the idea that men's dress is interlinked with the notion of utility and its purpose is practical rather than decorative. As we have already seen, this is qualified on several counts. In the first instance, men's dress has very complex meanings and even the most stoic of uniforms is on occasions transformed into decoration and intense sexiness in certain contexts including, for example, the strong sense of glamour and eroticism associated with American GIs dressed in their crispest uniforms. More importantly, the history of men's fashion has always shown significant attention to decoration and adornment for its own sake, though this is often juxtaposed with a more puritanical or conservative sense of status and tradition. It is also uncertain whether many of the actual forms of men's dress are indeed practical or convenient, as they often tie up the male anatomy in a myriad of fastenings and padding that restricts movement, is easily soiled or is simply uncomfortable. This more problematic aspect of men's dress in fact leads onto the final point.

Fifth, and finally then, men's dress has shown its greatest advances during the twentieth century particularly in moves towards increased casualness and informality in attire that is, indeed, of more comfort and use. The rise of sweaters, shirts with fixed collars in softer materials, and a whole array of more casual trousers and jeans, as well as the widening influence of sportswear, has created a near revolution in men's clothing. Much of this development was driven by the invention and mass production of synthetic materials after the Second World War, and even by the zipper, which in the 1920s started to revolutionise the way men held up their trousers, did up their coats and even went to the lavatory. These changes have also affected women's clothes, but the effect on men, whose history of dress was one of a drive towards minimalism until after the Second World War, is perhaps more challenging. Men have only very recently experienced the range of formal and informal, coloured and varied choices that have presented themselves to at least more middle-class women for several centuries, with all that entails in terms of freedom, personal expression and etiquette. It is, however, still the case that men's dress remains far more limited in form, style and design than women's dress. The rigidity of work and leisure expectations, let alone questions of looking "masculine", still remain, as a suit and tie, for example, is still the only socially approved office and City attire, whilst chinos or jeans with an open-necked shirt and casual jacket remains a near uniform for the weekend.

Perhaps more importantly, the development of more casual attire for men with its accompanying rhetoric reflects the increasing influence of North American culture upon clothing through the twentieth century. Whilst Europe, and Spain and Italy in particular, dominated design in medieval and Renaissance dress, and the fashion houses of Paris and Milan, as well as the sartorial and street figures of England, from Armani to Hamnett and Dior to Westwood, still dominate much of haute couture, the rise of the US in manufacturing and designing casual wear from sportswear to denim, as well as haute couture at the level of Calvin Klein and Ralph Lauren, is of profound significance. Calvin Klein's name, in particular, is now almost synonymous with designer casual wear as well as the colossally successful fragrance collections. This is of particular importance to menswear, where much opposition to casual wear came from its associations of effeminacy in comparison with more formal wear – a sweater did not invoke the same sense of seriousness. Importantly, then, the physically self-conscious and sporting looks of trainers and western jeans, for example, revolutionised the means through which men could still look like "men" without a suit and tie within the space of a generation. My own father was uncomfortable without a tie unless relaxing at home and never even possessed a pair of jeans. The turning point here in most western cultures was as late as the 1970s when the influence of youth cultures, the hippie movement and the technology of man-made fibres finally moved beyond subcultures into the mainstream. It also had something to do with shifting attitudes towards gender and sexuality following the rise of second wave feminism and gay liberation. These twin turbo developments in commerce and mores are also a key point in looking at the rise of a new "fashionability" for men in the 1980s to which we now turn.

New Man dandyism: the shifting fortunes and meanings of men's fashion

Recent decades have witnessed what appears as an almost exponential increase in interest in men's appearances and, more specifically, men's relationship to fashion. Most of this interest has focused on a series of apparently unprecedented and diverse developments starting in the mid to late 1980s. These include: first, the rise of designer fashions for men and the increasing inclusion of menswear collections on the catwalk and, more specifically, the making of some designer's names – particularly Paul Smith, Calvin Klein and Giorgio Armani – through their development of men's rather than women's fashions; second, the expansion of a whole series of interrelated markets for specifically male-oriented products, particularly in the arena of cosmetics and grooming, ranging from spa treatments to moisturisers and from aftershaves to hair styling, that have grown exponentially into international industries; third, the meteoric rise of self-conscious and glossy lifestyle magazine titles such as GQ, Arena and FHM aimed directly at men as consumers particularly in the UK and increasingly worldwide; fourth, the simultaneous increase in advertising targeting men as opposed to women of which the Bartle, Bogle and Hegarty "bath" and "launderette" commercials for Levi's 501 jeans remain prime examples; and fifth, the sense in which all of these developments increasingly constructed men as the objects of consumer desire, sometimes in blatantly sexual ways, as in the expansion of pornography aimed at women, the rise of male strippers such as the Chippendales, and the near endless parade of pictures of men with their shirts off, most particularly Spencer Rowell's "L'Enfant" photograph of a man holding a baby for the poster chain Athena. The "New Man" became a media driven shorthand for all of these developments that simultaneously encompassed an emphasis on narcissism and self-consciousness on the one hand with a concern around sexual politics and what all this meant for feminism on other.

From this distinctly mixed if not necessarily contradictory set of developments certain themes started to develop more academically. In Rowena Chapman and Jonathan Rutherford's pioneering, if eclectic, collection *Male Order*, the question of men's relationship to narcissistic consumption was raised primarily in terms of its impact upon sexual politics and framed in terms of its consequences for feminism (Chapman and Rutherford, 1988). Whilst the authors clearly differed in their opinions, the overall conclusion was that the aforementioned developments did not amount to some kind of sexual revolution. In particular, much work journalistically and academically concluded that what was witnessed in the 1980s were the same old wolves in designer clothing (Savage, 1996). More critically, these perspectives also tended to slide over the underlying causes and extensive consequences of the reconstruction of a new kind of narcissistic masculinity. In particular, some feminists questioned the extent to which the new man in designer clothing meant anything new at all in terms of sexual politics or just more competition for the use of cosmetics and toiletries (Moore, 1988). More seriously, some saw the rise of narcissistic masculinity as a defensive reaction against women, in increasingly asserting men's power visually and physically as a response to its increasingly precarious state socially and politically (Chapman, 1988a). Many of these claims were overstated as the majority of men practising the new narcissism were precisely those in *least* threat from feminism, operating in male-dominated professions and commanding huge economic privileges.

Later work tended to raise a different set of concerns more related to the question of the reconstruction of masculinity through consumption primarily for men themselves. Most of this work has tended to stress the significance of a series of increasingly plural and visual codes around masculinity where men are encouraged to engage with other men as consumers of style, whether in terms of a presentation of self, in terms of cuts of suits and logos on trainers or more widely in terms of their consumption of commodities such as cars, hi-fis, holidays and overall lifestyles. In particular, Frank Mort constructed an analysis that emphasised such developments as part of a wider cultural history. His work focused on perhaps an overly extensive array of shifting "narratives" around the sexual politics of style and fashion, the discourses of consumerism and advertising, and the role of space and place – particularly London – in considering all manner of factors, from gay culture to journalistic entrepreneurialism, and from Burtons in the 1950s to Next in the 1980s (Mort, 1996). Similarly, Sean Nixon equally stressed the visual significance of these patterns of consumption in shifting the male gaze from women to other men mostly through advertising and men's style magazines (Nixon, 1996). The primary thrust of these analyses was to highlight the supposed pluralism of identities and shifting terrains of masculinity away from more traditional models of conservatism and restraint towards something more consumerist and playful. As I have written previously, much of this was grossly overstated, neglecting the significance of quite specific demographic and geographic factors alongside an increasing sense of social divisiveness between those who were "in" and those who were "out" (Edwards, 1997). Whilst the miscellany of stores, products and services aimed at men had much importance for, and perhaps much impact upon, younger, single or city-dwelling men, many who were older, married or living in rural areas were effectively excluded.

More recently the emphasis has tended to shift towards the study of men's lifestyle magazines as a more empirical source of analysis of shifts in sexual politics, particularly in the wake of the New Man's apparent displacement by the anti-feminist beer swilling, pornography and football watching New Lad (Benwell, 2003; Jackson *et al.*, 2001; Osgerby, 2001). Again here opinion has tended to be divided, some sensing a degree of knowing irony or ambivalence in such developments whilst others, often more specifically feminist in outlook, have seen the New Lad as simply anti-women (Benwell, 2003; Greer, 2000; Whelehan, 2000). The difficulty here as elsewhere has been the lack of much empiricism either way and the tendency to "read off" meaning from magazines as unproblematic often muddling questions of production and intention (content analyses) with their consumption (men themselves), two factors that are often neither as simple as made out nor the same as each other. The one exception here was Jackson's study of men's consumption of lifestyle magazines, particularly the more "laddish" titles such as Loaded and FHM, that revealed a surprising degree of complexity of lay interpretations often pigeonholed into the author's attempts to critique other more content driven analyses (Jackson *et al.*, 2001).

Over 20 years since its inception, then, we are still left with the question of what this apparently meteoric rise of men's interest in their appearance actually *means*. There are ultimately only really three answers here: first, that men have responded to a crisis in their own masculinity, that crisis in itself partly forming a response to second wave feminism and women's increasing autonomy and partly centring on the decline of manufacturing and "real men's" or *man*ual work; second, that definitions of successful masculinity have shifted following a wider decline in the stigma attached to effeminacy itself following a greater acceptance of gay sexuality or, more widely, a blurring of the boundary of what constitutes gay and straight masculinities; or third, that these are primarily commercial developments that target men as the wealthier gender and attempt to make money out of men's concerns with their appearance alongside women's. There is some credence and evidence to support all these answers and ultimately much interrelationship of these three elements.

Perhaps more importantly, the "masculinity in crisis" thesis has come in for some severe criticism as anti-feminist in itself (Connell, 1995; Kimmel, 1987). There has also been some linkage here with the backlash against "men's movements" such as those promoted by Robert Bly in his book *Iron John*, seen by many more pro-feminist men as anti-women (Bly, 1991). As I have stated elsewhere, it is more simply overstated, as not all men have been affected by shifts in production or sexual politics equally, and the thesis also constantly muddles and conflates concerns with problems for men themselves (loss of power, confusion, competition with women) with an overall crisis of masculinity (definitions of success, uncertainties in identity, loss of traditional male values or roles) neither of which is a uniform phenomenon (Edwards, 2006).

Perhaps the more complex and immeasurable issue has been the blurring of gay and straight masculinities. Whilst following the Second World War the equation of effeminacy with homosexuality was relatively unproblematic, the rise of both an overtly "masculine" gay subculture and more positive image of gay sexuality, coupled with a growing acceptance of straight male grooming practices has led to some implosion of the boundary between the two to the point where it has now – as it were – become difficult to tell one from the other. The matter has become further complicated by the rise of "metrosexual" masculinities – a term first coined by journalist and critic Mark Simpson to connote a particularly metropolitan display of sexuality and interest in appearance that was neither "gay" nor "straight", but something more in its own right, which has now collapsed into "straight men who look gay" aka "the David Beckham effect" (Simpson, 1996). Simpson's work was sharply observed if not particularly well theorised and it is difficult to dispute that such self-presentations exist; much, as Mort and Nixon have pointed out, depends on shifts in the *way* men look at each other primarily as consumers of style (Mort, 1996; Nixon, 1996). Counteracting this, though, is a long tradition of male peacocks displaying their finery to attract female mates as well as the more contemporary example of the rapaciously heterosexual New Lad. Consequently, men's looking at other men as consumers and practitioners of style has as much, if not more, to do with heterosexual competition than homosexual desire – though one can never be sure. Also there *are* still limits here – men do not wear high heels, makeup or skirts – and those who do "have a go" either risk ridicule or are not "regular Joes" (pop stars, sportsmen, celebrities) or are openly gay anyway. The degree of outcry that ensues when men cross certain invisible boundaries, for example the pillorying of David Beckham for wearing a sarong or the current unease that surrounds men's use of hair straighteners, still testifies to the ongoing existence of the boundary itself. Furthermore, whilst male fashions have diversified massively in recent decades, certain defined limits and differences remain – men may well wear pink shirts but they will not wear pink coats and shoes to match, embroidery and embellishment remain primarily a female preserve, and fabrics such as silk and velvet tend again to get used as pieces and not as entire outfits.

What *is* unequivocally the case in all of this, however, is the money involved. Gyms, grooming products and men-only fashions are all now multi-million dollar, euro and yen industries that are growing year on year. The sense that there must be some kind of economic drive or financial incentive going on here is hard to deny even if it can clearly only be effective on the basis of a growing acceptance by men themselves of what it offers them. It is, then, perhaps, this coupling of economic initiatives with shifting attitudes towards men's appearances that explains the current resurgence of dandyism and male narcissism most fully. Conversely, the thesis that men's interest in appearance has been a response to the power of women or some kind of backlash against feminism – the framework by which it was first understood – appears to do little more itself than pin the tail on the proverbial feminist donkey.

One rather neglected angle in all of this is men's dress itself or the shifts in men's fashions. Indeed, this entire topic is something of a misnomer for men's *interest* in fashion rather than men's fashion itself. If anything the New Man miscellany of apparently unprecedented developments highlighted a series of issues that preceded it: first, that there has always been something of an oscillating tension between "playboy" and "puritan" tendencies in men's fashion or swings from dandyism to conservatism and back again throughout history. There is some economic explanation for this in Hoch's now aging study of masculinity in *White Hero, Black Beast* where he argued that more consumerist and playful masculinity correlated with affluence whilst moves towards conservatism and tradition were often coupled with periods of austerity (Hoch, 1979). Second, shifts in men's fashion and appearance are mostly inseparable from developments in consumer culture, sexual politics and wider concerns relating to masculinity past and present. Third, and most fundamentally, men are not one and the same, and fashion for younger, single men in particular has always differed from that for older or married men, and the concern for men's appearance is neither as widespread nor as extensive across other factors as women's – it never was and it may well never be. If New Man dandyism was symbolised by anything in men's dress *per se* it was not by denim or underwear – both of which, although exponentially increasing in their commercial importance, were marked more by a concern for branding than anything else – but by the shifting fortunes of the suit; it is to this vestment of masculinity to which we now turn.

Executive looks: masculinity, sexuality and the suit

The suit is perhaps the most misunderstood items of all men's dress, routinely perceived as dull and uniform (in all senses) and/or crudely equated with work. For the most part this is explained as a result of Flügel's overly simplistic assertion that the nineteenth century saw the separation of men and men's dress from all forms of fashion following their connection with the dandy culture of the late eighteenth century, or what he called The Great Masculine Renunciation cited earlier (Flügel, 1930). Central in this was the suit, seen as the nadir of indecorous dullness and constraint. There are several errors here. First, men as a group have never been entirely fashionable or unfashionable – younger and more affluent or higher status men have often shown fashion consciousness, and their dress has been used to reflect their status, youth and attractiveness whilst older, poorer and lower status men have often been too constrained in their resources to have an interest in fashion or to possess fashionable clothes. Second, this trend and variation continued through the nineteenth century which in many ways demonstrated an increasing, rather that lessening, diversity of styles and fashions for men, particularly those of the newly developing middle classes, from the expansion of sporting and riding wear through to evening dress. Once again this was heavily influenced by both class and status. The dour and dull association of men's dress is more accurately a reflection of lower status and working dress. Third, the suit is not and never has been purely worn to perform the function of work. The suit has, and always did have, a far wider range of functions and associations including romantic ones (proposals, dinners, dates, weddings), leisure (sporting wear, social visiting, evening wear), general smartness and dressing up (Sunday best) and even glamorous dimensions (Hollywood iconography, celebrity culture and increasing media variants on such themes) or sexual ones (gangster cultures, gambling and spiv elements), let alone its endless subcultural variants (zoot suits, teddy boys, mod culture). The suit is perhaps more accurately associated with money and power rather than work; hence the tendency of most monetary institutions such as banks, estate agents and law firms to be the most resilient to relaxing their dress codes, let alone the worlds of statesmen and politicians.

What is of interest here, then, is not the rise of the suit as some dull uniform phenomenon but the fragmentation and diversifying of the suit into a multiplicity of varieties in what would appear to be an underlying logic of form following function; as men's lives have increased in their complexity of roles and tasks so have their clothes. The near interchangeability of discussing men's dress and men's suits here also reveals a further significance, namely the extent to which the suit, in essence, is men's fashion or – to put it another way – the template for most if not all of modern western men's dress.

The suit is, in a sense, the very *essence* of men's fashion and, indeed, masculinity. It is what makes men's dress "masculine" and, ultimately, what makes men appear as men as opposed to women when clothed. The reason for this centres mostly on the design of men's suits which tends to echo the male form itself, fitting with varying degrees of suggestiveness the torso and legs and tending to construct a line running from larynx to crotch, crossing the chest along the way, itself displayed and accentuated via the placing of fastenings and, increasingly through history, the tie as opposed to the cravat.

Moreover, despite the so-called casual revolution in men's fashion, the suit remains a defining force in men's dress, still paraded in seasonal designs and worn for every important occasion from interviews for occupational positions to political address, and from boardroom meetings to dates for dinner. In addition, men's casual or more informal dress, from jeans and T-shirts to leather jackets and jogging outfits, tends to reflect a series of mutations of the suit's essential form of under-shirt, jacket or coat and separate trousers or bottoms that tend to fasten and cover or uncover the wearer in similar places. Historically, the only true opposition to the suit has come in the form of the shift or kaftan, still dominant in many eastern, oriental and traditional cultures, which is itself centred on the earlier and more unisex development of the tunic or dress which still tends to influence women's fashion. The suit, then, is also a predominantly, though not exclusively, *western* phenomenon. Slade's discussion of the rise of the suit in Japan is significant here, highlighting the importance of wider values of modernity and minimalism rather than any crude connection with industrialism (Slade, 2009).

It is my intention, then, to examine the nature and development of men's suits and to explain how and why they have come to occupy their present position. As a result, there are three sections: the first considers the history of the suit and its resolute, yet mutating, staying power; the second, a discussion of the differing interpretations of the complexity of meanings associated with men's suits; and the third, an examination of the importance of men's suits in the 1980s, particularly in the wake of a wider expansion of interest in the concept and practice of men's fashion. In addition, the emphasis is placed consistently upon the multiple and complex, rather than singular and uniform, nature of the meanings surrounding the suit in direct rejection of any simple or unilinear notion of dullness in men's dress.

In the first instance, it is necessary to clarify the definitions of certain terms and concepts. In keeping with Anne Hollander's insightful analysis of the suit, it is defined here in terms of an essentially tripartite structure of jacket or coat usually co-ordinated, though not necessarily matched with, trousers or breeches and worn almost always with a shirt and sometimes a waistcoat, tie or cravat (Hollander, 1994). Consequently, the suit does not apply only to pieces of clothing of the same material and is widened to include various co-ordinations of jackets, trousers and garments worn underneath these. This, in essence, emphasises the suit as a matter of *form* and design rather than textiles or materials. To define the suit in terms of matching materials is a far more specifically modern phenomenon. In the first instance, though, it is necessary to consider when and where the suit, and its series of powerful associations, has come from.

From Brummel to Bond: the history of men's suits

Arguably, the history of the suit is the history of at least western men's fashion in sum. From the extravagance of Louis XIV in the late seventeenth century to the classicism of the dandies in the early nineteenth century, and from the uniforms of the industrial revolution to the glamour of Hollywood idols, the suit has figured strongly in the fortunes and perceptions of men's fashion at the level of haute couture and mass market alike. The current reinvention of the mod suited styles of the 1960s, particularly in the work of Paul Smith, is a case in point that also demonstrates the processes of "trickling up" alongside the "trickling down" of design in men's fashion and dress (McCracken, 1988; Simmel, 1904). It is immediately a little odd, then, that the suit is sometimes such a *derided* form of dress, seen as everything from dull, uniform and uncomfortable to capitalist, corporatist and patriarchal. There is some truth in such assertions; yet as designers as diverse as Giorgio Armani and Ralph Lauren or Luccia Prada and Jean-Paul Gaultier do not give it up despite some outside pressures to do so, the suit has resolutely refused to disappear. Styles develop and mutate, fastenings go up and down, lapels narrow and widen, cuts increase in slimness or fullness, cloths and colours endlessly circulate, yet the underlying design and form of the suit remains. Some explanations for this situation are offered in the second section, yet a more fundamental question concerns quite where the modern suit has come from historically.

The modern suit is generally regarded to originate in the mid to late seventeenth century when the cloak, doublet and hose were gradually replaced by the jacket or coat, waistcoat and breeches. In short, the aforementioned tripartite structure or form of men's dress was born. The breeches were in many ways the first element to develop and yet the last to fully mutate into the modern suit's trousers; a mid-point form, namely pantaloons, were themselves not to arrive for over another century. Significantly, they were however gradually cut less and less fully and allowed to grow ever lower while ceasing to attach themselves to the upper garments. Also importantly, the shirt had the longest history of all, yet started its life as an undergarment, increasingly gaining exposure as the centuries progressed and home and work environments grew warmer. In addition, the jacket, which many sticklers for tradition will still call a coat, had its origins precisely as an article of protection or warmth rather than decoration (see, for example, Amies, 1994). This also partly explains the late adoption of the suit in many parts of Asia and Africa which retain cloak and tunic-like dress forms out of a greater need to maintain coolness. The suit as a signifier of civility and conservatism has a long history, therefore, that tends to predate its more contemporary corporatist connotations.

The modern western suit in its primary form, then, is represented in the dress of Louis XIV of France whose ornate finery of silk, cosmetics and perfume is as much a parallel to, or as far a cry from, the dress of the rest of his population as it is from the modern day attire of men in commerce. Herein lies one of most major difficulties in studying the genesis of the suit, for its earliest roots are almost entirely aristocratic whilst its more particularly modern form equally owes much to the working class dress of the industrial revolution. As a result, the colossal emphasis placed upon haute couture in many histories of fashion often distorts differing styles into a unilinear series of shifts, which may in reality have more accurately co-existed. The modern suit, then, has several foundations to its development of which the aristocratic example of Louis XIV is only one.

A second foundation lies more in the gradual mutations of men's dress through the late eighteenth and into the early nineteenth century. During this time male attire was slowly stripped of many of its adornments and whittled down to its essential form and elements of cut, cloth and colour. Whilst pantaloons were, in some aristocratic circles particularly, an increasingly luxurious and sometimes sexy or revealing adornment of men's thighs and legs in pale doeskin complementing plush and deeply coloured coats and waistcoats, the underlying form and stripping away of unnecessary decoration remained in evidence.

It is also this sense of minimalism, if not necessarily dullness, that informs the suit's meanings as a symbol of modernity – functional, effective, scientific even – reducing men's dress to something that displays no frippery and adapts to all requirements, clothing that *works* both practically and aesthetically. Consequently, it can be worn in lighter and paler variants for summer or heavier and darker in winter; coats, jackets, waistcoats and ties may be removed or added without requiring an entirely new outfit; and it moves with the body falling into line and not out of shape whether standing or sitting, moving or still. Interestingly, this cannot be said for many more contemporary and casual fashions – t-shirts and sweaters repeatedly ride up at the back, have to be pulled off upwards thus interfering with the head, hair or glasses and disrupting whatever lies underneath; jeans are effectively the same as trousers yet change their former shape in stretching and moving; only sportswear displays similar versatility, yet tracksuits, even in their massively expensive designer form, lack gravitas. Consequently, it is only the tie – the one decorative and entirely individual element of the ensemble – that can be said not to have a function and yet its aesthetic is functional: the suit does not look entirely complete without one and the tie itself cannot be worn with anything else. The sense in which sweaters worn over shirts and ties or suit jackets worn with jeans somehow do not look quite right or jar to the eye is not merely the result of a sense of social appropriateness but an aesthetic contradiction, like a table with one leg shorter than the others or a car with a door missing – form is everything and without one element it ceases to function, aesthetically if not practically.

A third foundation to the formation of the modern suit is the rise of an ever increasing diversity of men's dress with differing adornments for differing occasions during the same period. As middle- and upper-class men's lives in particular increased in their complexity, their dress equally started to reflect the differing functions of their roles. Therefore there were suits for dinner, the three piece suit for work, the two piece suit in which to "lounge", jackets for smoking, playing sports and so on. These in turn had their part to play in the formation of the modern suit. For example, the cut of the contemporary single-breasted jacket in buttoning around the waist and curving away across the pelvis is derived from the functional design of riding jackets; whilst the double-breasted style is similarly located in the styles of naval or reefer jackets of the nineteenth century. In addition, the blazer was aptly named to reflect its bright colour and sporting associations that came from hunting. There is an interesting sense in which form could be said to follow function here yet none of these styles were entirely dull or lacking in decoration and, as a consequence, the notion of the Great Masculine Renunciation is dependent upon one specific form of men's suits, namely the suit as worn for clerical or commercial purposes only, and it is to the question of where this particular example of suited attire comes from to which I now turn.

One immediate and important point to make is that formation of the clerical or commercial suit as a particular form of men's dress *per se* is primarily a development more strongly located in working-class modes of presentation in men's dress. Working-class men's dress, however, was *never* so colourful or fine as that of the middle or upper classes and, indeed, the use of decoration was an essential component of maintaining an appearance of wealth from the Renaissance onwards given the added costs involved in using embellishments, strong dyes, silks and so on. In addition, also worthy of consideration here is the more technological dimension to the formation of the modern suit for, prior to the advent of synthetics, the modern suit was primarily made of wool. As a result, the industrial revolution in England, which itself centred heavily on the mass production of woollen cloths particularly, also spurred on the adoption of the same material into men's dress. The difficulty, however, was that whilst many wools were hard-wearing and warm they did not, and indeed to some extent still do not, display deeply dyed colours in the way for example silk historically has, or even cotton. A certain dullness of dress, particularly when less costly, was consequently necessary. Indeed, much of women's dress of the same period, when in less expensive forms, was also often relatively dull in colour and sometimes as coarse as men's attire. As a result, the association of dullness in men's dress was a strongly class-related one.

In addition, men's dress, whilst centred almost entirely on the same modern form, was not a one-dimensional phenomenon and had many colourful, if primarily middle-class, aspects. These included not only the dashing and sporting developments already mentioned, rather also the formation of men's dinner dress, the top hat and tails as well as the tuxedo and, even more luxuriously, the crimson or emerald velvet smoking jacket as well as the seaside stripes. Indeed, middle-class commerce itself was hardly immune from such sartorial developments in the formation of the pinstripe suit accompanied by a bowler hat and a cane. Contemporary twists such as colourful linings, light reflective fabrics such as cotton satin, and an increasing emphasis on figure hugging tightness echo this. Consequently, whatever the suit was it was not a uniform or one-dimensional phenomenon and far from dull in at least some of its forms, even at the very height of the Victorian era in the nineteenth century. In addition, during the twentieth century, it is easily argued that men's suits gained yet more dashing dimensions as the smooth lounge suit, modelled so finely in the films of many Hollywood idols from Cary Grant to Rock Hudson, added some glamour and, on occasions, distinct eroticism to the shoulder widening and increasingly chest-exposing two-piece suit. Interestingly, the suit lost some of its "Englishness" at this point and was "Americanised" to some extent through the rise of the mass media and Hollywood in particular. In addition, the post-war Italian influence on design was felt in the mods' hardened, tightened and near phallic adoption of the suit in the 1960s which also opened up its appeal to youth cultures.

As a result, this discussion leads us clearly to the question of quite *why* the suit has since received such attack for its conservative dreariness. There are I think three reasons for this. First, as we have seen already, the modern suit of the nineteenth century was strongly associated with working-class deference and indeed work itself and, as a result, "sexy suits" are still usually those associated with advantage or wealth as in the case of boardroom directors or James Bond. Second, the casual revolution and the iconography of the 1960s particularly did much to damage the associations of the suit now increasingly seen as stoic and archaic compared with the jeans and T-shirts of Marlon

Brando and James Dean or the relaxed cheesecloth comfort of men in the hippie movement. Simultaneously, the suit was perhaps at its dullest at this time given its demob form that then mutated into the uniform of mass-produced sameness sold by Montague Burton in the UK and symbolised by the grey flannel of the 1950s in the USA. This sense of the suit's uniformity also has much to do with modern notions of democracy as we shall see in the next section. Perhaps most importantly of all, however, it was the definition of men's fashion and dress in relation to women's which lent it its dull reputation during the period in question. Whilst women's dress was increasingly decorous, mutated at greater and greater speed, and continued to adopt elements long removed from men's adornment such as cosmetics and a whole manner of entirely useless decorations from frills to jewels, men's dress was pared down to its most essential features and, as a result, the details of cut, colour and cloth were, and what is more still are, everything. The difference in terms of meaning or association of a man's navy blue double-breasted and striped wool suit cut wide at the shoulder and worn with a white cotton shirt and darkly coloured tie, compared with a softly tailored single breasted suit made from mohair or velvet and worn with a brightly coloured or silk shirt is immense, yet they retain the same essential form. From Brummel to Bond, then, the suit has endlessly mutated in meaning yet never entirely lost its eroticism or glamour. It is this question of the complexity of meaning of men's suits to which I now turn.

Meanings, myths and modernity: masculinity and men's suits

How, then, despite centuries of change and continents of variation, may we explain the power and resilience of the suit? One explanation comes from Anne Hollander who asserts with some force that, despite the disputes that surround it, the suit has come to stand for modernity itself as the *ultimate* in form and design, or the guiding principle, of the clothing of men (Hollander, 1994). Her point stems from a perspective drawn from studies in art history and design with the intention of demonstrating how the suit came to embody, quite literally, the ideals of modernity.

   Hollander's definition of modernity is itself decidedly woolly, often conflating notions of art or modern*ism* with social change or modern*ity*; the difficulty with such a perspective is that it sets up a notion of the suit as connected to a concept rather than a context. More importantly, it highlights an underlying tension in all studies of fashion that exists, sociologically speaking, at the level of structure and action. Whilst art historians endlessly complain that clothing does not simply reflect the society it comes from and has its own intrinsic worth, social scientists see its value as linked to, and refracted through, its social, historical and political context. Taking the suit as a case in point, there is some commonsense truth to each of these perspectives as the suit in general *does* tend to reflect the prevailing values of its time from commercial professionalism to self-restraint on the part of men particularly; yet equally the *precise* nature and meaning of more specific suits takes us onto the level of form and design.

In addition, the aesthetic satisfaction of a well-cut suit on an attractive man is not simply explained through crude reference to its associations of power or virility, though these do indeed come into the equation. Consequently, what we are confronted with is a sense in which the power and importance of the suit is not easily explained as some *ad hoc* effect of its underlying form nor understood as a kind of crude reflection of context, rather neither of these but both of them. The suit is, indeed, a most contradictory and complex, even paradoxical, phenomenon.

Jennifer Craik's solution to this conundrum is, for the most part, historical. In particular, she asserts that the notion of men's dissociation from fashion is essentially a figment of the late nineteenth-century imagination concerning dress and fashion (Craik, 1994). In addition, this is linked to wider and dif-fering definitions and perceptions concerning the roles of men and women in the wake of industrialisation. The dullness in men's dress, where it existed, was a reflection of definitions of masculinity that centred on work and production, thrift and control; rather than domesticity and consumption, decoration and expense which increasingly came to define more middle-class women's lives in particular. In the case of the suit, then, the difficulty that remains is one of over-simplification for, as we have already seen, men's dress even at the very zenith of dour industrialism in its differing forms exemplified many more decorative and sexual aspects tied up with its sporting and commercial associations alike.

Similarly, some feminists have wrestled with some of the wider meanings of men's suits, particularly when they are appropriated in the dress of women. For Lee Wright, the suit is the very epitome of capitalism and patriarchy in its representation of compliance with commerce and purposeful professionalism (Wright, 1996). As such, she equates the suit with masculinity, a connection I wish to explore in more detail shortly, and raises the question of what hap-pens to it when women wear it particularly for purposes of career progression. Converse to any sense of parody or piracy, Wright is scathing of women's use of men's dress, and the suit particularly, as an appropriation of male and/or corporatist aspirations asserting in the final instance that its adoption is: "a defeated purpose" (Wright, 1996: 159). As a result, Wright shows little sen-sitivity to the nuances of the suit or the complexity of its associations, asserting that its underlying form and meaning remain quintessentially "patriarchal", a term often in itself used to describe the oppression of women in rather trans-cultural and trans-historical terms.

Whilst differing with the underlying thrust of Wright's analysis, I wish to assert that the explanation for the power and endurance of the suit *does* lie precisely in its connection to the concepts and practices of masculinity. The suit is in no essential sense "masculine" yet its associations, particularly when worn upon the male form, are, in a very real sense, strongly associated with masculinity. There are several reasons for this, the first of which concerns the suit's interrelation with its wearer. What many analyses of men's dress tend to miss, Hollander's included, is the sense in which the importance and meanings of the suit crucially depend upon its interaction with the man underneath and, perhaps most fundamentally of all, the *way* it is worn. What makes actors as diverse as Daniel Craig, Cary Grant or the young Richard Gere often radiate when suited is not simply the suit itself rather their carriage and demeanour when formally dressed. It is precisely this near unconscious interplay of the suit and the suited that makes the suited man, in particular, more than sum of his adorned and unadorned parts.

This second aspect of suited masculinity takes us onto a wider and more cultural terrain, for what marks the suit out as different from any other form of male attire are its connotations and associations of success, maturity and money. The suit in this sense parallels that other accoutrement of masculine "having-made-it-ness": the fast car which is similarly caught up within the same mutually reinforcing triangle of associations of sexuality, wealth and masculinity. Suits, like uniforms and unlike jeans and T-shirts which children wear at play, connote not simply masculinity rather more importantly *manliness*, which explains why they often look out of place in miniature versions on children or even adolescents. These more cultural associations indeed have little to do with the suit's underlying form or importance as a mode of dress and far more to do with its social significance, although this is, again, an essentially "masculine" rather than "feminine" series of associations that run the gamut from managerialism to self-restraint.

This more social connotation leads on to the third and final element in explaining the suit's historic importance, namely its capacity to signify rank, status and group identity. Politicians, professionals, corporate representatives, news readers and indeed any men of any importance wear suits to perform their official functions. Factory workers, craftsmen, the caring professions and others who do not wear suits for working purposes usually perform their functions in other clothing for one of two reasons: the need for safety or practicality, as in the case of many uniforms; or to show allegiance to some other kind of value system, as in the example of social workers, for whom the formality of the suit is sometimes inappropriate.

Yet the suit's social importance for men particularly extends much more widely than mere work and professional roles. Pop stars often parade the latest fashions in suited styles, as do sports stars whose promotion of designer clothing extends considerably beyond their advertising contracts, whilst men in general will still wear suits at weddings or funerals, or to impress a particular sexual partner on social occasions; and, on top of this, others such as the Mods or Zooties will adopt particular suited styles to demonstrate some kind of counter-cultural allegiance (Polhemus, 1994). This is another severely underplayed aspect to men's suits – namely their role in *non*conformity.

The Mods adoption of narrowly cut suits, developed from more Italian rather than English designs, were worn as countercultural statements against conformity, whilst the zoot suit was often an inflammatory symbol of rebelliousness particularly given its association with black resistance in the US (Alford, 2009; Cosgrove, 2007; Hebdige, 1979). Much of this continues in the varieties of suits worn in the worlds of pop music from John Travolta's white suited disco dancing in *Saturday Night Fever* through to the New Romantics adoption of Antony Price suits in the 1980s. To put it more simply, men *communicate* through their suits, both in subcultural contexts and more widely in the competitive world of work. This is explicated most interestingly in Linda McDowell's study of gender mechanisms in the City and with more alarming fictional effect in Bret Easton Ellis's *American Psycho* (Ellis, 1991; McDowell, 1997).

What all of this adds up to in common is the suit's importance as a means of maintaining or presenting an identity, or image of self, in a way which is still quite unique. This is the sense in which the suit is truly a uniform as it remains profoundly important in providing a sense of collective togetherness, whether in displaying some kind of corporate power, music-land sex appeal or cultural identity. In addition, the suit, due to its essential mapping of the male form, remains unique in its capacity to adapt to a myriad of needs and functions giving it what Hollander calls its: "irritating perfection" (Hollander, 1994: 1). This also partly explains, perhaps, the collapse of attempts to oppose the suit such as those of the Men's Dress Reform Party which failed to develop a functional and aesthetic equivalent (Burman and Leventon, 1987). Following on from this, though, it is worth considering the suit's more contemporary significance as, in doing so, one also questions the very status of men's fashion today and, indeed, its importance for men themselves.

What are you looking at: sexuality and the suit in the 1980s

We all know that suit: double-breasted, padded shoulders, no vents, a bit boxy, with the lapels crossing in big, low-cut, diagonal slashes to show quite a lot of tie. A *Chancer* suit, an estate agent suit, a New City Boy suit. *The* suit of the mid/late eighties.

(York, 1995: 20)

The suit at the end of the 1970s was in increasing danger of losing all credence in the wake of its ludicrously wide-lapelled, tight-fitting and synthetically constructed styles. However, in the 1980s the suit returned with a vengeance against the associations of the 1970s in their entirety, epitomised in the swaggering guise of the yuppie. Suits were cut wide and a little loose, the jacket lapels slashed across the chest to accentuate the "V" of the torso, the colours and cloths of commerce from navy and pin-striped wool to deep red silk dominated the triumphant return of the corporate executive: young, hungry and well and truly "on the up". From Wall Street to London's Docklands the story was the same: monetary aspiration and unmitigated conspicuous consumption that was paraded, quite literally, in everything from the jacket swinging in the back window of the BMW to the mobile phone whipped out from behind the all important label on the inside breast pocket. Shirts gained bold stripes, trousers even bolder braces, ties grabbed attention, haircuts shortened and jaw lines hardened. Dominating all of this was the underlying importance of the executive *look*: a look that said "look at me", a look that said "look at my money", and a look that said "look at my masculinity", primarily to other men.

Several things are important here: first, the executive look was centred on a miscellany of products and not a single item, yet the suit itself remained constant and essential to its presentation; second, the look was not merely an image, it was importantly a process of looking particularly within competing male groups; and third, whilst much of this look and the processes of looking attendant with it were founded on the twin cam motors of conspicuous consumption and corporate display, more deeply, it remained fundamentally sexual or, to put it more precisely, phallic. Whilst the suit of the 1980s connoted corporate power or, more simply, money, it also meant male sexuality in a shoulder-widening, chest-expanding, crotch-thrusting sense of aggression.

These perspectives are often as seductive in themselves as the processes they seek to analyse, and there is some credence to the central notion that the 1980s witnessed the rise of a new essentially narcissistic form of masculinity most notoriously summed up in the concept of the New Man discussed earlier. Yet, as we have already seen, the history of men's dress and display is equally littered with highly sexualised presentations of masculinity from the dandies of the eighteenth century to the post-war cult of Hollywood idols, many centred on the use of the supposedly stoic and conservative suit. The developments of the 1980s, therefore, are not perhaps as new as they seem.

In particular, what this tends to highlight is the danger of generalising developments in men's dress and fashion across all groups of men. Narcissistic "new man", to the extent he exists at all, occupies a very specific demographic position as young, usually single, often gainfully employed and quintessentially in possession of a high discretionary income (Ash, 1989). This leaves open a gaping question of its divisive consequences psychologically as well as economically, and the impact of these developments in men's fashion may not be so benign (Edwards, 1997). Most importantly, it is this sense of a sloping playing field in men's fashion which leads Neil Spencer to snarl that: "More than ever, it seems, male Britain is divided into two breeds: those who wear suits to work and those who don't" (Spencer, 1994: 47).

What is interesting here is the rapid rise and fall of the double-breasted "double-barrelled" suit as described by Peter York at the start. Some of this was explained by the influence of designers such as Giorgio Armani who promoted a looser, floppier cut to the suit – what was often called the "deconstructed look" – yet it was really more at the level of the high street and certain big brands, namely Hugo Boss in particular, that it was promoted. The 1980s suit rose to dominance remarkably quickly and equally fell off the radar in the 1990s to be replaced by softer, narrower single breasted styles. As a result it came to symbolise, quite extraordinarily and directly, the values and excesses of the 1980s themselves – greed, ambition, the "power look". Thus, if not sexual politics or mere voyeurism, what *does* define the current position of men's fashion, and the suit within it, is marketing and economics. The enormous expansion of interest in men's fashion in the 1980s, which has continued into today, is premised first and foremost upon the formation of a market for its consumption. There are many elements to this from the top–down economic deregulation policies of the Thatcher and Reagan eras accompanied by the adoption of increasingly racialised flexible production methods, to the enterprising spirits of designers and the opportunistic seizing of the moment that came from magazine editors, not to mention the demographic and cultural shifts in the attitudes of men themselves (McRobbie, 1998; Nixon, 1996; Phizacklea, 1990). Yet what remains paramount in this complex conflation of factors is that it sustains itself in stimulating demand, and processes of self-presentation at all levels are of critical importance in this, which returns us, full circle, to the suit. The suit, whether as the underlying template for contemporary design, the key in the lock of successfully advertising masculinity, or the uniform for commercial negotiation, remains the nexus, the axiom or simply the lynch-pin of the perpetuation and development, production and consumption of men's fashion in western society.

Despite the capacity of many a suited hero to give many a heroine a serious dose of the vapours, it is to men themselves that the suit truly matters. The suit makes men look like executives, even when they aren't in any such position, it underpins their social interactions and ways of looking at each other and it informs their capacity to perform or execute their professional functions as men, from driving cars to carrying pens and credit cards, as trying to do any of these things in a kaftan defies any expectation of competence. The suit remains, then, fundamental to the execution of contemporary western masculinity.

Conclusions: the clothes maketh the man

In summary to this lengthy discussion, we are left to wonder on what exactly *are* the key factors in the evolution of men's dress. Whilst the emphasis placed upon the descent of decorousness into dullness is clearly misplaced, the importance of a shift towards minimalism remains alongside a wider sense in which men's dress has somehow come to accord with and express the values of classicism and modernity – form and function. Axiomatic in this is the rise of the modern suit not as some dull uniform rather as a template for men's dress that works for them in adapting to a multitude of situations, communicating status and seriousness and allowing them to perform their functions as men. The suit still dominates men's more public lives though it has been severely undermined in more private worlds of leisure and pleasure by the rise of a plethora of more informal and casual styles and garments. This emphasis upon modernity is, however, easily overemphasised, as what equally drives the evolution of men's dress is masculinity or, more precisely, that it should make men look like men and mark them out as different from women. It took many decades, and a major set of marketing initiatives, for men *en masse* to reclaim a sense of pleasure and desire around dress and, even now, the unease around whether certain styles or colours arouse feelings of effeminacy remains. Men's dress still relies on its assertion of masculinity and the modern dandy still risks ridicule. Daniel Craig's rise to the top of the elegance stakes has as much to do with his reinvigoration of the raw sexuality of James Bond as it does with his wearing of shoulder widening sharp cut suits designed by Tom Ford. To be dandy is still to negotiate a risk and requires a counter-attack against camp defences – the flashy suit gets discarded, undermined or even ripped just to prove it doesn't really matter – and in the twenty-first century men's dress and men's fashion have come a long way but still have a long way to go.

Chapter 4

The woman question

Fashion, feminism and fetishism

If men remain somehow marginal in relation to fashion, whether in theory or practice, then it is equally axiomatic that women remain central. The relentless contemporary emphasis upon appearances, unequivocally facilitated if not driven through the expansion of media and visual cultures more widely, has also "upped the ante" particularly for women who now no longer have to only consider what to wear, but also diets, exercise and plastic surgery, as increasingly men do too; yet the sense in which the male of the species is sucked into this world of looking, an almost nausea-inducing seesawing process of narcissism and scopophilia, does not detract from the pressures upon women, it merely adds to them. The problem here is not that genders are somehow becoming more balanced on their own swing; rather that the seesaw of vanity and voyeurism has got bigger and more powerful for everybody. In this slightly bizarre zero sum game of the genders, men have not taken from women; rather they have been added to them.

Aside from any religious – whether puritanical or Islamic – critique of women's decorousness, the only attack on this tyranny of mirrors has come from second wave feminism. However, the bra burning, women's libbing and beauty boycotting sisterhood of the 1970s has all but been defeated. Girls outperform boys in school and women routinely have careers, with or without children and husbands, but of course they can do all that and look great too. Today's woman is "everywoman" as Chaka Khan once sang "it's all in me", so being beautiful hardly holds you back; it just propels you even further forward. This is perhaps the key to the crisis in second wave feminism – femininity is no longer the problem but has become some kind of armoury or battle dress and that loathed object of subordination, the stiletto, has now become the "killer heel". It is this rather extraordinary sense of oscillating tension between seeing women as victims and women as warriors that informs this chapter and axiomatic within that is fashion and the conjunction of several factors: the construction of femininity, the role of fetishism and the critique offered by feminism – and this most unholy of trinities will form the focus of our investigation.

Butch, femme or lesbian: fashion and femininity

> Fashion and clothing were seen as constructing and reproducing a version of femininity that was false and constricting and that had to be escaped from or got out of. One way of getting out of the gender identity was to get out of, or to refuse to wear, the fashion and clothing that were constructing that identity.
>
> (Barnard, 1996: 133)

One of the greatest contributions of second-wave feminism has been the critique of femininity. Femininity – as both the concept and also the associated practices of a "feminine" personality of passivity, domesticity and duty to the male of the species – was slammed as either part of the unnecessary trappings of capitalist society or simply the result of centuries of patriarchy and male coercion depending upon the particular perspective in play. Contrary to this lay a rather more universal notion of femininity as repressed or womanhood as undermined (Rich, 1984). Second wave feminism emerged in the late 1960s and early 1970s as part of a wider rise in new social movements seeking to politicise various aspects of identity including sexuality (gay liberation) and race (civil rights). For feminism the primary concern was gender although there were variations on the theme, some emphasising the role of capitalism in the oppression of women, others positing a more trans-cultural notion of patriarchy (see Barrett, 1980; Eisenstein, 1984). Despite this, feminists at this point were relatively united in their condemnation of more traditional notions of femininity, whether in terms of its servile domestic dimension, its hampering of opportunity and career progression, or indeed in its emphasis upon appearance. It was not entirely surprising, then, that femininity as appearance was also attacked as supportive of a male supremacist and/or capitalist empire. If women now saw themselves as not wanting to *act* like the slavish women they were otherwise supposed to, then there was little reason to try to *look* like them either. Therefore, femininity was, in short, seen as wholly unnatural for women. The practice of this philosophy was, however, never so straightforward and the difficulty lay and still lies in the complex relationships of appearance, personality and practice.

At its simplest, the feminist polemic upon fashion and appearance stated that femininity, in terms of dress and cosmetics manufactured in the name of femininity, was not in any way natural or normal for women. Furthermore, men rather than women had been responsible for both producing the goods and inducing women to buy them. Women were, in addition, made to conform to the images prescribed for them by men in both the mass media and the press. Makeup, tight skirts and high heels, for example, were seen as hampering to women who otherwise required hard-wearing and practical, if not necessarily "masculine", clothing and styles to work and live in, and women did not, of their own volition, want to look "feminine". Primary academic examples of opposition to such formations of femininity came from Susan Brownmiller's radical feminist critique of femininity itself as a factor in the social control of women, and later in Naomi Wolf's powerful polemic *The Beauty Myth*, where the ideals of beauty and the regimes of feminine appearances were seen as the ultimate mechanism in women's oppression as part of a patriarchal post-feminist attempt to reinstate male supremacy (Brownmiller, 1984; Wolf, 1991).

Practical opposition to these constraints came in the form of the now notorious feminist apparel of the 1970s: cropped hair, no makeup and little jewellery other than politically correct earrings, no skirts, lots of trousers and jeans, and a certain penchant for Doctor Marten's boots. Many difficulties with this apparently simple line of thinking were, however, quickly discovered. First, it was difficult to prove that women did not want on some level to look like women, if not traditionally or stereotypically so, or that they took no pleasure *whatsoever* in certain facets of looking attractive or "feminine" as opposed to "masculine". In particular, Janice Winship's, Rachel Bowlby's and, more recently, Hilary Radner's use of psychoanalytic theory variously asserted that the feminine was neither a fixed nor an all-powerful category, and that women actively reinvented themselves through its multiple meanings and interpretations (Bowlby, 1993; Radner, 1995; Winship, 1987). This perspective was itself heavily derived from the reinvestigation of the role of psychoanalysis and, more widely, from developments in poststructuralism and cultural studies. Psychoanalysis, at least in its orthodox Freudian versions and, most particularly in relation to the notorious concept of penis envy, had initially been seen by feminists as part of the problem for women rather than the solution. However, major re-evaluations of psychoanalysis took place in the 1970s in the wake of second wave feminism and attempts were made to use psychoanalytic theory to explain their dependency upon men, women's subjective experience more widely and/or the reproduction of femininity itself (Chodorow, 1978; Mitchell, 1974). Similarly, poststructural theory sought to emphasise the diverse and polyvalent meanings of cultural commodities, including clothing, as far more complex and open to interpretation (Hall, 1997). For example, the stiletto – considered later in this chapter – could connote power as easily as it could subordination. Second, it was also difficult to deduce faultlessly that the desire to be feminine came simply from early socialisation or later from mass deception, as this rather implied that women merely soaked up the messages they were given until they equally and passively "saw the light". In addition, some feminists asserted alternatively that consumption itself formed a site of empowerment for women as an arena of female expertise where men were under-skilled and often excluded (Nava, 1992). Stereotypically, the case of the man shut out from the kitchen and the common complaint that whilst women may shop effectively for men, men were hopelessly ineffective at shopping for women, were examples of men's comparative lack of standing in relation to consumption. Third, this then led on to a slightly more empirical point of comparison with men, where it was apparent historically and cross-culturally that men have performed highly decorous and impractical roles similar to women's (see Chapter 3). In addition, men did not necessarily desire stereotypically feminine women. In sum, these points rather undermined the claim that there was any simple gender split in terms of either the desire or the function of clothing or appearance.

Many of these points were discovered over a process of time via women's own experiences and their attempts to explain their difficulties concerning their appearance theoretically and practically. The present predicament concerns a certain lack of resolution of these inherent tensions: if women do desire some degree of difference from men or some form of femininity or, more simply, enjoy dressing up as "feminine" women from time to time, then what is an appropriate form of dress or appearance for them, what is an appropriate form of political action against the pressures to conform to stereotypes and where does one draw the line? This also started to add up to a dichotomy of fashion as *expression* versus fashion as *oppression*, similar in kind to the pleasure versus danger disputes which developed around women and sexuality, to which there are similarly rarely any easy solutions (Vance, 1984).

Women today are presented with two opposed, yet dominant, images of themselves as femininity and anti-femininity, and their predicament concerns finding their way between these two extremes of the femme "Barbie Doll" and the butch "Diesel Dyke". As a consequence, women's appearance is often connected to almost existential questions of "who am I?" or, to put it another way, "butch, femme and back again". The difficulty lies, despite quite a daz- zlingly wide variety of styles and choices, in seeing and dividing forms of clothing into the "me" and the "not me", frequently according to the perceived forms of femininity involved, and selecting them accordingly. There is often quite a high degree of anxiety and difficulty felt in juxtaposing styles or recognising that different looks suit equally different aspects of personality. In short, there is a concern that any *one* appearance is personality – that the clothes maketh the woman most completely. This in turn depends upon the still all too prevalent judgement of a woman's worth through her appearance – something which is increasingly happening to men as well, but which has yet to attain the same overwhelming dominance of their gender. I will consider this point in more detail shortly.

Whilst the problem of fashion for women is often seen in terms of the enforced and fixed nature of femininity, a far greater difficulty often lies in the confusion and anxiety created by the high-speed turnover and diversity of styles for women. To put it more simply, whilst men on the whole know all too well how to look, women may not know well enough. Underneath all of this, though, is an increasingly fixed regime of physicality, often conducted in the name of health, that affects the sexes similarly if not equally. This involves the role of dieting and exercise for women and the issue of muscu- larity and strength for men. If there is an increasing variety of styles and accessories sold to the sexes then there is an equally increasing diversity of physical controls. Whilst successful, attractive and desirable femininity is often all about slimness, sexy and successful masculinity increasingly depends upon muscularity. This ultimately leads to a situation where all other variations are seen as potentially diseased, as slimness and muscularity are also meant to imply healthiness. This is, of course, partially false as intense dieting and/or excessive weight training are frequently ineffective, if not harmful, forms of health maintenance. If sometimes dubious in its effects, however, the relentless pressure upon personalities and bodies continues (Dutton, 1995; Goldstein, 1994; Scott and Morgan, 1993).

If feminism has formed a major critique of femininity and the consumption of fashion, then it has also launched an assault on the production of fashion. Fashion remains one of the most contradictory phenomena of contemporary consumer society in its dual aspects of "high speed and high spend", with "no pay and no end" to the exploitation of women, and represents the epitome of apparently postindustrial consumption and also the nadir of the most outdated forms of production (Fine and Leopold, 1993). Annie Phizacklea in *Unpacking the Fashion Industry* (1990) argues forcefully that the fashion industry could not have survived without the increasing use of Third World skills and materials, and the employment of ethnic minorities in western societies in conditions worse than the lowest white worker would tolerate. Put more concretely, the fashion industry, in lacking significant advances in technology, has survived through an equivalent deterioration in working conditions for its often women and minority workers (see also Chapter 7). Conversely, technology has developed rapidly in relation to consumption: telemarketing, direct mail and EPOS (electronic point of sale) information have created faster and more effective ways of selling products. In sum, then, feminism has provided a powerful critique of femininity, the consumption of fashion, and an equally strong attack on the production of fashion for its ruthless exploitation of women workers and racial minorities.

The often unhappy relationship between fashion and feminism took something of a new twist in the 1990s when "girl power" (or grrrl power when associated with the band Riot Grrrl) arrived. Rather like the New Man and New Lad/ette, girl power was perhaps more a media invention than anything else. Loosely starting with the "have it all" politics associated with Madonna it reached its pinnacle, or nadir depending on your point of view, with the rise of the Spice Girls, a five piece identikit pop act that proclaimed itself a proponent of "girl power". To the extent that it was ever fully defined, girl power referred to asserting one's right as a female to go out and "have a good time" meaning, for the most part, drinking and having sex "like men do". Whilst the emphasis upon independence, friendship and personal autonomy was fairly positive, the irony that neither the Spice Girls nor their legion of imitators actually controlled their music, managed their products and image or did much more than sing a bit, dance a bit and dress up a lot was not lost on some feminists. Whilst part of this centred on the "manufactured" nature of the music – the groups were quite literally put together by music industry moguls and then promoted through the media – the greater part of feminist concern centred on how they looked. In the UK this started with Germaine Greer's well-publicised spat with journalist Suzanne Moore, whom she accused of wearing "fuck me" shoes, in the *Guardian* newspaper, following Moore's allegation that Greer had had a hysterectomy. Greer's more informed attack on girl power, the Spice Girls and indeed wider debates on "third wave" or "post" feminism, came in *The Whole Woman*, a polemic that centred for the most part on the various abuses of the female body from dieting and beauty regimes through to IVF and HRT (Greer, 2000). Her discussion of girl power for the most part consisted of an acid critique of teenage girl's magazines:

> The language of independence conceals utter dependence upon male atten-
> tion, represented as difficult for a girl to get and all but impossible to keep.
>
> (Greer, 2000: 407)

Imelda Whelehan similarly slammed New Lad – and its sister Ladette – culture, also epitomised in the magazine *Loaded* as "retrosexism" or a nostalgic retreat into a notion of pre-feminist gender roles. Constantly underpinning all of this was a far from new concern with appearances. Whilst the Spice Girls asserted that wearing high heels, makeup and ridiculously short skirts were expressions of empowerment – or more simply female pleasure – Greer and the rest said otherwise:

> The ladette offers the most shallow model of gender equality; it suggests
> that women could, or should, adopt the most anti-social and pointless of
> "male" behaviour as a sign of empowerment.
>
> (Whelehan, 2000: 9)

It is difficult to know or define exactly what *is* new here, for something is, if not much, new. The feminist critique of femininity rests on three fundamental points: that it is male not female defined, that women do not enjoy it, and that it has negative consequences for them. Underpinning all of that more simply is the relationship between the subject (here the living female) and the object (the shoes, clothes and so on). The traditional "trappings" of femininity – heels, makeup, skirts, etc. – do not now simply equate with passivity. The meaning has now shifted as these are interpreted – not by men but by women themselves – as what they want and part of the means to their own pleasure not men's. Whilst the consequences may remain debatable (freedom or teenage pregnancies) the problem that still exists is that these objects and practices are not self-created even if they are re-appropriated. Without wishing to assert some kind of essential meaning, these aspects of femininity have for the most part been linked with the role of male designers and producers and hetero-sexual male rather than female desire. More politically it is equally difficult to know what is happening here other than the sense in which the critique of femininity has largely been lost. As students dress in ways in which their mothers would not have been seen dead in and the worlds of celebrity, popular culture and sex collide in an endless production cycle of hair straightened, overly made up and skimpily clad pussycat *dolls* cavorting around doing poses more suited to pornography than pop videos, the old feminist dialectic of expression versus oppression has simply imploded, as donning the guise of oppression is now simply an expression of success.

Fashion, fetishism and femininity: the subjective object of the gaze

Underpinning much of feminism's critique of fashion is the problem of sexual objectification or the idea that fashion creates, perpetuates or reinforces the positioning of women as (sexual) objects. Sexual objectification in turn depends upon the positioning of women more widely not only as objects but also as objects *to be looked at* by men. The problem of objectification is effectively a double one: first, in constructing the person as an object lacking in subjectivity and devoid of emotion and second, in setting up that person as passive and helpless, or at least disempowered, to resist that construction. The primary and most influential analysis of this process has come from film studies. Furthermore, the analysis of femininity and female subjectivity as being the object of the (male) gaze is premised almost entirely upon a critique of a single piece, namely Laura Mulvey's famous essay *Visual Pleasures and Narrative Cinema* (Mulvey, 1975). This has arguably been one of the most important articles of feminist writing in recent history and has, more particularly, defined an entire field of study ever since. That field of study is perhaps most aptly entitled the feminist analysis of viewing relations, giving its *prima facie* concern with the gaze as gendered and indeed sexualised.

The visual pleasures offered through narrative cinema for Mulvey are essentially two-fold: first, scopophilia or the voyeuristic pleasure derived through looking; and second, narcissism, or the pleasure developed from recognition and identification, yet the true cut of her perspective appears when these concepts are overlaid in gendered terms. Put more simply, men, the male subject and masculinity *look* whilst women, the female object and femininity are *looked at*. Clearly such a perspective correlates strongly with the parallel development of a broader feminist imperative to expose the sexual objectification of the female and women more widely (see, for example: Brownmiller, 1984; Greer, 1971; Millett, 1971). In addition, it also resonates strongly with the more widely theorised gender dynamic that equates the male and the masculine with the active subject and the female and the feminine with the passive object. The more particular problematic that then ensues is the idea that the male and the masculine "cannot bear the burden of sexual objectification" (Mulvey, 1975: 12). Similarly, narrative plotlines are themselves also seen to reinforce the activity of the male subject, often conceived as heroic or powerful, and the passivity of the female object who mostly serves the purpose of providing erotic interest alone. Similarly, the narrative itself often enhances wider processes of sadistic pleasure, given plotlines involving the heroic male conquest of enemies and frequent depictions of female suffering and distress.

Perhaps not surprisingly, Mulvey's work has since received a veritable barrage of criticism. This can be summarised as follows. First, it is seen to underplay the importance of female pleasure in looking and indeed the significance of women's spectatorship more widely (Mackinnon, 1997). Second, her analysis of looking relations is seen to be overly crude and simplistic in its emphasis upon a strictly polarised gender divide in viewing relations (Silverman, 1992). Third, the perspective she develops deflects attention away from more complex forms of identification that may exist (Neale, 1982). Fourth, following on from this, men as well as women may engage in masochistic as well as sadistic viewing relations and positions that exist *across* any strict gender divide (Neale, 1983). Fifth, the tendency to deflect the visual and sexual objection of men within cinema may be motivated as much, if not more, by the disavowal of male homoeroticism as by the heterosexual imperative to objectify femininity and women (Green, 1984). Sixth, her use of psychoanalytic theory both misappropriates some of its concepts and abuses some of its main tenets, particularly Freud's work around ambivalent identifications and polymorphous sexuality. Put simply, Freud's theory and concepts were far more complex, dynamic and fluid than given here and far less easily categorised in gendered terms (Rodowick, 1982). Seventh, and most severely, her analysis is overly westernised, middle class and racialised in its emphasis and examples (Gaines, 1986).

These are damning criticisms that expose the simplicity of Mulvey's analysis and question the role of psychoanalytic theory in understanding visual culture more widely. Yet Mulvey's primary assertion that the *way* men and women look and are looked at are fundamentally different still stands (Cohan and Hark, 1993; Jeffords, 1994; Kirkham and Thumin, 1993). In sum, *how* we look is often perceived as impacting upon *what* we are looking at and *vice versa*. Part of the problem here are the limits of the analysis itself. Indeed it becomes arguable that Mulvey's as well as some of her follower's work on the gaze set up as many problems as it provided solutions to the questions it raised. This is a point put most forcibly by Willemen, whose eclectic yet stimulating essays on film criticism and theory seek to challenge much of the orthodoxy of cultural studies (Willemen, 1981). As Meaghan Morris points out in her introduction to a major collection of his articles, Willemen seeks to develop discussion of the monolithic gaze into a wider analysis of *looking* and consideration of inflexible subject positions into the fluid world of *frictions* between moving parts (Morris in Willemen, 1994). Key within this is the concept of the fourth look. The first three looks are contained within Mulvey's essay: first, the look from the camera to create the film; second, the look from the audience to the film; and third, the look between the actors within the film. The fourth then focuses on the more abstract look at the viewer than comes from within the film. This more reflexive form of positioning centres on making the audience increasingly self-conscious of its own looking is demonstrated through a discussion of some of the films of Dwoskin. In particular, one scene in the film *Moment* is considered. Here the camera is fixed on the face of a young woman lying on a bath mat and the audience is required to "fill in the blanks" of what is happening to her. Her expression suggests this to be possibly intimate or sexual but it is never proven one way or the other. Thus, the fourth look of the actor looking at the audience is invoked. It is perhaps arguable that the fourth look is only truly applicable to more avant-garde art forms yet Willemen's wider intention is to undermine the overly simplistic separation of audience and any given cultural form. What is often at work here is a more philosophical, if not existential, question of the relationship between text, context and audience or to what extent any text, or even image, exists without an audience (Hall, 1997).

If analysis of sexual objectification has been informed by an often heady mixture of feminist politics and psychoanalytic theory, then much the same applies to understandings of fetishism. Fetishism is often, if not exclusively, seen as a one dimensional and one directional phenomenon. From heels and lingerie to uniforms and corsets, almost all of the most commonplace examples of fetishism are female that are in turn fetishised exclusively as part of male desire not female. To put it more simply women do not have fetishes, men do, and those fetishes relate wholly to female or feminine items. As I point out in Chapter 6, however, this is something of a misperception – or perhaps even a blind spot – concerning fetishism, yet my primary concern here remains with the relationship of fashion to the feminine. Whilst it is commonly assumed that men are fetishists and women are not, this may more accurately be perceived as a continuation of the invisibility of a more active female sexuality. Thus the issue remains the marginalisation of woman as *desirer* rather than *desired*. There is indeed significant, if rather implicit, commonplace evidence of female fetishism – from the well known love of men's bottoms to the desire for a man in a well cut suit, leather jacket or a pair of crotch hugging boxer shorts, female and fetishised desire does exist yet often under the surface and left of centre. Clearly we are on much the same terrain as when considering gendered looking relations or the problem of sexual objectification – fetishism is a masculine phenomenon "put upon" the passive female by the active male. The problematisation of fetishism thus primarily exists on two levels: the first is a wider moral or pejorative perspective that says that fetishism is unnatural or a pathological response to sexual intimacy thus setting up naked and fetish free sex as natural, normal or healthy, and sex involving dressing up or the use of objects, barring prophylactics, as abnormal and deviant or even downright wrong; and second, a gendered one as this is something that men do to women. Much of the so-called evidence for either viewpoint extends from the legacy of psychoanalytic theory to which we now turn.

Understandings and definitions of fetishism must necessarily start with the work of Freud. Having said this, despite its prevalence, Freudian theory of fetishism is far more limited than commonly assumed. Its definition originates in Freud's *Three Essays on the Theory of Sexuality*:

> What is substituted for the sexual object is some part of the body (such as the foot or hair) which is in general very inappropriate for sexual purposes, or some inanimate object which bears an assignable relation to the person whom it replaces and preferably to that person's sexuality (e.g. a piece of clothing or underlinen). Such substitutes are with some justice likened to the fetishes in which savages believe that their gods are embodied.
>
> (Gay, 1995: 249)

Thus fetishism essentially depends upon: first, the eroticism of objects – or objectifying of one part of the human form – rather than the sexuality of complete human subjects; and second, the substitution of the fetishised object for the human subject in the pursuit of sexual pleasure. In this respect, Freud does not depart from earlier sexology that attempted to document, detail and list every desire ever known in the late nineteenth century often in ways that were later seen as sexist and or heterosexist (Coveney *et al.*, 1984; Jackson and Scott, 1996; Krafft-Ebing, 1965). As many commentators have pointed out since this also had the effect of creating a myriad of sexual identities, not least homosexuality (Foucault, 1978; Plummer, 1981; Weeks, 1985). Whilst the desires were perhaps universal, the setting up of a specific type of person as a "homosexual", a "masochist", or indeed a "fetishist" was nineteenth-century invention. More particularly:

> The situation only becomes pathological when the longing for the fetish passes beyond the point of being merely a necessary condition attached to the sexual object and actually *takes the place* of the normal aim, and, further, when the fetish becomes detached from a particular individual and becomes the *sole* sexual object.
>
> (Gay, 1995: 250)

There are two immediate problems here: first, the setting up a dialectic of "normal" and "pathological" sexual desire within which fetishism slithers rather uneasily; and second, the linkage of fetishism with male desire for female objects. This second factor is reinforced through Freud's use of examples that focus wholly on male fetishes of which the desire for a woman's foot or shoe is later seen as key in his discussion of Leonardo da Vinci. His justification for this comes from a more empirical point concerning the lack of available data on female desire, something he makes clear in his discussion of the "overvaluation" of sexual desire or the sense in which it is increasingly seen as existing outside of genital satisfaction.

Some of these ideas were challenged through the work of David Kunzle on the corset. Through a primarily archival study of journals and letters, Kunzle argues that the late Victorian desire for corsetry and tight lacing was not simply an imposed constraint, rather an expression of female desire. Thus: "the rebellion/restraints of tight lacing is not merely a masochistic reflection of socio-sexual subjection of women by man, but a submissive/aggressive protest against that role" (Kunzle, 1982: 250). Perhaps not surprisingly, not all feminists agreed, seeing corsetry and fetishism as yet more evidence of patriarchal oppression (Daly, 1979; Dworkin, 1981; Wolf, 1991). Valerie Steele's significant documentations of sexuality and fashion through her discussions of women's clothing and indeed fetishism as a costume historian rail against such prescriptive judgements, tending to celebrate the plasticity of fashion, its linkage to sexual and psychological motives and – more implicitly – the importance of the pleasure of clothes (Steele, 1996). We are returned with *Groundhog Day* like repetition to the feminist critique of femininity and its tiresome oscillations from seeing fashion and fetishism as unadulterated domination, to perceiving it as unmitigated empowerment. Neither are that helpful and oversimplifies the relationship of production and consumption.

One attempt to develop a more sophisticated understanding of female fetishism comes in the work of Lorraine Gammon and Merja Makinen. In *Female Fetishism: A New Look*, Gamman and Makinen are keen to stress the sheer existence of female rather than male fetishism and indeed women's activity in engaging with it in various ways, ranging from female fandom and the collection of memorabilia, the common linkage of femininity with food, and particularly chocolate, through to their participation in the sexual fetish scene (Gamman and Makinen, 1994). There is something of a commonsense statement of the obvious going on in this although the authors are right to highlight that for every (at least heterosexual) male fetishist there does quite literally need to be a willing female participant, and stilettos and corsets would mean rather little or certainly a lot less if not seen on the female form, and unless one is to assume that women are entirely duped and controlled in such processes it seems logical to imply that they might get something from it themselves. Moreover, the more radical feminist critique of fetishism and sexual objectification itself becomes part of the problem for it simply will not allow a female subjectivity other than one that is either "false" or that of a "victim". Gamman and Makinen however struggle to grasp the central tension that still exists between seeing women as *either* active desiring subjects *or* passive objects of male desire. Thus, for example, their discussion of fashion sees them slithering towards a more orthodox feminist critique:

> The objectification of women's appearance is now so central in Western culture that the relationship of women to fashion appears in itself to be fetishistic, or at least fixated on certain parts of the female body.
>
> (Gamman and Makinen, 1994: 61)

Indeed, one could argue quite easily, at least within a more contemporary western context, that women's fashions are precisely predicated on their relationship to their bodies in ways that go well beyond merely reflecting the female form. The relentless emphasis, particularly in younger women's clothing, upon nakedness via rocketing hemlines, plunging necklines and one strap, thin straps or no straps alongside clinging, shimmering and shining fabrics that hide nothing have no parallel in menswear, bar perhaps the tightly fitted white T-shirt. Gamman and Makinen's squaring of the circle here centres on the invocation of postmodernism. In drawing on the work of Baudrillard, they argue that clothing brings together both commodity fetishism and sexual fetishism:

> Fetishism of clothing may include "orthodox" sexual fetishism, that is orgasm from an article of clothing which becomes the fetish object. But clothes can also function as icons of commodity fetishism, because consumerism uses sexuality, or more particularly, codes of the sexual erotic, to give fashion *meaning*.
>
> (Gamman and Makinen, 1994: 59)

It is this question of meaning that is central here. Clothing of any kind does not mean anything of and in itself; rather it becomes meaningful when encoded within a particular culture. For postmodern theorists this process also develops a stage further into the complete separation of sign, or meaning, from object, artefact or even form. Moreover, that meaning is then displaced into the world of the commodity. Thus the meaning of Gucci, its sexual frisson, does come from the inherent "Gucci-ness" of the clothing, or even the relationship that exists between a real person buying or wearing a real piece of Gucci clothing, but "hyper reality" or a media driven swirl of imagery and advertising that gives it that meaning and, more insidiously, constructs a kind of Gucci subjectivity that the otherwise voided human subject can "buy into":

> In postmodern terms this means that gender is the perfect simulacrum – the exact copy of something that never existed in the first place.
>
> (Gamman and Makinen, 1994: 217)

There are strong links here with my argument concerning the rise of celebrity and designer label culture in Chapter 8 but in the meantime it is perhaps useful to work these themes through by concrete example and there is none more powerful or provocative than the stiletto.

Achilles heels: female sexuality and the stiletto

When thinking of fashion, one commonly thinks of clothes. Footwear is thus an often neglected area of dress, yet – like clothing – performs the fundamental function of protection of the physical form. Consequently it is, or should be, equally significant. Part of the difficulty lies in its specificity – it only functions in relation to the feet or at least the lower leg whereas clothes relate to the entire human frame – yet the wider reason for comparative disinterest perhaps is the ordinariness of much footwear itself. The significance and status of shoes is almost exclusively related to their impracticality – tottering heels, hopelessly inadequate straps, open toes, flimsy but decorative fabrics; when they become practical they often become *boring* – sober in style, dark in colour and hard or heavy in material. The one exception, the brightly coloured and rubbery sports training shoe, is a modern and limited exception that tends to prove the rule. It is precisely this oppositional juxtaposing of functionality and decoration that marks footwear out as separate from the rest of dress that may do both at once, as in the case of the well-tailored suit or attractive dress. Of course, the other key defining factor here is gender. If Flügel's concept of the Great Masculine Renunciation was otherwise largely misplaced in understanding men's dress then it remains far more successful in relation to understanding their footwear (see Chapter 3). Whilst women's footwear can be found in every conceivable colour and material from crimson silk to black plastic, from flats to house-like heights, from no substance to yards of leather and strapping that reach the top of a woman's legs, men's footwear is either brown or black, formal or casual, and hardly anything in between. Of course this was not always the case, men used to wear buckles and bows and cover their calves in sumptuous hide but when the renunciation happened it was the shoes that went rather than the clothes. This point is picked up to some extent by Chris Breward who argues that, rather like the suit, the male shoe under the industrial revolution became a symbol of class and manliness and, as it were, the devil is in the detail:

> In the delicate balance between function and aesthetics that continues to dictate the pattern of stitching on a black Oxford or the number of eyelets on a brown Brogue, there still persists the residue of older discourses on manliness, nationhood and class.
>
> (Breward, 2006: 207)

The study of footwear is similarly mixed and distinctly gendered. June Swann has provided the most major and exhaustive historical work into who wore what when and where in her studies of shoes (Swann, 1982). More analytic work has tended to focus on the wider symbolic significance of footwear particularly in relation to gender and culture. Riello and McNeil's collection of essays provides the most extensive analysis of these dimensions through a series of lavishly illustrated case studies on footwear as diverse as Chinese slippers, men's industrial boots and the American sneaker or training shoe. These essays in sum illustrate the shifting meanings and histories of various forms of footwear that are never quite as simple as they seem (Riello and

McNeil, 2006). For example, Zamperini's study of Chinese footwear illustrates a history of such shoes as part of religious rituals and ceremonial gifts, not merely symbols of female subordination (Zamperini, 2006).

There is also a powerful historical mythology surrounding shoes that illustrates similar themes. The Golden Lotus is an ancient symbol within Chinese culture, possibly dating as far back as the tenth century, that celebrates the smallness of the feet – here to less than three inches – and led to the notorious tradition of foot binding in order to reduce the size of an adult woman's foot (O'Keefe, 1996). What is of interest here is precisely the intertwining of status, sexuality and gender as the small foot was symbolic of both aristocratic status and intense eroticism – for women's feet that is. The wider theme of status through impracticality was perhaps a little less gendered as aristocratic footwear for men in many cultures at many times is less practical, less comfortable or simply less hardwearing than it is for their more working class counterparts. Despite this, gendered difference in footwear is pronounced, nowhere more strongly than in the Cinderella story where the unhappy servant girl gains her prince and her happiness for no other reason than having feet small enough to fit the slippers. Similarly, *The Red Shoes*, originally as a Hans Christian Andersen fairytale and then as the famous Michael Powell film, tells the story of the spell of a pair of red shoes that won't stop dancing and effectively take over the life of their wearer, a theme re-examined through the work of Kate Bush in her single and album of the same name and her mini-movie *The Line, the Cross and the Curve*. The wearer in each case is of course female and transfixed by the sexual allure of the shoes. The potency, particularly of female shoes, is central here and cuts across a multitude of examples, including the stiletto which we will consider shortly. What is immediately apparent, however, is the relationship of the shoes to their female wearer – they have the power to empower her, to express her innermost desires and invest her with sexual allure, yet simultaneously entrap, cripple and subjugate as if by magic. That magic in itself however echoes the active–passive dichotomy that dominates women's relationship to fashion and their position as both fetishists and fetishised objects outlined in earlier sections of this chapter. It is also this polarity that underpins understandings of the stiletto to which we now turn.

The stiletto is, in essence, a high heel. As such, it is – and is not – new in the ways in which it illustrates the meanings of footwear and the relationship of those meanings to their wearers. The wider role and history and high heels is decidedly mixed – ancient Egyptian butchers wore them to raise them above the meat and blood they were working with, they were adopted as a practical grip in stirrups for horse riding men, and first found mass manufacture in the United States in the 1880s. None of this of course equates with their more contemporary significance as a symbol of female sexuality: a theme that has its origins more in the rise of the Venetian chopine during the Renaissance. As Vianello illustrates, the chopine most probably developed from the clog into the more infamous cork or wooden wedge that both literally and symbolically enabled women to walk tall, albeit with difficulty (Vianello, 2006). It is this enabling/disabling dimension that links the chopine with the stiletto, the high heel that somehow empowers a woman, makes her taller and gives her phallic sexuality – and indeed a fatal weapon – yet can cripple her on an uneven pavement or see her toppling down a flight of stairs. The chopine more specifically is a forerunner of the modern platform that, interestingly, was relatively gender neutral in the 1970s given Glam Rock's adoption of platform heels for men, most notoriously in the towering stilts worn by Elton John. The platform is however different in its effect on its wearer who clumps around in an ungainly fashion, whereas it is the high heel more specifically that creates an issue of balance and wobble for its female wearer. For some, following Freud, this echoes the quiver of orgasm (Steele, 1996).

The stiletto, as Caroline Cox demonstrates in her lavishly illustrated history, in its more specific and modern form has its origins in the rise of increasingly consumerist femininity that developed rapidly in reaction to the austerity of the utility wear of the Second World War (Cox, 2004). Strongly interlinked with Dior's "New Look" which spearheaded the development of a wider form of female glamour centred on accentuated breasts, tiny waists and yards upon yards of chiffon skirting, the stiletto formed the aesthetic icing – or perhaps more accurately the pedestal – for the ultra-feminine cake. As a partly Parisian and partly Italian design centred on the work of Vivier in France and Ferragamo in Italy, the stiletto symbolised the burgeoning of a new form of femininity, domestic yet sexy, glamorous yet accessible, modern yet classic:

> Thus women were being encouraged to participate in the new culture of consumption to create an unambiguously Francophile femininity though the use of clothes and cosmetics.
>
> (Cox, 2004: 38)

And shoes. Crucial in this was the role of design, for the stiletto was not just a high heel but a shapely sculpture carved to a point and echoing the curves of the female form. More importantly it also depended upon the newly developed technology of incorporating metal into the heel rather than wood, allowing for far greater weight to be placed upon a far smaller area. The stiletto in this sense was a feat of engineering not unlike Concorde. Of course the other key dimension in its history was its promotion through the media – the rise of advertising, the expansion of cinema and other visual media, and – at the epicentre of all of that – Hollywood. Within the space of little more than a decade, the stiletto had gone from an unknown to something seen on the feet of every female celebrity from Sophia Loren in Italy to Marilyn Monroe in North America. There was of course a more sinister aspect to this, namely the reconstruction of a femininity centred on looks and consumption in the wake of women's activity and productivity in the Second World War, yet the notion of a conspiracy is perhaps misplaced for the success of the stiletto also rested on the fact that women wanted it and were prepared to go to often quite insane lengths to get it, hurting their feet and learning to walk on something that threw their weight unnaturally forward. The stiletto was also grabbed with both hands by the growing youth culture of the 1960s that saw many young women embrace it as a symbol of sexual liberation:

> An object of consumption, the stiletto embodied the pleasures and dangers of the city street and had become a pivotal part of a new vocabulary for girls who walked on the wild side.
>
> (Cox, 2004: 81)

Despite this, in the 1970s the stiletto became an emblem of second wave feminist ire with Germaine Greer castigating its links to sexual subordination and Brownmiller, in her fierce critique of femininity, comparing high heels with leg irons (Brownmiller, 1975; Greer, 1971). In addition, the stiletto was increasingly exposed as a more and more tawdry object of sadomasochism paraded on the heels of bunny girls and porn stars, each drawing to some extent on the wider fetishism of female footwear in Sacher-Masoch's infamous novel *Venus in Furs* (Deleuze and Sacher-Masoch, 1989). It was also this sadomasochistic angle that was reclaimed in the punk era when young women would adopt spikes and ankles chains, heels and laces in an assertion of sexual aggression or, to put it more crudely, turned "fuck me" shoes into signifiers of "fuck you". This was also echoed in the "killer heels" of the 1980s' shows such as *Dynasty*, with the likes of Joan Collins conflating commerce and sexuality to hysterical – in every sense – effect, and the infamous use of a stiletto heel as a murder weapon in the overheated sexual politics of the film *Single White Female*. What dominates this discussion is the constant connection of the stiletto heel to female sexuality whether as a crippling symbol of their subordination or as emblematic of their empowerment. This polarity of meanings repeatedly mutually reinforces from one to the other – the stiletto as pleasure, the heel as danger – that echoes far wider debates concerning the ambiguous status of women's sexuality (Vance, 1984).

All of these elements go some, yet not all, of the way in explaining the current renaissance of the stiletto heel. During the past decade, and particularly since *Sex and the City*, heels have become like skyscrapers in Dubai. The question has become – how high can they go? And like Corbusier's shining towers they symbolise phallic mastery. All of which rather raises the question – who is the master and who is the slave, the shoe or the woman? The show's heroine, Carrie Bradshaw, was a highly successful journalist living independently in New York, yet she was equally enslaved to her love of shoes, quoted at one point as having spent $40,000 on her obsession. This obsession and the show's parading of its four female characters in an endless array of outfits and heels also brought in a further element, namely the shoe's importance as a designer label. In another episode for example Bradshaw is mugged but protests far more strongly about having her Manolo Blahniks stolen than anything else. As various commentators have noted, *Sex and the City* effectively made Manolo Blahnik a household name. Similarly in Lauren Weisberger's novel *The Devil Wears Prada*, also made into a successful movie starring Meryl Streep, the narrator and lead character Andrea describes in detail the imperative placed upon all female employees for a leading fashion magazine to wear high heels and their slavish attention to the designer in question (Weisberger, 2003). At various points she also invokes the complex series of meanings attached to this predicament from fury and helplessness to awe and admiration, and documents numerous employee attempts at subterfuge under the regime of the Head from Hell, aka the Devil, Miranda, commonly understood to be modelled on US *Vogue* editor Anna Wintour. To argue, therefore, that the stiletto or high heel has a single meaning let alone one that is fixed as oppressive to women is, quite simply, wrong. Its more contemporary meaning perhaps has as much to do with designer label culture more widely as it does to gender politics, yet the caveat here is that the extremities of any obsession with fashion and labels, with the possible exception of gay men, are nearly always female (see also Chapter 8). In addition, what is also illustrated here is that the stiletto's constant connection with female subordination has much, if not more, to do with the lack of choice involved. Indeed, the pleasures and perils of the high heel have much to do with whether the wearer chooses to wear them or is somehow forced into doing so. Similarly, cheap ill-fitting or poorly made shoes whether high or low heeled and made for men or women may also be crippling to the wearer. The heel is an important yet not the only factor. Design is crucial here as it is not only the height of heels that concerns women but their width and overall stability, and it is also this factor that begins to inform our understanding of the contemporary stiletto.

The high heel of the twenty-first century is in many ways far removed from the stiletto of the 1950s in its meanings and indeed its design. First, it's a good deal higher – designers such as Gina, Blahnik or Choo regularly turn out shoes with five or even six inch heels whereas Monroe rarely wiggled at much more than four inches above her natural height. Second, it's also strappier – whilst the slingback was well in evidence decades earlier the current trend for spindly, strappy and even see-through shoes has a lot less precedent. And third, much of the sculpture of the stiletto heel has gone to be replaced by something closer to a spike – narrower, longer and altogether sharper. The impact of this is to make the stiletto even more potent and completely crippling – "limo heels" as worn by US *Vogue* editor and well-known fashion Stalinist Anna Wintour – shoes quite literally unwearable beyond stages, carpets and a few hundred metres. These three design elements also play into its shifting meanings. Whilst the original stiletto was sexual yet stately, powerful yet feminine, the new heel is often just plain blatant. The problem here is deceptively obvious, namely the increasing conflation of women's high street fashion with the media sex industry. The emblems and symbols of pornography have become increasingly incorporated into the mainstream, which is precisely what enrages Elizabeth Semmelhack alongside Greer and Whelehan in their condemnation of girl power outlined earlier:

> At the turn of the twenty first century, popular rhetoric equating female sexuality with power was concomitant with the ascendancy of fashion inspired by strippers and sex workers in both haute couture and ready-to-wear markets.
>
> (Semmelhack, 2006: 245)

Contemporary patterns of dressing up for young women – skimpy dresses, long hair, lots of makeup and preposterously high heels – are remarkably akin to pornographic imagery that has long relied on certain well worn symbols of available female sexuality – a lot of hair, a lot of makeup and cripplingly high heels. Alongside the rise of plastic surgery that quite literally did not exist in any mass market sense in the 1950s or 1960s, the emphasis upon women's appearance as pornographic has increased, stepping out of Playboy clubs onto city streets and into primetime television. Women may have always been the objects of the male gaze, sex objects even, but they have not been until more recently near replicas of porn stars and sex dolls. This is perhaps nefarious enough, yet to reclaim such imagery as the epitome of hedonistic female emancipation is frightening. The feminist project, for all its faults in over simplifying female subjectivity and offering solutions duller than the sink water they sought to remove women from, remains unfinished.

Conclusions: the woman question

In attempting to pull these matters – and indeed polarities – together it is tempting to ask the oft-quoted Freudianism "what do women want?" In contemporary western cultures at least, many young women appear to want – and actively promote – the trappings of what one might call an increasing "pornographifica-tion" of fashion consisting of long silky hair, a lot of makeup, skimpy skirts and "fuck me" heels. It is difficult – in fact impossible – to proscribe against this unless adopting Islamic dress codes that in themselves only control women's appearance in public for the argument that is repeatedly made – including by Cambridge University students wishing to conduct beauty pageants – that this is about women's rights to pleasure, to self-expression and, somewhere down the line, sexual gratification. To which one may well say "fair enough", yet for the sticking point – and it is indeed super gluey – that these "trappings" were, and are, for the most part not of women's making and are male defined.

In addition, the question of "what women want" remains mostly unanswered due to the sheer invisibility of female subjectivity. Whether many young women now aspire to having plastic surgery, careers in modelling or celebrity lifestyles that *may* be an expression of their innermost desires or equally it may *not* be – we do not know. The problem here is the lack of opportunity, facility or space even for any kind of ground-up as opposed to top-down female subjectivity to develop. The fashion industry itself is perhaps less a concern here than the media – magazines, reality TV, popular culture – that quite literally drown out any attempt to think clearly. Unfortunately, feminism for the most part has not helped here either in prescribing unrealistic limits, offering few alternatives and making killer heels the jam jar on the top shelf. Thus the need to open up a space – or indeed a pot – in which female subjectivity can be formed, and answers to the question of what women want can be developed, is more pressing than ever.

Chapter 5

Who are you kidding?

Children, fashion and consumption

The study of consumption has grown almost exponentially over recent decades. This expansion has developed over an increasingly multidisciplinary terrain including anthropology, economics, history, geography and literature as well as sociology, covering topics as diverse as shopping and identity, processes of commodification, marketing and the role of psychoanalysis, the critique of utilitarian economics, and the relationship of consumer culture to postmodernism (see, for example: Bowlby, 1993; Featherstone, 1991; Fine and Leopold, 1993; Jackson et al., 2001; McKendrick et al., 1982; Miller et al., 1987; Slater, 1997).

Despite this, empirical research in the area of consumption remains relatively under-developed, although perhaps addressed more fully through the recent launch of the *Journal of Consumer Culture* and the ESRC's *Cultures of Consumption* initiative, of which more later. One key exception has been Bourdieu's study of Parisian lifestyle choices in *Distinction* (Bourdieu, 1984). The influence of Bourdieu in the area has been immense and, in particular, his analysis of the role of cultural intermediaries such as designers, advertisers and magazine editors in defining styles, social groupings and social divisions centred on consumption practices (see, for example, Cronin, 2004; Nava et al., 1997; Nixon, 1996). A second and recent dimension of research into consumption has had a primarily ethnographic focus, particularly on house-holds and domestic consumption, seeing consumption practices and meanings as generated within and out of household relations (see, for example, Miller et al., 1998).

This chapter draws on a jointly held research project entitled *New Consumers: Children, Fashion and Consumption* funded by the ESRC/AHRB under its Cultures of Consumption Initiative, conducted between 2003 and 2006. The project sought to draw on each of these strands of research through an analysis of the role of cultural intermediaries such as buyers and retailers, including formal interviews, and through a more ethnographic and long-itudinal investigation into the consumption of children's fashion within a small sample of seven families. In doing so it aimed to provide some insight into the overall "loop", or interconnected nature of, production and consumption, seeing children's consumption of fashion as resulting from both push (advertising, marketing and lifestyle initiatives) and pull (pleasure, desire and appropriation) factors as part of an overall "circuit of culture" (Johnson, 1986). Within this the study also aimed to investigate some of the processes of inclusion and exclusion that underplay children's consumption of fashion goods according to key variables of social class/income and geography/access. Following this emphasis upon the "looping" of the production and consumption of children's fashion, this chapter draws on interviews conducted with representatives of the fashion industry including store managers, product managers and company buyers. Fifteen interviews were conducted during the period of 2004–6, composed of five interviews with supermarkets and the so-called "value end" of the market, four with the independent, top or designer label driven end of the market, two with sports shops, two with leading high street multiples, and two with those involved with the marketing of children's fashion more widely.

Despite immense media interest in children and fashion, most notoriously in the rise of the so-called "tweenager", and a growing market in children's clothing and accessories now estimated to be worth around £6 billion in the UK alone, social science literature and research on fashion shows a glaring neglect of children and fashion (Mintel, 2008). This is mostly due to its heavy emphasis upon gender, whether in the form of feminism (Craik, 1994; Entwistle, 2000; Wilson, 1985) or the New Man (Edwards, 1997; Mort, 1996; Nixon, 1996) or alternatively upon youth subcultures (Hebdige, 1979; McRobbie, 1989; Nava, 1992). The exception here has been marketing and retail management driven studies of consumer behaviour which have increasingly turned their attention toward the role of children in relation to branding, product choice or wider family dynamics (Elliot and Leonard, 2004; Grant and Stephen, 2005; Harper, Dewar and Diack, 2003; Hogg, Bruce and Hill, 1998). The limits of such behaviourally driven studies for social science analysis are clear as they tend to either under-theorise the subject and or imply a rational choice model that elides wider consideration of social and structural constraints.

The study and analysis of children's fashion is, to say the least, disparate. Recent years have seen an expanding literature on the sociology of childhood, major developments in the study of consumer culture and a small, but well-established and interdisciplinary, analysis of fashion. Despite this, consideration of children's fashion or even children as consumers remains rather thin with some exceptions (Hood-Williams, 1990; James, Jenks and Prout, 1998; Kline, 1995; Swain, 2002; Wyness, 2000). One key example here is the work of Dan Cook which I will consider shortly (Cook, 2003, 2004). However, there would appear to be several reasons for this situation. First, the study of fashion is – as cited in Chapter 1 – rather split between the analysis of dress, or what people wear when and how, and the analysis of fashion *per se* as a phenomenon of social change, or the processes by which style and taste shift and develop in relation to any number of goods, commodities or services (Craik, 1994; Edwards, 1997; Wilson, 1985). The difficulty here is that it also reflects a wider disciplinary rift between seeing fashion as a matter of dress (as seen within the arts and design) and seeing fashion as a phenomenon of social change (as seen within the social sciences). Within this, children's fashion as a topic *per se* is almost entirely lost as either an un-theorised subsection of costume history or as a tiny variable within a wider sea of social and economic analysis. It is particularly remarkable that the study of fashion has in many ways almost entirely neglected questions of aging. Given its relationship to the body this is striking; yet the body itself often maintains a near absent presence within the analysis of fashion as Entwistle has noted (Entwistle, 2000).

A second dimension here is the tendency of literatures on consumption to construct the category of the consumer as unproblematic (Edwards, 2000). Whilst variables of class, race and gender are often considered, once again age is often left out other than to consider the particular plight of the elderly as an excluded group or possessors of "grey power" in market terms (Cahill, 1994). This is only partly explained in relation to children's relative lack of autonomy as consumers and is more a reflection of the wider tendency of sociological literatures on consumption to treat consumers as a homogenous group. More deeply, as I have argued previously, analysis of consumption is often caught between more economic and more cultural explanations that emphasise either class and income or identity and style as key variables (Edwards, 2000). All of these variables, however, are problematic in relation to children whose position in all respects is often inextricably bound up with that of their elders and, furthermore, considered only in those "adult" terms.

Third, one might expect the sociology of childhood to move the topic forward here but there is a strong tendency for the analysis of children to become caught up in wider debates about agency and structure whereby children become either the plastic constructions of history or seen as increasingly significant agents of some sort. In neither case is children's uniqueness as "clothes wearers" particularly apparent. The study of childhood often shows a tendency towards overly macro considerations of the role of children as merely the constructed subjects of history. Studies such as those by Aries and wider applications of the work of Foucault strongly emphasise the historical construction of childhood itself as an essentially modern and western phenomenon, bound up with the advancement of industrialisation and the role of the state (Aries, 1962; Ashenden, 2004). Whilst such studies play a crucial role in undermining the attempt to either render childhood a universal and biologically driven entity or as an inherent state of innocence they also tend to render children passive objects of history with little subjectivity or agency. A more recent sociology of childhood has begun to challenge these notions and to understand childhood as a more unique and rounded part of human development (James, Jenks and Prout, 1998; Wyness, 2000). The tendency, however, for the sociology of childhood to inculcate debates concerning the power and agency of children often sheds little light on the importance of dress or children's relationship with clothing.

One exception, perhaps, is the work of Dan Cook (Cook, 2004). Through a thorough-going analysis of trade journals and similar retail sources throughout the twentieth century in the US, Cook attempts to simultaneously construct and unpack the intertwining of the rise of the child as an agent and as a separate group that potentially has rights and needs protection from other groups, and childhood itself as a commodity enmeshed within the growth of the market in advanced western industrial capitalist societies. Fundamental in Cook's analysis is the assertion that the economic, moral and political dimensions of constructing the child and childhood are inseparable: "a view of the child consumer as always, already embedded in market relations" (Cook, 2004: 5). This potentially sets up a notion of the child consumer as a mere passive victim of market forces or what Cook calls "market invasion" perspectives. Implicit within this is Cook's repeated, yet rarely unpacked, use of the concept of "discourse" to understand the construction of childhood and the child consumer. Thus, although rarely made explicit, Cook's perspective is fundamentally a Foucauldian analysis of the construction of the child and the consumer and thus, in essence, not far removed from the work of Aries (Aries, 1962). What is more unique here is his emphasis on the enmeshing of moral and economic dimensions and his clear demonstration of these connections through archival research. The subjectivity and agency of children, however, develops into little more than a ghostly presence here. Thus the problem that remains, over and over again, is one of agency and structure in understanding children as passive or active consumers, a theme echoed in some of the findings from the work carried out with the fashion industry to which I now turn.

New consumers? Industry perspectives on children's fashion

> I think it's going to continue to grow for a while but then obviously there's going to come a saturation point.
>
> (Elizabeth, design manager)

This chapter presents some preliminary findings from research conducted into the significance of the childrenswear market and children's fashion. In particular, it draws on interviews with representatives and cultural intermediaries from the childrenswear industry in the UK. These findings are presented under five clustered headings: first, the significance of the childrenswear market in retail terms; second, a consideration of the significance of demographic, geographic and more "psychographic", or lifestyle and attitude-defined variables in the market for children's fashion; third, the role of branding, whether in terms of designer labels or more generic brands; fourth, the balancing of questions of supply and demand within the childrenswear industry and how this is played out in patterns of decision making and shifts over time; and fifth, perceptions of the influences upon childrenswear both within and outside the fashion industry itself. More specific concerns, often located in the media, relating to the rise of the so-called "tweenager", "pester power" and "fast fashion" will also be considered along the way.

All interviews were conducted on site in stores or head offices, and were semi-structured to cover a range of issues rather than set questions. They were tape recorded and fully transcribed, and lasted from half an hour to several hours in some cases according, quite simply, to the time constraints of the interviewees. Pseudonyms are used to cover questions of data protection and anonymity. Perhaps not surprisingly the main difficulty was one of access. Retailers, managers and other store workers had little incentive to spend time talking to university researchers other than the promised pay-off of seeing the results. An additional difficulty here was accessing the correct person, given endless tendencies to pass correspondence or calls on to someone elsewhere that then led to no response. Interestingly, companies varied in their levels of accessibility – Gap for example simply dismissed all contact saying that all decisions were taken in the United States, yet London's most famous and renowned department store Harrods readily agreed to take part. It was thus more internationally and strongly branded companies that were most hard to access. The study received significant support from the Leicester-based company and leading fashion retailer Next, for which it remains immensely indebted. As a result, the makeup of the sample was as follows: five interviews were conducted with supermarket or "value end" retailers, four interviews were conducted with "top end", designer or independent retailers, two interviews were conducted with designated sports shops, two interviews were conducted with mid market multiple chain stores, and two interviews were conducted with leading industry experts or marketing analysts. This reflects the difficulties in accessing the brand-oriented mid-market, particularly where it is international, yet shows success in gaining access to the key concerns of children's fashion: value or fast fashion, and designer wear. The focus is of course on the UK and it is perhaps difficult to generalise more widely yet the sense in which many western societies appear to experience similar, if hardly the same, developments remains important. In particular there are parallels to be drawn between the UK and US markets, both of which are brand and multiple dominated unlike some European markets such as France and Italy which have a stronger independent sector.

First and perhaps foremost, all of those interviewed, from higher to lower organisational levels, were almost unanimous in their feeling that the significance of children's fashion had been exaggerated by the media. Contrary to media opinion, the market for children's fashion in the UK has not in fact grown at a rate in excess of other sectors of dress and its growth is both lower than suggested, at between 2 and 4 per cent per annum, and in tandem with the retail market for fashion in the UK more widely (Mintel, 2008).

Where concern was expressed this was in relation to the more detailed make up and nature of the market for children's fashion *per se*. In particular, the rise of the value end of the market, popularly called the "walmart effect", was often noted and seen to be significant, though most of those interviewed still acknowledged an inevitable limit to expansion here:

> I think there will be more casualties in terms of other players within the market and I think you'll end up with a very, very strong value market and a very, very strong branded top end market and quite a minimal middle market.
>
> (Stephanie, product director)

Similarly, it was felt – even by those working at the high status and design-led areas of the children's fashion market – that the rise of "designer" children's fashion in particular had also been over played. This is also evidenced in market research information that estimates the independent (and usually more top end) sector of the market only accounts for a very small part of the market, usually well under 5 per cent, particularly in volume terms (Mintel, 2008). This is in some ways a peculiarly British phenomenon, as the fashion market in the UK is dominated by large high street multiple outlets and chain stores, particularly when compared with many of its other European counterparts, whilst there is some similarity between the UK and the US markets. Thus, change was felt to be occurring more *within* the makeup of the childrenswear market with a particular squeeze on the middle end of the sector coming from the rise of supermarkets and discount outlets offering children's fashion, rather than in terms of any wider change from *without* that was particular to children's fashion in the UK.

Second, when investigating more complex demographic and geographic changes within the nature and significance of children's fashion in retail terms, some surprising responses were found. Without exception, those interviewed dismissed most major demographic and geographic variables:

> I'd say the differences are more age orientated. In terms of a geographical change we don't do individual ranges for individual areas with the exception of England, Wales, Scotland T-shirts or St. David's day outfit. What I would say though generically ... is that there are certain cities that sell fashion earlier than others so you have a far more city profile.
>
> (Stephanie, product director)

In addition, this was also often to seen to relate to the working of many companies whose policies on design and distribution were similarly centralised and kept "in house" according to a core brand identity. Thus whilst many companies sought to gain feedback, and therefore "loop" their day-to-day decisions concerning the control of stock levels and ranges from one store to another, this was not equated with any wider demographically or geographically informed policy. Thus such factors as class, socio-economic grouping, regional, racial or ethnic variations were routinely dealt with at a level of little more than needing more Newcastle-branded T-shirts in Newcastle. The sole and significant exception to this rule was gender:

> Girls are more fashion conscious. Boys are difficult. They won't try, they're very non-committal. They put things on and "Do you like it?" "Yeah" "Well do you want it?" "Yeah".
>
> (Annie, store owner/manager)

Most of those interviewed highlighted differences according to sex as significant not only in terms of the obvious variations in the products sold but in terms of being a key variable around which wider decisions were made. Consequently, children's fashion was clearly divided into boys' wear and girls' wear with decisions concerning design, distribution and marketing often being taken in relation to each semi-autonomously.

Interestingly here the balance in emphasis between the two markets, both in economic significance and in wider cultural terms, was seen to be quite finely played with the split rarely being any more than 60:40 in favour of girls and sometimes less. This was partly accounted for by the relatively higher cost, but lower volume, of boys' wear and lower cost but higher volume of girls' wear, with expensive branded sportswear for boys being the most notable example. It should be noted that this emphasis upon gendered difference was often largely inseparable from wider variables of age. Retailers varied widely in their cut-off points and segmentation of the market with some consensus around a pre-school, or under five, age group and another market niche set in the later teens or adolescence. There was, however, no real consensus concerning the age at which children were seen to become more "fashion conscious" (this ranged from three to twelve!), and a distinct sense of fuzziness around the beginnings of so-called "tweenage" at seven or eight. There was some consensus, however, that girls became more fashion conscious earlier than boys. On a more specific note, some mention was made of the significance of two demographic groups in terms of the top end or designer brand driven dimension of the childrenswear market: first, a metropolitan elite, particularly in relation to London, where fashion conscious parents sought to dress their children in the same or similar clothing; and second, a more regionally based "footballer's wives" fraternity that was strongly label conscious and willing to spend very large amounts of money on particular brands. This tendency towards an emphasis upon a "mini me" culture is significant yet demographically appears quite limited. More importantly, in neither case does it demonstrate a growing fashion consciousness or demand from *children* themselves but rather changing buying patterns in their *parents*.

Following on from this, discussion of branding was a major theme within all the interview work with industry representatives. However, what quickly emerged here was a distinction between what one might call "generic" branding, where high street chains, multiples and supermarkets would consciously try to maintain a strong brand profile of their own, and a more international or "independent" brand significance relating to a variety of products sold across a diversity of outlets ranging from Nike and Ted Baker through to Dior and Dolce & Gabbana, sold through small regional outlets or large metropolitan department stores.

> They know what we stand for, we have a reliable brand and we don't need to be told.
>
> (Lorraine, design manager)

> I think branding tends to be more about international brands so for instance things that you would see elsewhere – Nike, Adidas, maybe Ben Sherman – whereas I think designers are very unique.
>
> (Elizabeth, design manager)

Given the nature of the children's fashion market in overall retail terms, the former is the perhaps more significant development, yet there was also some sense in which the two dimensions of branding could be seen to mutually reinforce a wider culture of brand significance. Interestingly, although some customers – such as those designer label oriented buyers mentioned in the discussion of demography earlier – were seen to be wholly loyal to a single brand, others clearly juxtaposed needs for "special outfits" for parties and treats alongside routine demands for "ordinary" clothing. Thus whilst loyalty to a single brand might lead to higher or more top end purchasing patterns, wider "pick and mix" patterns of purchasing feed strongly into the expansion of the value end of the market and these are not necessarily incompatible. One factor considered here was the particular nature of children's clothing compared with adults. Children are generally much harder on their clothes than adults and of course grow out of the products in ways in which adults do not. From the point of view of commonsense, this would seem to lead to a stronger emphasis on price consciousness for children's clothing which – one could assert – is evidenced through the strength of the value market, but others in the industry returned to the counter significance of a "mini me" culture where parents would refuse to dress their children in anything less expensive than themselves, or perhaps spend more on their children's clothing than their own. In either case, though, it was the influence of the *parents'* fashion consciousness rather than the children's that was highlighted and this theme will be returned to shortly.

One slightly different aspect that was also considered were the processes of decision making and, to a lesser extent, production that were involved in the retailing and selling of children's fashion in the UK. With the exception of small, independent businesses and one rather unique department store, this was a process that was overwhelmingly centralised and decisions concerning product ranges, design and so on were usually taken at the head office level nationally or even internationally. Most large multiple and chain store companies operated a policy of "looping" or gaining feedback from their stores more individually, particularly concerning lines that were selling well or poorly:

> We communicate more and more with the stores. Obviously, we get figures daily, sent through and we collate them weekly. And then what we do we have a weekly meeting and look at the current best and worst sellers.
>
> (Elizabeth, design manager)

There was some evidence of store managers and shop floor workers having some control over such factors as display but much of this existed within defined limits set by head office personnel and particularly the product director, or equivalent, for childrenswear. One, less easily evidenced point to note was that the stronger the brand image, whether "generic" or "independent", the more likely it was that decision-making processes were centralised. Thus middle to upper end chains and multiples were particularly unlikely to allow their individual outlets a say in any decision-making process, whilst the value end of the market was strongly driven by connecting feedback from shop floor levels to those of head office. Independent and top end sectors of the market operated with more free rein but were subject to the policies and indeed supplies of global brands.

One factor that may explain some of this difference is fast fashion, or the pressure to cut lead times and the gap between identifying a trend and producing the goods, which was noted by all to be an issue but generally more strongly felt by those operating at the value end of the market. Consequently, the factors of branding, fast fashion and decision making often interconnect in different ways at different levels of the childrenswear market. Thus many value end retailers are also leaders in fast fashion and operate intensive systems of communication between the shop floor and management in making decisions, whilst more mid market retailers are often driven by a more a static emphasis upon maintaining brand image that is centrally controlled; top end retailers are also often subject to less formalised interactions with more powerful suppliers. Importantly, this produces a more complex view of the power relations involved in the retailing of children's clothing; neither designers nor managers, shop workers nor suppliers were wholly in control of what got to be sold to children but were rather often caught up in differing processes of decision-making that varied according to the level of the market at which they operated. An important and connected factor here is the significance of value versus volume elements in sales. Lower priced and fast fashion relies on volume sales to make profits, leading to a greater need to connect with stores, whilst higher priced and branded clothing is sold more according to value and thus controlling the brand and its promotion becomes critical.

The final area highlighted by the industry interviews was the question of the most major influences upon children when it comes to their clothes, tastes and desires for fashion. Perhaps not surprisingly, there was a mixture of responses here. Most attention centred on the role of the mass media, and particularly children's television such as Saturday morning pop programmes which were generally seen as more significant in stimulating demands and desires than magazines:

> When Kylie sort of had her revival all the little girls wanted to look like Kylie and obviously on boys' wear it's very much about the latest football star.
>
> (Elizabeth, design manager)

Product directors for childrenswear were curiously unwilling or unaware of acknowledging their own role in marketing childrenswear or stimulating demand for fashion products, and repeatedly saw themselves as merely responding to consumer demand. One wider trend that was broadly noted was that of "adultification" or the tendency of children's clothing to mimic or quite literally downsize adult clothing:

> It is very much a mini me, especially at the age group I am buying which is up to ten years ... If the parents wear those brands they will buy those brands for their children.
>
> (Carol, buyer)

One example cited was the trend towards ponchos for women a few years ago, something that was simply repeated in smaller sizes for pre-adolescent girls. This was again seen to be tied up with the demands of parents to dress their children like themselves rather than as any kind of industry-led policy. When asked about questions of the potential sexualisation of children's clothing, particularly for girls, none of the companies spoken to had any policy beyond a loose question of good and bad taste.

> No we've obviously got safety guidelines for a purely safety point of view to the British standards so for instance entrapment and so that they don't harm themselves but no for ... I mean, it's a question of taste and it's really, you know, it is very woolly.
>
> (Elizabeth, design manager)

Thus decisions concerning the appropriateness of children's clothing were taken on an *ad hoc* basis by senior buyers and directors in most companies.

It was often the case that many retailers claimed that they themselves did not sell such goods as "boob tubes" or asymmetric tops for eight-year-old girls but that someone else did. To be fair few, if any, of the stores interviewed appeared to be selling overly sexualised children's clothing. This raises the question of where young girls in particular might be accessing such items. There are two suggestions here – one is that girls themselves, with or without their elders, are visiting more adult stores and buying teenage or adult clothing in small sizes, and/or even altering clothing to fit themselves, and another is mail order where there are fewer restrictions on what can be purchased other than those applied by parents. It was unfortunate here that access to some children's and girls' wear specialists in particular could not be attained.

Whilst it is beyond the scope of this chapter to consider the data gained from the work conducted with children and families in detail, some points are worth noting. First, the work with parents and their children displayed an equally mixed picture of results within an overall framework of what one might call the triangulation of parents, children and consumer culture. The worlds of advertising, branding and consumption were emphasised both by parents who experienced a sense of pressure to conform and from their children who increasingly started to articulate their identities in relation to such dimensions. Thus children would express strong opinions on brands or styles whilst their parents would feel under pressure to either keep up with the Joneses or resist their children's demands. This did not, however, equate with any kind of slavery to advertising or brands. Parents did for the most part resist their children's demands, and in some cases even quite young children actively resisted commercial or media images they were presented with them-selves or via their parents, advertising or their peers. Similarly, factors of comfort, fit and diffuse notions of taste such as liking or disliking a particular colour remained crucially significant in any decision-making process concerning children's clothing. Thus whilst growing fashion consciousness or pester power was sometimes in evidence, it was neither uniform nor uncontested. Much of this discussion centres on the recurring theme of children's agency and power, or lack of it. Some of the industry representatives interviewed alluded to such concepts as the "democratisation" of the family and family relationships and the rise of children as persons within their own right with their own needs, wants and opinions. Yet there remains a very real sense in which children cannot be considered as autonomous consumers as, at least until later adolescence, they have little or no economic power with which to make their own purchases or decisions. The purchasing and indeed appro-priation of children's clothing is fundamentally relational, not only between producers and consumers, but between children and their parents or even peers and elder siblings. Thus in a very real sense children *are* rather powerless. However, their powerlessness does not render them without subjectivity and the tendency of much of the literature on childhood in particular to equate agency with subjectivity is misleading here. The work with fashion industry outlined earlier highlights the complexity of much of this – children are not simply autonomous agents that pester their parents for what they want and neither are they merely products of history or victims of markets; rather they are relatively powerless but often pretty opinionated consumer *subjects*.

From mutton to lamb: fashion and aging

At the risk of stating the blatantly obvious, children's fashion and clothing are not the same as adults' on several counts. First, children outgrow clothing and "consume" clothing at a faster rate as they are harder on clothes, both through the rough and tumble of play and the fact that their bodies quite simply grow. Second, its meanings are also different – far more of children's clothing is aimed at or centred upon the importance of play, leisure and incorporates more emphasis upon dressing up in the theatrical sense, whilst conversely little of children's clothing is centred on work other than perhaps for the school uniform, and most children's clothing at least prior to adolescence is not defined as "sexual" or intended to have the function of enhancing sexual attraction – indeed it is this sexual *intentionality* that often defines dress as "adult". And third, children's clothing is consumed differently to adults as most children do not buy their own clothing rather it is bought for them, and whilst often involved in decision making processes children are not autonomous consumers and any aspect of the selling and retailing of children's fashion is often as much about engaging with adults, parents or guardians as much as it is about the children.

The current and repeated concern with the "sexualisation" of children's clothing centres on the second point here – that children's clothing, unlike adults, is not intended to be sexually attractive or it does not have that function. Thus the *sexualisation* of children's clothing, particularly that of girls, is inextricably bound up with its "*adultification*" or the tendency to dress children as adults. As outlined in the empirical discussion in the last section, much of this centres on the rise of a "mini me" culture that reflects the desires of parents as much as, or even more than, the needs of children. In addition, there is also something of a historical paradox here as prior to the late twentieth century and in non-western societies, a separate category called "children's clothing" has been – and continues to be – far less in evidence. As Cook has noted, the construction of a category of "children's fashion" goes hand in glove with the construction of childhood as a defined and separate part of the life cycle and its commodification and absorption into wider patterns of consumer culture (Cook, 2004). The selling and marketing of clothing or fashion – and indeed anything – relies upon the process of expansion through diversification: day wear, work wear, evening wear, children's wear, etc.

Interestingly, it is also precisely some of these dimensions which return at the other end of the age spectrum in clothing or fashion for the elderly. Once again, clothing loses much of its association with both sexuality and work roles and becomes primarily centred upon leisure activities. The consternation surrounding the scantily clad teenage girl is on a remarkably similar terrain to the scandal when her grandmother is deemed to be dressed too sexually provocatively or as "mutton dressed as lamb". In addition, in both cases it is the role of the body that is central – particularly the baring of too much flesh – although the difference here is aging flesh is seen as unsightly or even downright ugly whilst youthful flesh is conversely simply "too hot to expose".

However, in either case it is female flesh that is the primary concern – whilst eyebrows may rise at tight jean and T-shirt-wearing male pensioners or leather-jacketed teenage boys it is nothing compared with the outcry concerning a teen girl's rising hemline or granny's cracking red lipstick. It is of course the case that recent years have witnessed an increasing emphasis upon the sexual attractiveness of "older women" from the über fit body of Madonna to the apparently ageless Joan Collins, yet what dominates such discourse is an emphasis upon *youth* rather than age as sexually attractive – the fact that such stars do not *look* their age, rather than some re-definition of female attractiveness. There are, as Dinnerstein and Weitz note, also discourses of naturalness versus "working at it", and whilst the naturally youthful-looking woman is simply admired, a more "worked at" aging femininity can lead to accusations of desperation (Dinnerstein and Weitz, 1994). In sum, the mores and values surrounding aging appearances and attempts at youthful style, particularly those for women, are often harsh and far from emancipatory. Thus, it is the passing as *younger* here which is key. Similarly, marketing campaigns aimed at the older woman are dominated by youthful and stereo-typically beautiful examples and models rather than some new-found eroticism centred on lines, rolls of fat or cellulite. Thus the recent Dove, Levi's or Simply Be advertising campaigns may well use much older models but retain remarkably similar codes of attractiveness and beauty – toned if more curvy bodies, long hair, smooth skin and so on. The only true latitude here appears to relate to the making of more fashionable clothing for older women "who can get away with wearing it" or in larger sizes. In sum, then, there is a strong sense in which fashion, if not clothing, is primarily an *adult* phe-nomenon that tends to exclude both the child and the elder at least in most western societies.

Conclusions: who are you kidding?

Throughout this chapter I have emphasised the extent to which the significance of a growing fashion consciousness amongst children, whether coupled or not with a demand for designer clothing in particular and/or wider patterns of pester power, has largely been exaggerated and is not borne out by the data found in this study, whether with children, their parents or representatives from the fashion industry. In summary, the media interest in a new form of children's fashion was often seen to be largely false, particularly in its emphasis upon more designer clothing which still only makes up a small percentage of the market for children's clothing. Perhaps surprisingly, the overwhelming key variables were age and gender and not class, geography or ethnicity in the market for children's fashion in the UK. The most significant development within this was the rise of value and supermarket fashion retailing. In other senses, though, this is to be expected. Children have always required clothing; the overall historical trajectory towards an aging rather than young population, alongside the more specific practical demands placed upon children's dress, counterweighs a sense of major change taking place with respect to clothing, in western societies at least. What is perhaps newer here is the rise of a more adult sense of fashion consciousness in the children's clothing market, whether in terms of the wishes of some parents to dress their children more fashionably or in terms of wider trends towards a "mini-me" or status conscious culture amongst some families. This was however in many ways demographically quite limited. It is also interesting to note that again this is not without precedent. Historically, children have had a far greater tendency to be seen as, and to be dressed as, miniature versions of their parents. The construction of a new category of children's fashion has much to do with the construction of a new category of children *per se*. As Dan Cook has noted much of the anxiety here concerns the struggle to define childhood itself and the power relations around that (Cook, 2004). Data gathered from interviews with industry representatives similarly did not support a notion of simple top-down market driven initiatives, but rather a mixed network of power relations within and across the retail sector that varied often according to the level at which they operated. Where decision-making processes were more centralised this was also often tied to the question of branding, whether generic and in house or more international in focus. It is perhaps this emphasis upon branding, of whatever kind, that is most distinctive and new here. However, this is a process that cuts across many sectors of consumer culture, affecting a wide variety of goods and services, and is not an insidious targeting of children in particular. Similarly the demands, and vulnerabilities, of children in relation to consumer culture are as old as sweets. One is left then with the sense in which the anxieties concerning children's fashion are inseparable from the worries that surround childhood more widely, from paedophilia to toys at Christmas. Western societies in their struggle to define, locate and regulate children and childhood are, rather inevitably, equally embattled with trying to work out how they should dress their smaller, younger selves.

Chapter 6

Express yourself
The politics of dressing up

The politics of fashion are essentially two-fold: first, in relation to its production, historically exploitative and more recently racialised; and second, in connection with its consumption. The former is mostly considered in Chapter 7. Here we will consider the politics of fashion's consumption. For the most part this centres on the politics of identity or the series of ways in which aspects of our more contemporary identities such as class, gender, race or sexuality have become more politicised in the wake of new social movements such as black protest, civil rights, feminism and gay liberation. A second dimension centres on questions of subcultural style or forms of mostly youth driven resistance towards more dominant or mainstream forms of self-presentation. Common examples include mods and rockers, the punk movement, goth culture and some aspects of black style such as Rastafarianism. The two dimensions connect significantly in relation to questions of class, race, sexuality and gender. Thus, the differing aspects of the politics of fashion are also interconnected: class-driven *and* gendered, racialised *and* sexualised. As a result, the first two sections of this chapter consider these dimensions in turn. A final section shifts attention to issues of work dress which display similar yet differing tensions around conformity, individuality and identity.

Fashion and identity politics

For a long time, fashion has been seen as an apolitical phenomenon, outside of politics, and of little concern to politicians. It is still the case today that politicians rarely involve themselves in decision-making processes that impact on fashion – although the rise in VAT on adult clothing in the UK, sales taxes in the US and similar policies in parts of Europe, plus the impact of interest and exchange rates nationally and internationally all have some effect. Fashion is, however, now a very political phenomenon. This is due, for the most part, to the various social movements of the 1960s and 1970s that sought to politicise appearance as part of an overall politics of identity.

The perception of fashion as an apolitical phenomenon has also been a partial *mis*perception as fashion and appearance have always played a key part in the politics of difference. The politics of difference here refers to those politics which effect, reinforce or even invent difference within groups and societies whether according to class, age, gender, race, sexual orientation or, more simply, the politics of bodily regulation. For example, sumptuary laws were used periodically – and particularly in the wake of the Reformation and later periods of Puritanism – to regulate perceived extravagance, which usually meant expenditure on personal appearance and fashion (McCracken, 1988). This still persists today in the rather mixed series of attitudes towards fashion, and particularly haute couture, often seen as wasteful, superficial or worse. Often what is implied in such attempts to regulate extravagance is a sense of moral, as well as economic, control in maintaining class distinctions, an attempt to stop people "putting on airs and graces" or "getting ideas above their station in life". Sumptuary laws were rarely applied at the top of the social ladder and were aimed primarily at the middle classes as a defensive gesture from the aristocracy (Barnard, 1996). Similarly, the style-conscious or fashionable person is often seen in rather ambiguous terms – sometimes as admirable and worthy of emulation but at others regarded with suspicion, accused of narcissism, idleness or wastefulness.

What is perhaps less apparent in the application of such morality and legislation is the issue of gender. The stereotype of the extravagant and wasteful person overspending time and money on their appearance and fashion was usually a woman. As with most stereotypes, this was not merely the production of myth, as middle and upper class women *were* often the primary and conspicuous consumers of fashion, particularly in the late nineteenth century. If women of leisure were often mocked and portrayed as superficial and passive, then men who adopted similar modes of living were often equally condemned. The primary examples of this process at work were the dandies of the early nineteenth century who were often seen as excessive, effeminate or morally suspect (Laver, 1968). This sense of unease concerning dressed-up men continues into the present day as very well dressed men, unless pop or film stars, are often seen as narcissistic, silly, homosexual or all three, whilst their female counterparts are more likely to be perceived as stylish (see Chapter 3). However, the situation concerning the interpretation of fashion increased in complexity in the 1960s when the politics of identity shifted many perceptions.

Politically, the 1960s saw a radical discontinuity with the past. This primarily came from a whole series of minority, and not so minority, movements: feminism, youth and student protests, peace campaigners, gay groups, civil rights, rising tensions around racism and, in particular, hippie culture which was also welded to the rise of youth culture and "sex, drugs and rock 'n' roll". Hippie culture was perhaps the most influential of all these movements as it was the most loosely focused and encompassed most groups and issues – free love, self-expression and spirituality were woolly concepts that could incorporate pacifism, youth culture, homosexuality and even some forms of androgynous feminism all at the same time.

The impact of hippie culture on fashion was, as a consequence, immense. Jeans, cheesecloth, velvets, beads, bangles and long hair ultimately, if briefly, became the uniform of almost the entire western population under the age of 40. The significance of hippie culture upon fashion was, ultimately, threefold. First, it fuelled a near revolution in casual clothing and emphasised formal dress as being for the middle class, middle-aged and conservative only; second, it created an intense interest in dress and appearance that went hand in glove with a rapid increase in mass-produced cheap products and a second-hand market; and third, it led indirectly to the creation of a very strong sense of politically correct dress centred particularly on an anti-middle class and anti-formal rhetoric. This last factor is tied up with the simultaneous development of identity politics.

Identity politics at their most simple state that identity is not neutral, it is socially shaped and, most importantly, it is political (Edwards, 1994; Rutherford, 1990; Weeks, 1985). Identity itself is often tricky to define other than as a social sense of one's own individuality and location in the wider society or as the process of self-definition and self-presentation in everyday life. There is an intense sense of conflict here as identity is often seen on the one hand as something of a fixed entity, something one *is* whilst it is equally experienced as contradictory and awkward, or something one may be, could be or would like to *become*. Identities also tend to multiply and change according to time and place – I am not the same here as there, or the same now as I was. This is also what informs more "postmodern" interpretations that tend to argue that identity is multiple, fluid and fragmented rather than uniform, fixed and coherent, and – if it exists at all – a matter of almost theatrical performance (Butler, 1990).

At the heart of all of this is the tension of the individual and the social, a sense of oneself as the same and yet different to others, as fitting in and as standing out, and as shaped and yet creative. It is, moreover, not surprising that the swirling world of fashion should have so strong a connection with the equally dynamic world of identity, and as the patterns and shapes of the clothes on models mutate in front of us we are also confronted with the three-dimensional kaleidoscope of ourselves. This sense of fashion's connection with identity and its resulting tensions informs the final section of this chapter where I consider dress at work. Whilst attitudes towards dress in many other areas of life – particularly those relating to leisure activities such as dining out or going to the theatre – work remains something of a battleground concerning clothing, exemplified in the controversy surrounding the rise of more casual business attire and so-called "dress down Fridays". For some, this sense of fashion's increasing complexity is taken further to lead to connections to postmodernity and fashion as the epitome of a consumer-oriented, image-driven society where meanings are increasingly less fixed and more chaotic (Baudrillard, 1983; Evans and Thornton, 1989; Kroker and Kroker, 1988). This current view of identity politics and its relationship to fashion is in many ways new and the result of a collapse in whatever sense of political unity existed previously. To unpack this further necessitates a more detailed consideration of some of the unities and tensions concerning dress, appearance and fashion that existed within some of the political groups and movements of the 1960s and 1970s.

The 1960s saw a radical politicisation of many aspects of identity including gender, race and sexuality in the wake of new social movements such as feminism, civil rights and gay liberation. The impact of feminism upon questions of gender or, more particularly, femininity and fashion, was considered in detail in Chapter 4. The issues of race and ethnicity, rightly or wrongly, tend to implode – at least more academically – into the study of subcultures given the enormity and diversity of Asian, African, Caribbean and Oriental styles throughout history and more recently. Some of these are therefore considered in the following section on subcultural style which leaves us with the issue of sexuality.

The politics of identity as they relate to fashion are perhaps at their purest in relation to sexuality for sexual desire, preference or orientation – unlike gender, race or ethnicity – is primarily invisible save for factors of self-presentation, dress and or demeanour that are, in turn, often matters of choice and/or interpretation. If feminism provided a powerful critique of femininity and fashion for women, then it was up to gay men as "outsider men" to provide a similar set of insights into masculinity and fashion for men. These insights were distinctly mixed and heavily derived from the historical position of male homosexuality. Male homosexuality was, and to some still is, seen as almost synonymous with effeminacy: limp-wristed, lisping and dressy queens of high, and low, culture. This conception of homosexuality as masculinity "in crisis" has a very long, if very varied, history starting with Greco-Roman and Muslim notions of passivity, developing through the molly-houses of the seventeenth and eighteenth centuries, and culminating in the very definition of homosexuality itself in the late nineteenth century as an "inversion" or a "feminine soul in a male body" (Bray, 1982; Edwards, 1994; Eglinton, 1971; Tapinç, 1992; Weeks, 1977).

The problematic relationship of homosexuality to masculinity and the part myth/part reality of effeminacy, although mixed up and undermined in various ways throughout the centuries, has never quite been severed. As a result, it was not entirely surprising that those asserting the positivity of gay culture from the late 1960s onwards should also assault the association of homosexuality with effeminacy. The difficulty lay, and still lies, in which way to shove it: a camp masquerade of self-parody typified in drag where effeminacy is pushed all the way into an enactment of femininity, or an attempt to prove once and for all that gay men are real men too, if not more so.

This latter position, on occasions, led to a sending-up of masculinity itself as the "hyper" masculinity of clone culture where leather biker jackets were worn across muscled torsos or white T-shirts whilst tight, button-fly Levi's jeans accentuated sexual availability. This sometimes ended up as something bordering on self-parody (Bersani, 1988; Blachford, 1981; Gough, 1989). The problem undermining this, though, was the very welding of masculinity to sexuality, on occasions literally, as the gay clone was not only the epitome of the appearance of masculinity, he was the epitome of masculine sexuality in concept and practice (Edwards, 1990, 1994). Quentin Crisp's dreams and desires for a "dark man" were hardly dead; rather they were extolled and expanded upon as the muscular clone was precisely what many gay men desired and dreamed of and, what is more, this figure now cruised the streets inviting partners to revel in lookalike sex (Crisp, 1968; Lee, 1978; Rechy, 1977).

The difficulty in interpreting the degree of seriousness or silliness involved in all of this led to a series of unresolved discussions throughout the 1970s and 1980s. For some, this intense masculinisation of gay culture represented a triumph of sexual expression and political opposition to heterosexual ideology, whilst for others it meant attempted conformity to oppressive stereotypes of sexual attractiveness and practice. The difficulty lay partly in the interpretation of appearances as, for some, the macho gay clone was precisely a clone, an android and not a "real man" at all, only a man who *looked like* a man (Bristow, 1989).

However, drag queens regained significant attention in the early 1990s when the Vogue Movement was highlighted in the media. The Vogue Movement referred to an underground network of posing and impressionist dancers taking place in New York and some other major cities where young, gay and often black men would don the costumes and appearances of many cult icons, including Hollywood idols and some, more contemporary, hegemonic images of femininity and masculinity. These were then paraded in front of audiences on the street or in bars and nightclubs, as if in a fashion show, and often set to music as part of a particular contest or competition. The men were otherwise deeply oppressed as outsiders racially, sexually or simply in terms of their effeminacy and poverty, and the practice of voguing partly parodied and partly affirmed the aspirational dreams of the famous magazine and, in particular, their desires for the front cover. Moreover, the matter of voguing gained media-wide attention and controversy when Madonna, herself an icon of pastiche and parody, released *Vogue*, a highly successful single and video featuring black men dressed in 1940s suits voguing to the record whilst Madonna herself imitated a collection of cultural icons from Bette Davis to Marilyn Monroe via a series of stylised "front cover" poses. This then spread, diluted, into disco-land where dancers desperately tried to pull off the same effect with a series of hand-on-head dance routines. Controversy concerned whether the wealthy Madonna had exploited an oppressed minority movement or given it the media attention it deserved, as much of the original message was lost in a sea of hand gestures (Schwichtenberg, 1993).

The potential of the Vogue Movement remains partially untapped, as an adherence to the parody and display of cultural icons has not generally led to an equal parody of the traditional styles of masculinity. This was particularly apparent in the 1980s when the proliferation of images of maleness – from naked torsos and Levi's 501s to 1950s iconography and pinstripe suits – was wide open to parody and take-off, yet in practice led to little more than an increased sense of theatricality. However, there is some readily witnessed evidence for the idea that the impact of this movement has supplemented the increasing diversity of styles displayed in the gay male community, which now includes more sporting, work-related and design-led fashions in addition to the perpetual proliferation of fetish, leather and clone looks. As a consequence, the 1980s affected some continuity and change in the gay community's relations with fashion as the intense masculinisation of gay culture finally gave way to some variations in style. Interestingly, drag culture also enjoyed a more populist renaissance in the 1990s through the cult hit movies *The Adventures of Priscilla, Queen of the Desert* and *To Wong Fu, Thanks for Everything, Julie Newmar*, and the current style situation represents a jostling sense of change and stasis.

Shaun Cole's detailed study of the diversity of "gay" styles during the twentieth century clearly illustrates this sense of continuity and change (Cole, 2000). Underlying this, as Cole notes, is the linkage of sexuality and gender – the effeminate queen and the macho clone stand at opposite ends of an oscillating continuum that swings from skinhead hardness to new romantic softness and back again – almost at the same time. Cole struggles to make his analysis stick here and the reason, I would suggest, is the confusion of understanding clothing and styles with reading looks and meanings or, to put it more simply, what makes gay men look "gay" is only in small part a matter of *what* they wear and rather more to do with the *way* they wear it and, furthermore, how they read the looks – in all senses – of others. Key within this process is self-consciousness. Whatever "gay style" is, it is neither un-thought-out nor thrown on – this is in fact a feature that defines the most rugged forms of heterosexual masculinity – but somehow *knowing*. It is gay men's skill in understanding fashion and style as communication that is most fundamental here – that matching your shirt and tie a little too perfectly is possibly a giveaway. Of course, as Cole also notes, in the twenty-first century, many gay men could not care less or choose to avoid communicating anything at all through how they dress and thus become absorbed into hetero-normativity, which in itself may be evidence of social acceptance. Yet of course the end result is that they don't then "look gay", whilst the increasingly self-conscious efforts of their straight counterparts *do*, leading to the endless discussions concerning metrosexuality outlined in Chapter 3. Thus, the issue for the politics of dressing up is one of choice in display – to dress up or not – a choice that does not for the most part exist in subcultures that, by definition, are all about making something known.

From subcultural style to street style: the shifting politics of fashion

Dick Hebdige's highly influential, if problematic, analysis of subcultural style in *Subculture: The Meaning of Style* (1979) provided the basis for an analysis of fashion *per se* as a political phenomenon. He attempted a semi-semiotic analysis of style and its significance for subcultures and, in particular, punk, asserting that it disrupts dominant codes of communication, understanding and commonsense. This was both a Marxist and a linguistic analysis of fashion that saw style as a language, and subcultural style in particular as parallel to a foreign language, a counter discourse or conversation in conflict (see Chapter 2):

> Style in subculture is, then, pregnant with significance. Its transformations go "against nature", interrupting the process of "normalization". As such, they are gestures, movements towards a speech which offends the "silent majority", which challenges the principle of unity and cohesion, which contradicts the myth of consensus.
>
> (Hebdige, 1979: 18)

His work followed heavily on the heels of Stan Cohen, Stuart Hall and Paul Willis, all of whom attempted essentially variant Marxist analyses of various phenomena under the auspices of the new deviancy theory (Cohen, 1972; Hall and Jefferson, 1976; Willis, 1977). Consequently, teddy boys and Bowie-ites were all seen as reacting equally against the dominant culture and against a society which structurally subordinated them in relation to economic position, unemployment, housing and so on. In a sense, all of these style cultures were then seen as "noise" or "interference" in the semiotics of a dominant culture that ultimately incorporated these movements into the culture as a whole on two levels: first, through the commodification of subcultural signs into mass-produced objects as, for example, in punk safety-pins seen on the catwalk; and second, through the labelling and social control of subcultural activities as "deviant" via the state and the media. The immediate difficulty with this lay in the assumption of a strict division of "dominant" ideology or culture from "subordinate" ideology or subculture, further problematised by the dominant culture's implied one-way control of its subcultures, when it could be argued that the reality is more fragmented, less hegemonic and also more mutually influential.

Interestingly, the fashion system itself was seen as central in incorporating outsider or street styles into the mainstream forms of dress and appearance. In particular, the likes of Mary Quant, Zandra Rhodes and even Vivienne Westwood were seen as "hijacking" street culture and, in particular punk, into haute couture. Punk itself was seen as the epitome of style in revolt, or "revolting style", against dominant culture. However, the teddy boys' transformation of Edwardian style was seen as a more subtle subversion or "bricolage" of the original image:

> More subtly, the conventional insignia of the business world – the suit, collar and tie, short hair, etc. – were stripped of their original connotations – efficiency, ambition, compliance with authority – and transformed into "empty" fetishes, objects to be desired, fondled and valued in their own right.
>
> (Hebdige, 1979: 104–5)

Hebdige did, then, acknowledge a variation in degrees of resistance and conservatism in the styles involved. However, he never escaped the sense of separation, if not divorce, of dominant culture from subordinate culture or subculture. More problematic still was his constant interpretation of style according to class rather than any other factor, as the suit, for example, was automatically equated with conservatism, when in concept and practice its meaning is more varied; and coupled with this there was a serious neglect of gender in defining meaning. For example, in considering skinheads, he states: "The boots, braces and cropped hair were only considered appropriate and hence meaningful because they communicated the desired qualities: 'hardness, masculinity and working-classness'" (Hebdige, 1979: 114). This is, however, precisely the problem with such imagery: its ambiguity. Whilst skinheads reacted violently and successfully against middle-classness, their aggressive acts and looks gave away a profound conservatism, if not reactionary hostility, in terms of gender. There was an added twist here as the skinheads' epitomising of masculinity and hardness consequently found many admirers in the gay community who incorporated the look into wider processes of sexual fetishism and sadomasochism. Similarly, punk, whilst effectively utterly chaotic and confrontational, often reinforced traditional definitions of masculinity in tight jeans, jerking of phallic guitars, and glorification of nearly all forms of aggression.

This gender dimension was addressed in Angela McRobbie and Mica Nava's *Gender and Generation* (1984), something of a misnomer for a feminist collection of essays that provided a successful critique of femininity but failed to address masculinity or gender more generally – later considered more successfully in McRobbie's *Zoot Suits and Second-Hand Dresses* (1989). This second collection also raised the significant factor of racial and ethnic variation in the use and interpretation of street style and fashion. From the Zooties of the 1940s in their dressed-for-success suits and the pinstripe hipsters of the 1950s, to the later revival of Rastafarianism and dreadlocked reggae culture in the 1970s and 1980s, and even the current crusade of techno-rappers: racial and ethnic minorities have had a long, varied and influential history of association with fashion. This history has, however, tended to suffer serious neglect in the face of the white, western fashion system.

Afro-Caribbean and Indian, as well as Oriental styles and designs, have been ruthlessly plundered and played out upon the catwalk, often without acknowledgement, and portrayed as weird, exotic and primitive when they are acknowledged. Kobena Mercer and Isaac Julien have, separately and together, provided detailed critiques of both the representation of racial variation and of stereotypes of black masculinity as potent and primeval, primarily exemplified in Robert Mapplethorpe's homoerotic photographic exploration of black masculinity via various displays of their penises (Mercer and Julien, 1988). The fact that the fashion industry brutally exploits the Third World in selling its otherness as exotica or pornography, in stealing its customs and designs, and in exploiting its labour and skills, is well known and easily acknowledged. What is less well understood and consequently significant is the fact that it gets away with it in a way that even Barclays Bank could not in South Africa. Naomi Campbell's well-publicized squabbles in the world of supermodels, where she accused agencies of racism for not hiring her because she was black, are a case in point. Being black for the fashion industry means no more than being tall or short, blonde or dark, or a size zero and, in this sense, the fashion system is quite insidiously asocial. The analysis of fashion and racism, then, tends to reflect the concentration of the expression of racial difference within music and style cultures – often without paying equal attention to its connections with wider, or even international, society, other than in economic terms (Phizacklea, 1990). The key question of the role of racial and ethnic minorities in exploiting and undercutting dominant styles, for example in voguing, and in turn the wider exploitation of their own particular cultures and styles through mass culture and high fashion, remains open to interpretation (however, see Hebdige, 1987).

The relationship between race or ethnicity and fashion is, to say the least, problematic. As previously outlined it raises questions of exploitation in relation to the production of fashion (see also Chapter 7), yet its consumption remains equally complex. It is now typical for an increasingly global variety of styles to be worn by both black and white and western as well as non-western groups, rendering the question of what constitutes "black style" almost unanswerable. Thus analysis tends to collapse into either a reinforcement of binary and biological difference – for example analyses of black hair – or subcultural resistance where dress, style and bodily adornment are seen to express counter-cultural values against a more dominant culture. Despite some more recent analysis in the work of Mercer, Tulloch and others, this is for the most part an assumed rather than demonstrated assertion given the lack of empirical research involved (Ebong, 2001; Mercer, 1999; Tulloch, 2004). Much of this centres as ever upon the question of fashion's *meanings* – the sense in which we may, or may not, agree on what a style or mode of self-presentation means and, more particularly, what it means for the observer may not equate with that of the observed. It is perhaps this sense of the increasing slipperiness of defining fashion's meanings that also informs the rise of more "post-subcultural" approaches centred more upon the concept of streetstyle.

In his analysis of style cultures entitled *Street Style: From Sidewalk to Catwalk* (1994), published to accompany the Street Style exhibition at the Victoria and Albert Museum in London, Ted Polhemus points to the contemporary tendency to plunder the fashions of the past in faster and faster succession as a "supermarket of style", where one is a Mod one day, a Punk the next and a raver in the evening with an equal sense of parody or authenticity in each case. This perspective, he asserts, also ties up with the theory and practice of postmodernity. Yet the difficulty with this is that, whilst style cultures have proliferated, they have yet to infiltrate society as a whole and remain rather confined to youth groups and disco dancers, whilst bankers continue to go to work in pinstripe suits and everybody wears jeans at the weekend. The end result of this is that street style is perhaps tending to plunder and parody itself rather than anything else.

As should already be clear, Hebdige's account of subcultural style has come in for a veritable barrage of criticism since its inception in the late 1970s. Most of this centres on, for the most part, the documentation and formation of "post" subcultural studies in turn based on "post" modernism. Muggleton's work has been key within this and he defines postmodern subculture along the following lines: first, the problematisation of group identification whereby individuals cannot be assumed to have an automatic allegiance to any group of which they may appear to be a part, by nature of their personal style or patterns of consumption; second, a sense of the increasing implosion of any boundary between a dominant or hegemonic culture and any given subculture(s); third, the tendency of more contemporary subcultures to be transient and dynamic rather than long lasting or static; fourth, following on from this, stylistic display itself tends to become more fluid and less directly connected to any one subculture, so subcultural styles may interweave, overlap and appear less distinct; fifth, more politically, the values of any given subculture become more based upon *celebration* of a particular set of values or mores rather than *opposition* to another, most commonly more dominant, set of ideals. Thus the aim of many subcultures becomes one of perhaps, quite simply, "having a good time".

It is worth unpacking some of these points more fully and also delineating some more general themes. The most important and perhaps even pivotal point here is that subcultures have become, in essence, less politicised. As a result, dress and personal style themselves also become less "political" or "oppositional". Whilst the punk movement promoted values that were fundamentally "anti-establishment" – in terms of a rejection of individualist careerism, property and monetary aspiration in favour of a more collectivist, anarchic or simply non-conformist viewpoint, that was in turn expressed through the adoption of black, ripped, chained and fetish oriented clothing, combined with bodily piercings, outlandish hairstyles and/or makeup – contemporary subcultures, where they exist, express little more than a preference for a type of music or style of dress without necessarily any further or more radical agenda. A second, and particularly significant, point here is that subcultures merely become consumer groups in buying, using and appropriating commodities and in ways not dissimilar to any other market niche. Again the comparison with the punk movement is germane here. Whilst punk produced its own DIY form of style, dress and music that could not, at least in the first instance, be bought, more contemporary subcultures merely buy or adopt clothing or music that has already been provided by the existing market. The key point of active subjectivity here becomes one of *appropriation* of goods and services rather than their *production*, thus contemporary subcultures will choose to buy certain clothes or wear them in certain ways but not actually create them. The difference becomes one of assembling an image out of what has already been given rather than ripping, pinning or distorting that impression or even making a look out of new materials such as refuse sacks. What this clearly begins to set up is a distinction, or even boundary, between "modern" and "postmodern" fashion where the former is seen to have a fixed meaning determined by pre-existing structures of understanding – a business suit as symbol of commerce and conservatism – and the latter centres more on a sense of surface, ambiguity and shifting boundaries – the suit becomes parody or theatrical costume. It is this sense of artifice that underpins Polhemus's notion of a "supermarket of style", cited earlier, where fashion becomes something "pick'n'mixed", chosen, used and thrown away with little sense of permanent consequence – thus the office secretary by day becomes a raver by night and a cyber punk at the weekend. What seems key here is the shift in terminology itself for Polhemus's work also documents the shift from subcultural style to streetstyle. Streetstyle is precisely *not* subcultural style – it is as mixed up, meaningless or meaningful, and ephemeral as the high street itself. It's as if one were trying to film the population walking along any given major city street for 24 hours, then playing it back on a large screen and attempting to say that such a kaleidoscope of everything from the downright ordinary to the totally outlandish means something quite specific when clearly it doesn't. Conversely, certain difficulties clearly do arise here: first the distinction between modern and postmodern subcultures like the distinction between dominant and subordinate culture that it plays upon is overplayed in itself. The supermarket of style is not, in essence, so very far removed from Hebdige's original notion of bricolage. The problem, then, is not so much empirical as political. It cannot be assumed that mods or rockers, hippies or punks were automatically dedicated followers of alternative value systems any more than it can be assumed that today's all consuming cynics, geeks and technos have no sense of oppositional or counter cultural allegiance at all. Second, and this is key, most of the current work on "post subcultures" works with and builds upon a wider prevailing literature of "post modernism" including Maffesoli's and Bauman's work on tribes and neotribes, Butler's work on performativity, and – to a lesser extent – Bourdieu's work on cultural capital (Bauman, 1990; Bourdieu, 1984; Butler, 1990; Maffesoli, 1991). Thus whilst Muggleton and others are right to notice a wider consumerist and depoliticising shift in the use of style and fashion they are constantly working within the parameters of two overly opposed and overly polarised concepts, namely modernism and postmodernism. Importantly, fashion and dress have arguably always had the tendency to both individuate and collate, to conform and to oppose, and to express a true self or parody it, and – in the end – the sense of conflict of the two is as fake as the straw cats it stands between.

Well maybe, because the annoying factor that won't quite go away here is the sense in which the supermarket of style, unlike its parent subcultures, is precisely an institution of consumerism. To return to the question of racial and ethnic difference this is itself de-politicised as a matter of consumer taste and market niche. It may mean something subversive or it may not and much here depends upon context – Rastafarian dreadlocks may cause "noise" if worn by bankers at work, yet cause less "interference" when witnessed in music clubs, but this is a point already largely raised within the original "Hebdigean" analysis of subcultures under the umbrella of "incorporation". The politics of fashion have, in essence, imploded. There is no haute couture and no subculture in dialectic relation to it, whether that be trickle up or trickle down. There is in essence designer and status wear, conspicuous consumption *par excellence*, and the rest. The only difference, such as it is, is between the real and the fake, the genuine and the copy, the original and the knock off; yet when celebrities boast of their love of high street cheap even that disintegrates. What remains is an ever increasing, ever fast moving world of design and sell, copy and buy, and design and sell, and copy and buy again, and again, and again ...

Dressing for success: clothing at work

Given that now, at least in western cultures, almost anything goes anywhere – there is no longer any clear dress code for attending operas, theatres, dinners or much else, and little sense of outrage at an increasingly wide variety of styles as witnessed on any journey on any city metro – the one area in which consternation and even legislation are invoked is the world of work. As Rubinstein has noted in her study of contemporary American culture, dress is fundamentally an expression of wider social symbols and codes (Rubinstein, 1995). Consequently, dress is different from fashion:

> When consumers reorder their choices, those styles become the fashion. Consumer relevance, not designers, turns a style into a fashion. Unlike clothing signs and symbols, which tend to be somewhat stationary, fashion reflects the sociocultural dynamics of the moment at a more frenzied pace.
>
> (Rubinstein, 1995: 15)

To paraphrase Saussure, if dress is the *langue* – or linguistic structure – then fashion is the *parole* – or speech – and whilst the former is relatively fixed the latter is dynamic. The workplace tends to heighten this distinction setting rules – or dress codes – that are then interpreted and adapted by workers. For Rubinstein, this is mostly about presentation of self, particularly public self, in ways that show both an understanding of the symbolic meanings of dress – for example, the suit as a uniform and repression of personal desire – and then interpret it to maintain some sense of individuality. Whilst this process is perfectly observable it also tends to obfuscate some of the more obvious basics of dress at work. I wish to argue that dress codes, or written and unwritten rules defining appropriate dress and adornment, fall into roughly three forms and apply at approximately three levels in the world of work.

First, in uniforms, where the strictest codes are adopted for what is often a confused mixture of practical and aesthetic reasons – thus nurses, surgeons, the police, military, fire fighters, many shop workers, industrial and factory workers, waiters and front line customer service representatives from bank clerks to those selling McDonald's hamburgers are required to wear set – often pre-given – clothing, and even maintain particular hairstyles, clipped finger-nails or wear regulation shoes in the name of safety, protection or more simply corporate identity. The two functions also often interconnect, as whilst parti-cular clothing may protect a person from harm there is no reason why it equally could not be designed – or simply look – different, and still perform that function. Of course the other dimension – or even function – of any uni-form is more democratic. Uniforms make people look the same and undermine individual difference and, therein, social divisions.

Second, in more formal or informal – as in written or unwritten – codes of what is acceptable or appropriate self-presentation, bodily adornment or dress in a particular work context. The key example at work here is the office where men are often required to wear suits, or at least shirts and ties, maintain tidy head and facial hair and are not allowed to wear jeans, sportswear or casual shoes; whilst women are involved in what is often a wider yet still restricted notion of appropriately "formal and feminine" attire that includes wearing what are clearly women's – not men's – suits, adopting skirts or dresses, donning high heels or stylised shoes, and applying at least some makeup. The emphasis in either case is upon a particular executive *look* or a corporate identity. Interestingly, the underlying theme of the uniform remains in place here as some argue that the suit is essentially a uniform. The problem here, as pointed out in Chapter 3, is that this undermines the complexity of the suit and its meanings. Uniformity is indeed one of them – exemplified in the suit's structured form – yet its diversity in details, cuts, cloths and so on opens up a Pandora's Box of nuance and personal expression.

Third, in more informal work contexts where the dress code is, in effect, a rejection of all other dress codes through the adoption of more casual styles. This includes many more creative industries and services – at least when behind the scenes – some parts of education and social service work and what might loosely be called more "left wing" or at least less corporate institutions such as charities or pressure groups. Of peculiar interest here is the sense in which many occupations in this last group "invert" the codes of the first two through imposing an expectation of "uniform informality" and casual attire – thus to wear a pinstripe suit as a social worker or advertising creative is often seen as inappropriate for no other reason than its association with conservatism, commerce or formality.

There is some parallel here with the work of Roach and Eicher who distinguish functionally *mandatory* uniforms (as in necessary to perform the work in question such as fire-fighters dress) from functionally *utilitarian* uniforms (as in more rule governed dress such as that of maids or nurses) from functionally *symbolic* uniforms (based on the need for recognition as in the case of the police), factors that now clearly blur significantly (Roach and Eicher, 1973). Craik also echoes this in her discussion of quasi, corporate and informal uniforms centred mostly on a study of airline and academic dress (Craik, 2005). Curiously, in either case the role of the suit as the template around which much of this revolves is scarcely considered.

However, what is more lacking here is an unpacking of the wider tensions of individuation and conformity that dominate all forms of work dress. Of greatest significance within this is the second group, where the "art of getting it right" or "looking the part" is often a source of anxiety and consequence from minor levels – strange looks or personal comments – to major ones – missing out on promotion or even facing dismissal. What is often at stake in all of this is the importance of "fitting in". Uniforms – whether formal or casual – are precisely a symbol that subordinates individual difference in favour of wider collective identity. This is of course one of the reasons why they are adopted in schools as preparation for what will follow. What is important here is not the clothing at all, rather the imposing of discipline, the restriction of expression and the minimising of display that is invoked in the process of adopting a set dress code. Thus underlying all of this are the aforementioned tensions of identity, the sense in which we dress – even under our own volition – to fit in and stand out, to express parts of ourselves and repress others, to feel unique and also to belong. In occupations where there is no uniform, this tension, this politics of dressing up – or down – is ratcheted up through a multiplicity of notches, so the young executive seeking their first promotion frets to the point of anxious distress over what to wear to work. Moreover, there is a history to these developments. As service industries have taken over from manufacturing and as competition has increased at all levels in the wake of the rising costs of labour, this process has intensified, spawning a multi-billion dollar industry of guides and books on how to look the part, magazines to keep you up to date, and style consultants and personal shoppers for when you end up completely lost. What is also clear here is the sense in which this anxiety has been, and continues to be, at its most intense in the United States. There are perhaps several reasons for this – America's position throughout the twentieth century as both an economic superpower and at the epicentre of many image centred and media driven industries, its comparative lack historically – with the possible exception of the motor car – of a manufacturing base, and its ongoing cultural emphasis upon conformity and collectivity as part of the "American way of life".

Academic attention to the question of dress and work and its significance is, for the most part, surprisingly lacking. This is curious given the dominance of work in everyday life, past and present, and the obvious importance of dress as both symbolic and functional in any given work context. This predicament has shifted, a little, in the light of increased concern around the casual–formal divide in clothing at work and the increasingly "litigious" nature of dress at work, where anything from uniforms to crucifixes has caused conflict. France's recent outright ban on the wearing of all religious symbols in the wake of both rising Islamic and Christian fundamentalism is a primary case in point. Perhaps not surprisingly most of analysis of dress or fashion in the work place has come from the study of organisations and management. Here the rise, and fall, of what is often called "business casual" is central. It is difficult to assess exactly where this phenomenon came from other than it was most definitely one that started in the United States in the 1990s. Some analysts have argued that the rise of business casual (blazers, polo shirts, chinos, etc.) as opposed to business formal (the suit and tie) reflected a more particular development in the dot.com revolution and Silicon Valley, as computer workers have historically dressed more informally. Others have highlighted, I think more accurately, a shift in cultural values away from the power dressing excesses of the 1980s towards a softer, more relaxed approach in the 1990s and onwards. The economic recession of the early 1990s and the fall of Reaganomics in the US and Thatcherism in the UK at the same time did much to sway opinion against the 1980s and the dress that went with them – suddenly shoulder pads, pinstripes and the double-breasted double-barrelled "power look" were out. Of course the question this then raised was one of what to put in its place. This initially started through companies adopting "dress down Friday" policies, where employees were encouraged to dress more casually on one day of the week, almost as an experiment in itself to see what would happen. Initially, the impact was seen as positive in fostering greater productivity and more harmonious working relationships. This was, however, often centred on little more than personal perceptions or interpretations and little hard evidence. As many other commentators then soon noted the trend was ultimately doomed to failure for three key reasons: first, no-one really knew what to wear and ended up confused and anxious for themselves, with each other and with clients; second, they were suddenly confronted with finding a "third wardrobe" that wasn't work wear and wasn't leisure wear but was something in between involving considerable time, money and effort in itself; and third, in some cases business casual just became an excuse for business scruff or sloppy dress, poor presentation and a lack of professionalism. Formality has tended to return, though perhaps with a little less rigidity as a simpler and more effective answer to the question of what to wear in the workplace.

A second factor in increased attention to occupational clothing has centred on the legal status of dress at work. In essence, there are few – if any – state or national laws concerning what one wears to work. However, an increasing number of individual applications have been made under case law. What is often at stake here are wider questions of civil liberties, constitutional crises and/or matters of discrimination on the grounds of sex, race or religious belief. Uniforms or set dress codes clearly *can* both infringe individual liberty and play into problems of discrimination, whether in banning turbans and other religious symbols or in demanding what can be deemed to be gender stereo-typed dress, such as disallowing trousers for women workers. Consequently, dress at work has become an increasingly contested terrain legally and politically and one where overly rigid dress codes are difficult, even risky, for companies to enforce. Having said this, the decline of casual dress particularly in more commercial occupations since the 1990s indicates that western socie-ties are a very long way away from saying that anything goes in dressing for work.

Conclusions: the politics of dressing up

At the start of this chapter I asserted that fashion was widely seen as an *apolitical* phenomenon and there is a sense in which this is still correct. Fashion is, perhaps uniquely, free from overt forms of political constraint. There are significantly few laws, regulations or rules relating to fashion and yet our appearances are deeply located within an unwritten series of conven-tions on how to look: the politics of dressing up. In particular, there are few actual *laws* governing what we should wear to work, to the theatre or to take part in other formal or informal activities, and yet we all somehow and very expertly know how to look: that a pinstripe suit is appropriate for the City, an interview or a formal dinner, and jeans are equally fitting for shopping, washing the car or sitting around.

The question raised is only partly one of *how* we know, as this is clearly a process of imitation and picking up cues; it is, more to the point, a question of *why* we continue to stick to such conventions so meticulously and with so little sense of compromise. For example, the power of street cultures to shock and upset the applecart of appearances lies precisely in the very fixed nature of conventions of style and fashion themselves. Despite the apparent plethora and ephemerality of all the ways one *could* look, the question of *how* to look is heavily constrained in contextual dependencies that act like a set of chains on the potent opportunities that dressing up offers for self-expression and, ultimately, social change. The capacity to develop and change depends on the fact that we never get it quite right, that we make mistakes and that in doing so consistently we turn the tide in the sea of conventions. The politics of dressing up, whether related to identity or not, represent a conscious attempt to force the issue further and to make these mistakes correct; yet as these opportunities continue to open up, new constraints develop to control the outcomes, and this forms the focus of the final chapter.

Chapter 7

From rags to riches

Fashion production

Fashion production is the ugly sister to its Cinderella fantasy, consumption. Indeed the study of fashion production compared with its consumption is relatively neglected. Costume histories and analyses of advertising, designers or signifiers significantly outnumber empirical investigations into manufacture, training or even retailing. There are perhaps several reasons for this situation: first, fashion production is particularly complex, involving the coming together of a number of fragments – weaving and dyeing is not in the same arena as cutting and sewing, let alone retailing or distribution; second, the production of fashion is politically sensitive and difficult to access – designers and retailers have a vested interest in concealing at least some of their sources whilst the often grossly exploitative working conditions that surround the cutting, sewing and finishing of garments are equally intentionally hidden; and third, it is nauseatingly unattractive – discovering one's gorgeous gown was once no more than a set of rags in a grubby garment factory undermines its mystique to say the least. There is indeed something here that echoes the relationship of dream and nightmare or fantasy and reality. Fashion, even in its second-hand market versions, is sold according to illusion or the notion that dresses, jackets or shoes are somehow invested with the transformative magic to make us more than what we are, that clothes may somehow make up for what we lack or more simply help us to fulfil our fantasies. Fashion's production is a grim reminder that they are no such thing, that they are just materials assembled and sold, often at a rip-off cost to our pockets and at the expense or the exploitation of someone else.

Fashion production *is* exploitation – the culmination of sweatshops, under-paid designers, industrial turmoil and now increasingly racialised as well as sexist methods that exist alongside the abuse of child labour. Documenting this is hardly necessary – we all know it without even having the evidence put in front of us – the more interesting question is *why* and perhaps following that why we apparently do not care, cease to care or simply don't care enough. The answer to this question, or at least some of it, I will argue, lies in the idiosyncrasies of fashion itself, what defines it as different, and what characterises it as quite unlike anything else.

The defining features of fashion production

The defining features, or what one might even call the idiosyncrasies, of fashion's production rest on five fundamental factors.

First, fashion, or at least clothing, is a fundamental necessity of human life. Even disregarding its significance as a fairly universal form of non-verbal communication or symbolic language, clothing is needed for warmth, protection and – in most cultures – some form of modesty. It is therefore not in the same category as cars, gadgets, music, television, the vast majority of what we use in the home, or anything else other than shelter and food. Comparisons with these last two other examples are interesting. Food is the most fundamental consumer good of all – we will quite literally die without it – this also makes it the fastest moving of all consumer goods, consumed and disposed of at a rate unparalleled anywhere else. A similar imperative applies to shelter; yet this operates in precisely the opposite direction as the slowest moving of all commodities too cumbersome, too expensive and too quite literally inert. Of course the contemporary tendency within western cultures to invest food and indeed housing with the vagaries, the movement and indeed the oscillations of fashion as similar matters of "taste" is increasingly significant; yet neither can remotely match it – the former moves too fast and the latter moves too slowly. With the possible exception of cars that are generally subject to some kind of annual or bi-annual registration cycle or mobile phones that generally get superseded in under a year, nothing turns over with the speed of clothing.

Second, fashion is therefore a fast, if not the fastest, moving consumer good. This speed is only partly explained as a result of industry imperatives to make us throw away perfectly good clothes and only partly the outcome of the connections of fashion as dress with fashion as social change. To state what is already clear, clothing and accessories – let alone other forms of adornment – are *worn* and indeed therefore *wear out*. They require repeated cleaning, risk shrinkage and damage, and get sat on, rubbed up against, dragged through doors, sweated in and so forth. Whilst a well-made suit or an extra special dress may last a lifetime with care, they are the exception rather than the rule. Whereas cars, white goods and so on also increasingly wear out and are subject to processes of what is sometimes called "built in obsolescence" in order to ensure productivity and profit, nothing other than perhaps a pupil's pencil wears out at the same rate. A connected factor here is the linkage of clothing and dress to the performance of an ever increasing array of functions – a suit for work, a dress to go out in, sports clothes to sweat in, a coat to keep warm in and so on. The seasonal shift from autumn and winter to spring and summer is not just a fad invented by fashionistas – one needs warm sweaters and overcoats in winter, light cotton clothing and sunhats in summer.

Third, what this is truly about is fashion's relationship with, indeed fundamental dependence upon, the body. Bodies themselves change – in the first instance they grow, then they change shape, they also shrink and expand in varying places over a lifetime, they are made to do different things at different times – eat, work, sleep and so on – and finally they wither and die. The idea that one or two outfits will see one through from forceps to stone is therefore a nonsense. These processes – growing, maturation, ageing, putting on weight or dieting – also increase the need for clothing to adapt and change. It is also this bodily dimension to dress and adorn that accounts for much of the wear and tear everything – from movement and exercise to sweating and creasing, or the process of wearing – creates. Of course, children are the hardest on their clothes, yet the main issue of dress and accessories having to adapt to the impact of its use is fundamental. Whilst everything from carpets to mp3 players is worn out through its use we are perhaps harder on our clothes than anything else, and this in some way accounts for its colossal turnover.

Fourth, it is also the physical nature and uses of fashion and dress that underpin some of the difficulties in its production. Not only are technologies involved in making clothing and particularly textiles to withstand pulling and stretching, heating and cooling, cleaning and washing but they are also involved – ideally – in making it *fit*. Yet the very infinite variety of individual measurements and shapes militates against mass production, standardisation or technological solutions. Thus, despite centuries of human adornment, it took until the twentieth century for mass production of clothing to truly happen and, whilst the processes of weaving and dyeing cloth were mechanised much earlier, the processes of sewing and finishing remain effectively stuck in time. Thus up until the early part of the twentieth century clothing fell into two forms – the hideously expensive and labour intensive realms of haute couture for the rich and the processes of making up and making do that underpinned clothing for the rest. It was not until the invention of templates in the nineteenth century, which in turn depended upon developing adequate systems of measurement, that the means of cutting *en masse* as opposed to cutting *per capita* could start and mass production of clothing take place, processes that took decades to perfect and operationalise. It is also this templating process that still exists today, and which dominates the complaint that a litany of high street stores from discounters to designer fashions don't produce clothing that will fit vast sections of the population. It also explains why a Savile Row suit may have a price tag twice the national average pay for a UK worker for an entire month, yet still ends up hardly covering the costs it took to make and relies on the near religious dedication of its makers.

Fifth, of course underpinning all of this is the connection of fashion as *dress* or adornment with fashion as *social change*. It is this driving force that renders perfectly adequate clothing in all of the four senses already outlined redundant. The difficulty that is raised here is that whilst processes of restless innovation and shifting tastes exist for most commodities or services, why is it clothing, accessories and dress that demonstrate such a process *in extremis*? The answer, as I have indicated elsewhere, lies in the peculiarly *personal* importance of dress, its connection with ourselves and identities. Whilst similar tendencies may exist for cars, phones or other technologies, the intimacy of the relationship of clothing and accessories to their wearers is particularly intense. At the crux of this is the interplay of subject and object which is again both bodily and symbolic. To put it more simply, one's relationship with one's toaster, television or settee is not the same as one's relationship with one's shirts, shorts or shoes. Apart from a fundamental sensory element it is the role of clothing and accessories as an extension of self which is often critical here. Whilst many may feign utter disinterest in what they look like or what others think, they are also unlikely to be willing to wear just anything on the basis of what it means or indeed how it feels. Thus the selection process – comfy old pair of slacks from pink lycra – is equally a tactile one and a symbolic one, which is precisely the same dynamic that underpins identity both as a bodily expression of what we are or consider ourselves to be with what we think that means more symbolically to others. All of these elements go some way to explain the uniqueness of fashion and dress as commodities or objects to produce as well as consume. Indeed it is also a demonstration of how consumption informs production and vice versa. What it does *not* do, however, is explain *why* that process or interaction is so exploitative, for which one has to investigate the elements of fashion's production in more detail.

Investigating fashion's production in more depth primarily means at least beginning to see it as an *industry* made up of various parts completing an overall process that sees pieces of untreated material end up as completed items of clothing, which someone purchases and then wears. These processes comprise roughly the following: first, the creation or extraction of raw materials, whether natural as in the case of wool, cotton and silk, or chemical as in the case of synthetic fibres such as polyester; second, the spinning, dyeing and weaving of those materials to make cloth or textiles; and third, the designing or patterning, cutting, sewing and finishing of those clothes or textiles into completed items. In the first instance it is necessary to separate the production of fabrics or textiles from the production of clothing. Clearly fabrics and textiles are used for all sorts of things – soft furnishings, carpets, curtains and so on – and not just clothing, yet equally clearly the production of fashion depends upon the production of cloth as its raw material. There is indeed an almost anthropological sense in which the raw becomes cooked through the process of fashion – untreated, undyed and uncut materials are turned into clothing through a process of cooking, or making, which finally becomes served up at table, or shop, as fashion (Levi-Strauss, 1964).

As numerous commentators have pointed out, the two industries in question – textiles and clothing – do not have the same histories or the same dimensions (see for example Ross, 1997). It is the differences in some of these histories and dimensions that go some way to explain why the production of clothing is what it is, and indeed why it is so exploitative of at least parts of its workforce. The creation and production of fabrics or textiles is essentially capital intensive – that is to say it requires significant investment in machinery, premises and raw materials to get started. Productivity, profit margins and economies of scale are then essential in off-setting the initial investment. Not surprisingly, then, the textile industry gained greatly from the advances of the industrial revolution and indeed rises in mechanisation and automation since. In contrast to this, the clothing industry is not capital intensive but labour intensive – that is to say it requires little investment in property or equipment, yet relies on enormous amounts of skill and work from a willing workforce. Thus, the making of clothes did not start or even advance through industrialisation but rather began more as a cottage industry made up of workers using hand stitching and then sewing machines in their own homes. More importantly, as Fine and Leopold have argued, the fashion industry never truly benefited from the advances of industrialisation or indeed mass production and has effectively remained "stuck" at the level of casual, flexible and smaller scale manufacturing (Fine and Leopold, 1993). It is of course also true to say that the workforce in question was often made up of women, and the original definition of a spinster was not an unmarried woman but rather one who worked as a spinner of fibres. The invention and development of the spinning jenny in the late eighteenth century was a prime example of a form of mechanisation that went so far as to make a single worker more productive yet hardly advanced mass production. The development of the sewing machine, patented by Singer in 1851, around a hundred years later similarly speeds up the production process yet remains reliant on one worker per machine to make it work. As a consequence, the production of fashion remains – even today – both labour intensive and low in capital investment. Its openness – if not vulnerability – then, to fast-paced, poorly contracted and unprotected entrepreneurial initiatives is therefore immense.

A second factor here then is that it is *fashion* production rather than textile production that has benefitted *least* from advances in technology. Whilst significant advances have been made in the creation of raw materials – not least the invention of entirely synthetic fibres from chemicals – and the industrial revolution led to advances in the mechanisation of processes of spinning, dyeing and weaving, the processes of design, cutting (to a lesser extent) and sewing and finishing (to a greater extent) remain almost entirely dependent upon manual skills and workforce labour. This problematic situation is also arguably compounded by the relative technological advances in fashion retailing and consumption including the rise of EPOS (Electronic Point of Sale) information allowing faster communication between retailers and suppliers, the exponential advance of advertising and marketing techniques, and the rise of the internet allowing greater, wider and faster processing of orders across all parts of the fashion distributing, merchandising and retailing chain. These developments have for the most part empowered the retailing or demand chain at the expense of the manufacturing or supply chain.

This also partly explains the inequalities in careers and jobs that exist across the fashion industry. Whilst managers and CEOs of profitable cloth and textile manufacturers may typically do well at the expense of both their workforce and suppliers alike, the cutter, sewer or pattern maker simply remains exploited. Similarly, retail buyers for large companies and brands are some of the most powerful and highly paid members of the entire fashion industry, whilst sales floor workers are far less privileged though far better off than their sweatshop counterparts. Importantly and interestingly, the position of the designer is complex and mixed – opportunities for art school graduates are often extremely limited, the creative space for designers in large chain stores is frequently constrained, and the go-it-alone entrepreneur may sink or swim whilst iconic and creative designers from Tom Ford to Vivienne Westwood exist at a level best described as celebrity. Underpinning much of this success or failure in the design industries is the correct mixing of commercial and creative vision. In sum one has to know what will sell as well as what will assemble.

To summarise this section then, the fashion industry is not merely or most effectively understood as a matter of consumption driving production; rather it is defined by some fundamental features of its own. These include the primary necessity of clothing for human life which stimulates and perpetuates demand, its dependence upon the human form which makes it difficult to standardise, its tendency towards fast moving and disposable status due to the sheer variety of functions it has to perform, the relative intensity of its use, and its tendency to simply wear out or spoil, again stimulating all aspects of its demand. These demands of various kinds are then offset against difficulties in creating mass production methods to keep up with those demands, an ongoing and heavy reliance on a workforce that is in turn open to sweatshop-style exploitation due to the low levels of capital investment required in the first instance and its origins – and arguably continuation – as a near pre-industrial cottage industry. These difficulties of monstrous yet volatile levels of demand predicated upon an intense dependence upon both natural and labour resources, difficulties that are in turn almost unsolvable due to the impossibility of providing any kind of mechanised or standardised "one size fits all" answer or solution that the demand for fashion creates, may make it unsurprising that the fashion industry appears both so outmoded and so ruthlessly exploitative. However, it is worth considering other and wider explanations for this situation in more detail.

Explanations of exploitation: perspectives on fashion production

The ghost of Marx, and Marxism, haunts the study and analysis of fashion production, particularly more sociologically. In the first instance, Marxism as the most complete and incisive economic and political analysis of the industrial revolution, as the explication of exploitation through the extraction of profit via the underpaying and undervaluing of the workforce provides the most fundamental and convincing understanding of fashion production

(Marx, 1975). The exploited cutter sells her skill to her owner and manager who extract a profit. Of course this has not stopped the attempt to revise and develop alternative explanations particularly in the wake of the wider decline of the left, communism and socialism or indeed the rise of flexible post-industrial working methods. In many ways part of the problem for fashion production here – and indeed Marxism – is that it existed first as a pre-industrial cottage industry and has now ended up as a post-industrial set of fragments without ever truly fulfilling the criteria of industrialisation. It is perhaps this odd sense of misfit of Marxism and fashion production that explains the difficulties in perspectives on it that we will now explore.

As stated at the outset of this chapter, the study of fashion production is at least relatively speaking rather limited. Perspectives on it roughly divide into three sorts: politically informed polemics, revisionist forms of economics and analyses of fashion as a form of cultural industry. Exposés of the exploitation involved in contemporary fashion production are relatively well known. Naomi Klein's *No Logo*, for example, is considered in more detail in Chapter 8. The primary thrust of most of these analyses is to expose the gap in prices paid for fashion products versus the wages received by those used to make them or, in short, the chasm that separates fashion consumption from fashion production. This effectively cuts in two directions: the worker who is paid a pittance for producing goods and the consumer who is effectively also exploi-ted as they are over-charged. Given consumers have some choice in whether to purchase certain items or not, or at least pick and choose among them, the greater concern often lies with the ruthlessly exploited worker. In Klein's analysis Nike trainers epitomise this process, as consumers pay inflated prices purely for a shoe with the famous "swoosh" logo on it whilst the workers who assemble them are paid often only a few pence or cents per item. As is common with many such accounts, the direction of the interrogation is then to recommend direct action and in particular the boycotting of leading brands. The problem is that this does little to explain *why* fashion goods figure so largely in such accounts or why, even when at least semi-consciously knowing the conditions of production, consumers continue to purchase the items *en masse* regardless. The additional difficulty is that such preaching often has a very indirect relationship to practice unless to those previously converted.

One example of this kind of perspective is Annie Phizacklea's study of the fashion industry in the midlands of the UK in the 1980s (Phizacklea, 1990). She argues with some force that more orthodox Marxist perspectives are inadequate to explain more contemporary developments within the fashion industry: "What we are unpacking, therefore, is no simple capital–labour relationship. The "capitals" in question are sometimes multinational, others hand-to-mouth enterprises that compete for orders from giant retailers, while at the same time being locked into a subcontracting stranglehold" (Phizacklea, 1990: 5). More fundamental in this is her argument that contemporary expan-sion of the fashion industry has directly depended upon wider patterns of racism and racial discrimination in employing immigrant workers, a problem that is then compounded by sexism:

> Finally, it is imperative to recognise that it is racism and racial discrimination that constrain choice and force many men into the entrepreneurial option and thus minority women to work for them. In the clothing industry the only way in is usually at the bottom of a dog-eat-dog, subcontracting chain, which means up to 200 per cent mark ups for retailers and paltry sums for subcontractors and their retinue of workers and homeworkers.
>
> (Phizacklea, 1990: 93)

Whilst not disputing the realities of such practices and experiences such a perspective, however, does little to explain how or why "racism" should affect the fashion industry more particularly as opposed to any other sector.

More explanatory power is found in an eclectic range of essays edited by Andrew Ross in *No Sweat* (Ross, 1997). Underpinning much of the discussion is a concern with the deleterious effects of globalisation as this shifts attention away from specific factory managers towards diffuse and giant retail consortiums or, to put it more simply, if you wanted to complain then where would you go? Michael Piore highlights other elements such as the difficulty of mechanising work with textiles, as cloth, unlike metals and resins used in many goods, is pliable, perishable and plastic under varying conditions. In addition, a key factor linked to the rise of global rather than national production has been the simultaneous decline in protective regulation and unionisation: "The return of the sweatshop in recent years thus appears to be primarily the product of the decline of government regulation and diminishing union strength" (Piore, 1997: 140). Similarly other authors such as Wark and Smith highlight the deleterious effects of an increasing emphasis upon "fast fashion" or clothing items that are designed, manufactured and sold at escalating speed in smaller volumes (Smith, 1997; Wark, 1997). Paul Smith in particular highlights the role of what he calls "mass customisation" through the example of Tommy Hilfiger, where the emphasis is placed upon ever-increasing product variety and turnover with a lower inventory that is in turn fuelled on the other hand by the rise of credit.

The role of credit in relation to fashion is interesting here. Credit has long existed in some form or another even if only in primitive forms of exchange; yet the rise of credit cards during the late twentieth century indicated a wider shift in consumer culture. In particular it has fostered a "have now, pay later" culture and arguably made debt more acceptable. The problems of credit card culture are potentially, as Ritzer argues, also a good deal wider: increasing debt both personally and globally, an escalation in fraud and similar monetarily related crimes, an increasing concern with the invasion of privacy and the role of financial data, and the overall homogenisation and perhaps

"Americanisation" of culture itself (Ritzer, 1995). Of course the recent collapse of credit on a worldwide scale may well question many of these assumptions; yet what is the connection of credit to fashion? As Smith highlights, fashion constitutes a major part of credit spending. People may well purchase their food and pay their utilities in hard cash or its equivalents, yet purchase fashion items on credit. Clearly what underlines this is the increasingly slippery distinction of luxury from essential goods, and fashion, with its connotations of excess and desire, tends to fall into the former category. It could be argued, although it is nearly impossible to demonstrate, that the fashion industry itself now directly depends upon credit card culture and the rise of store cards (as brand or retailer specific credit cards) that in themselves evolved out of much of the deregulation of financial services in the 1980s have been key within this. Whilst store cards do exist in other areas they predominate in fashion and clothing retailing. This is not surprising and again relates to the specific rather than universal characteristics of fashion goods – their perception and invocation of luxury, their ephemeral nature, their speed of turnover and their more personal seductiveness. The phrase "I've got to have it" rarely applies to the other goods the way that it applies to fashion and clothing. The same feeling may be invoked by cars, yet few can afford to buy them at whim, or food, yet unless extremely excessive this is easily afforded. The nearest equivalent – phones and other personal technologies – are themselves increasingly sold and indeed *experienced* as fashion accessories. This necessarily affects fashion production in increasing demand at higher speeds and with more immediacy; yet this "looping", connection or even impacting of the consumption of fashion with or on its production is rarely touched upon within most fashion literatures.

One potential exception to this situation is Fine and Leopold's historically informed study of the development of the fashion industry in *The World of Consumption* (Fine and Leopold, 1993). The primary thrust of their analysis is, in common with this chapter, to highlight the peculiarities of fashion in terms of its production and consumption through what they call a "systems of provision" model. This involves looking at individual commodity groups such as food, white goods or indeed fashion as having their own specific conditions of production and consumption. It is a perspective very much set up against others, whether Marxist or postmodern, that tend to see commodities, consumers and producers as relatively homogenous and therefore concern themselves with their similarities to provide a more "horizontal" form of analysis. Fine and Leopold stipulate that not all commodities are produced or consumed under the same conditions and therefore require a more "vertical" perspective that follows the process for any given commodity from production to consumption, therefore emphasising the significance of its differences and uniqueness. Fundamental in this is the sense in which the market for fashion suffered from early segmentation due to the variability in demands for clothing that in itself came from the varying needs of different groups, and that this process happened *prior* to any form of mass production. Thus the manufacture of fashion was from the outset set up as a form of cottage industry that had to continuously adapt to differing demands and increasing turnover. Thus they argue: "The resulting contradictions and tensions this has created are unique to the clothing industry and have had a profound influence on the pattern of consumption" (Fine and Leopold, 1993: 92). Their analysis therefore seeks to emphasise the ways in which the nature of the industry has informed fashion, rather than the ways in which fashion has simply made its own industry. Interestingly, their study then depends upon an increasingly *gendered* analysis that sees the expansion of men's dress, primarily through tailoring, as distinct from women's, mostly centred on dressmaking. Thus the development of men's clothing historically depended more upon its functionality and the need to perform particular working tasks; the manufacture of suits or Levi's 501 jeans for example benefitted from standardisation and the rise of easily adapted made to measure templates more than dressmaking, which still relied on the individual cutting, sewing and finishing of whole dresses that did not lend themselves to such processes and remained far more dependent upon a single worker making up an entire garment. Such modes of working also left the manufacture of women's clothing far more vulnerable to the rise of flexible production, subcontracting and other insecure working conditions.

Convincing as this at first seems it opens up a greater gap in connecting the consumption of fashion to its production. To put it more simply, why did *women* particularly either want, or submit to, the vagaries of fashion and not men, who apparently remained content with more uniform clothing? Fine and Leopold's answer to this, of sorts, is that variations in *design* came to form a substitute for mass production in women's clothing so whilst women's dresses could never be made in vast numbers they could be made in vastly numbering forms to stimulate demand. However, whilst a thousand suits may be made according to the same template yet with a multitude of outcomes according to cloths and minor details this does not account for the desire of men to look essentially the same whilst their female counterparts apparently demanded completely different outfits. Feminine horror at being seen in the same dress cannot be entirely explained by the differing production techniques used in making it and the assumption that a diversity of designs could automatically inculcate a slavering of desire is overly crude. Consequently, the study of fashion production remains stuck in a chicken-and-egg-like ricocheting from supply to demand. Part of the difficulty here is the failure to recognise the peculiarities of *clothing* – as aside from the whims of fashion – as part of the driving force in their consumption *and* their production. The concern here is also repeatedly with a reified notion of "fashion" as a form of social change that is seen to apparently control everything – from whichever end one looks at it – to do with clothing, a point also made by Fine and Leopold in their critique of "trickle down" theory (see Chapter 2).

The role of design, or at least the designer, is also what informs Angela McRobbie's work on the contemporary British fashion industry (McRobbie, 1998). McRobbie's study is set in the UK in the early to mid 1990s in the wake of debates concerning what were sometimes called "the new culture industries" following the rise of a series of entrepreneurial initiatives in the 1980s. Through a series of interviews with art school graduates and designers in the UK she argues that the fashion design sector has undergone a series of changes that are otherwise barely recognised:

> The image of the fashion design sector which has acted as a central motif thought this research, is of a skimpy, silky dress, carelessly tossed between two pillars of support, but always threatening to slide to the ground in a crumpled heap. The dress itself is the underfunded, under-rated design industry, a fragile flimsy thing of some beauty and some importance. One pillar represents the world of the art school, and the other the commercial world of women's magazines.
>
> (McRobbie, 1998: 14)

What also becomes clear is that the skimpy dress in question also belies an industry that is equally precarious and exploitative offering few secure, let alone lucrative, opportunities despite media promotions to the contrary. Thus: "No single graduate student had avoided the extraordinary long hours, the low pay, the bad employer who wouldn't issue a contract, or the anxiety of mounting debts and the recognition that there was a whole string of factors over which they had little or no control" (McRobbie, 1998: 88). Interestingly, McRobbie avoids the tendency towards crass exposés of exploitation, seeing the fashion industry as structured around a highly dynamic if wholly unstable mixed economy that incorporates both pre- and post-modern production methods. Underlying this are both the peculiarities of the fashion industry in the UK and the wider sense in which it echoes global processes of deindustrialisation. This returns us rather to where we started with a strong sense in which fashion production is both uniquely idiosyncratic in its history and development as well as being, for the most part, explained as a cottage industry that developed into a post-Fordist economy without every truly benefitting from mass production or industrialisation. In light of this it is difficult to see how the fashion industry ever was, or ever could be, one that is not predicated upon at least some serious forms of exploitation. The question that remains is whether this is likely to change or will, in the end, get better or worse, for which it is worth considering some more specific contemporary developments.

The Primark effect: fast fashion and value fashion

Recent years have witnessed a significant resurgence in the market for low cost or value fashion, a phenomenon that has also depended in part upon the rise of fast fashion or the increasing speed of turnover in fashion production. It is worth considering in this section the implications of such developments for fashion production, fashion consumption and the fashion industry more widely.

The expansion of low cost or value fashion sold at often very low prices is sometimes called the "Walmart effect" given the significance of the Wal-Mart company in the US and its increasingly global expansion, particularly in light of its takeover of Asda superstores and supermarkets in the UK. The connection here with supermarket culture is also significant. Recent decades have seen supermarkets offer a greater and greater range of goods under one roof including electrical and computing items, a far wider range of household goods, and – more particularly – clothing. The development of "one stop" shopping has a long history, particularly in the United States where supermarkets and shopping malls developed at a far faster and far earlier rate and on a far more epic scale than anywhere else, mostly due to three factors: first, North America's massive economic expansion and rise to "Super Power" status during the twentieth century; second, its largely outspread geography both requiring and facilitating greater car ownership, travel and the formation of major out of town shopping sites; and third, its relatively untrammelled and uninterrupted development of consumer culture comparative to its European counterparts during the twentieth century, due in part to its lesser involvement in the two World Wars. However, "one stop" supermarket shopping initially simply meant shopping for groceries and basic household goods not clothing. In the UK particularly, since their inception in the 1970s, supermarkets have become increasingly engaged in price wars, meaning that grocery prices have tended to stay artificially low with equally low profit margins. The solution to this situation came through selling a wider and wider range of goods to increase profits and turnover. Thus, the UK's number one and increasingly globalised supermarket Tesco is also the largest seller of other goods, and indeed has developed its market dominance through the profits it makes on non-grocery and non-household items. Asda works along similar lines and most supermarkets now offer fairly extensive ranges of fashion and clothing items. The effect of such developments on the market for fashion more widely is significant and also considered in my more empirical discussion of children's clothing in Chapter 5. In more general terms, the development of value fashion has led to a significant "squeeze" on the middle of the market for fashion whilst top end, prestige and designer label fashion has also expanded, although not to the extent commonly assumed. One immediate point to make clear here is that such developments have had a very variable impact according to differing fashion markets more internationally. Thus their significance in many European countries is far less than it is in either the UK or the United States. This is due largely to the historic dominance of major multiple retail chains in these countries such as Marks and Spencer or the Arcadia Group (Burtons, Debenhams, Dorothy Perkins, Topshop/Topman, etc.) in the UK or

J.C. Penney and the Sears Group in the United States. Such chain stores exist in all major towns and cities, selling a wide range of clothing and fashion goods for women, men and children alike. Consequently, it was once estimated that Marks and Spencer alone accounted for over a third of all clothing purchases in the UK. The effect of the expansion of value end fashion has been to undermine the dominance of such multiples and whilst the fashion market overall has shown only small growth in recent decades, discounters and supermarkets in particular have majorly increased their market share (see Chapter 5).

Primark is a primarily yet not exclusively UK-centred company with its headquarters in Dublin, Ireland, where it trades as Penneys. Interestingly, Primark's parent company is Associated British Foods which also controls the upmarket fashion store Selfridges. The company is famous for its extremely cheap yet relatively well-designed and fashionable clothing, particularly that for women, although it also sells childrenswear and menswear. As such it spearheads so-called "fast fashion" that relies on trend spotting and tracking what is selling in stores with rapidly increased production or "lead times" from design to shop floor, and an equally fast-paced attempt to discontinue any line seen as not selling quickly enough. It also relies on near zero advertising, a relatively low cost shopping experience (minimal service and store decoration), selling lines in popular sizes only, and sheer volume for its profits. Of course what also underpins this is a repeated concern with the use of sweatshops and workforce exploitation. Despite joining the Ethical Trade Initiative (ETI) in 2006, a trade organisation that monitors most of the UK's top retailers, Primark – along with Tesco, Asda and other value end stores – has consistently scored poorly on all scales relating to ethical trading. Definitions and exact indexes of ethical trading are diffuse to say the least involving questions of wages, subcontracting, sourcing of materials and so on. This situation hit its nadir in 2008 when the BBC broadcast a documentary exposing Primark's use of child labour in subcontracting across the Indian subcontinent. Although staunchly defensive, Primark was then effectively forced to withdraw its ETI advertising in stores. Despite this, further allegations were made in 2009 concerning its use of sweatshops, this time on home ground in Manchester. Moreover, despite this, Primark's profits have continued to soar, reportedly making a 20 per cent increase during 2009. There are perhaps a couple of points to make here. First, fast fashion – and Primark is no exception – uses its own turnover precisely as a mechanism to stimulate demand. Shoppers, or more accurately women, will hurtle towards such stores afraid that they will run out of stock, a fear well founded as they frequently – and I would add – *intentionally* do. Second, and this is key for our analysis here, shoppers *know* that what they are purchasing is the result of sweatshops and other forms of exploitation. Thus to return to issues raised in the previous section, the difficulty with what one might call "exposés" of the fashion industry is that they imply people do not already know what is going on when they quite clearly do – in fact I would argue that one would have to be very unthinking indeed to imagine that such cheap clothing *could* be sold at profit *without* such forms of exploitation. Thus we are forced to ask the question again – why do people still purchase such items knowing, at least semi-consciously, the serious levels of exploitation involved. This is ultimately a question for studies of consumer psychology. Yet one might suggest a few answers: first, consumers of fashion resent paying more than they have to and seek to resist the high prices set further up the market; second, they cannot afford to pay more or at least not without giving up other things or without simply reducing the frequency with which they purchase them; and third, they know what they are doing, yet consciously or subconsciously disengage from any feelings of guilt or responsibility that may prohibit them from making such purchases.

Once again what emerges here are the peculiarities of clothing and fashion – shopping for fashion is precisely *not* like other forms of shopping and invokes a greater sense of self, emotionality and sometimes even sexuality in the decision-making process. Hopeless levels of excitement may attend purchasing gadgets, for example, yet one cannot have twenty different phones or televisions for precisely the reason that one cannot use them all. With clothing all one has to do is to wear it once – or even to just imagine doing so – for the point of having yet another one to be seen. With the possible exception of the consumption of aspects of pop music which invoke equally intoxicating mixtures of personality, attachment and sexuality, nothing is – or can be – consumed in the same way as clothing and it is this sense of desire becoming need that drives the fashion industry. The difficulty that ensues here is then in seeing where this need comes from – to assume that it is merely the result of aggressive advertising is far too simple and Primark for example has no advertising; yet to see it as somehow "inherent" is equally problematic, and it is to this question of the desire for fashion that we turn in the last chapter.

Conclusions: from rags to riches

Throughout this chapter I have consistently asserted that the exploitation attendant with fashion's production is only explained in reference to the peculiarities of fashion itself. The rags to riches analogy is germane here for it is precisely the creativity and the desire invoked in making rags into riches that stimulates demand and is, in effect, what fashion production – and the fashion industry – *does*. The fashion industry is *not* inherently more exploitative than any other; rather it is able to operate in such a way due to the nature of the objects it is selling and the subjects to whom it is selling them. This includes the problematic dependency of clothing and fashion upon the body, the lack of an ability to standardise, and the ways in which both of these factors have consistently undermined any attempt to mechanise, automate or develop mass production. Perspectives upon this situation are at their most effective when considering these idiosyncrasies – and indeed the various histories of the fashion industry – and are least useful when most prescriptive. The advancement of fashion's production depends for the most part on the development of some form of technology – as yet not invented – that can effectively mechanise if not automate production whilst allowing sufficient if not infinite flexibility and variety in design. The problem here is less about the raw materials or textiles and more about the assembling process of cutting, sewing and finishing. Effectively what is necessary is a made to measure service for all clothing, not just tailoring, at a less prohibitive price yet that appears, to say the least, some way off yet. Whilst major advances are happening in the consumption of fashion through the internet, tracking of sales and other forms of electronic information, the production of fashion remains stuck somewhere between a cottage industry, a Victorian sweatshop and a third world factory, for the spinster and her children.

Chapter 8

Desiring subjects

The designer label and the cult of celebrity

In recent years, wannabe fashion has almost become synonymous with designer labels – from pop stars to urban elites, just about anybody who is anybody, or wants to be somebody, aspires to labelled goods whether cars, dresses or technical devices. This "desire to aspire" is, in some senses, nothing new and as old as the finery of European kings, queens and figures of state whether secular or religious. Yet its growth into something way beyond the preserve of the few and into a mass market of an ever increasing array of fashion goods requires some investigation and indeed explanation. In addition, the world of aspirational design and high end yet mass market fashion is now next to inseparable from celebrity. Magazines, television reports and advertisements are full of who's wearing what and where and how you can have it too, even on the cheap. Of repeated pertinence here is the fact of the desire itself – the near lust for status transposed onto all sorts of commodities that somehow thrill, enrapture and entice in one almighty seductive "come on".

My point here, as will become clear as this final chapter develops, is that desire itself is increasingly separated from what one might normally see as its more usual targets – other human beings or subjects – into a fascination with, longing for, and sometimes downright obsession about – objects. This is hardly an entirely original argument – it is one made by Marxists, new and old, along the well worn theme of alienation and the separation of subject and object under capitalism (see Chapter 2). Yet there is something of a twist here – for fashion has always fascinated, if not all then at least many, and that process started way before the industrial revolution.

In addition, from the other end of the telescope, the contemporary aspirational vortex into which most western, if not all, societies find themselves sucked has a far more insidious feel about it, precisely because it hardly stops at wanting objects but becomes about wanting (to be) other people. We come, in a sense, full circle – in losing the contact with desire for "real" people we put it onto objects but those objects become human subjects in themselves. Thus it becomes, in an example played out year on year in my classes with numerous students, not "here's an advert for razors that shows a picture of David Beckham so I want to have them because if they're good enough for him then they must be good enough for me" but "buy this razor and *be* Beckham". Thus it is not the razors that are being bought and sold but Beckham or perhaps more accurately "Beckhamness". A further twist of the knife here is the way this world of wanting object–subjects turns into an entire lifestyle, a set of values, or morals and codes to live by – hence Chanelle Hayes of Big Brother fame in the UK wanted not only to look like Victoria Beckham but be her and find her David. The increasing tendency of many an advert to tell you next to zero about the product but to try to sell you an idea of something that goes with it is further evidence of this tendency, namely abstracting desire. This terminology draws on, yet develops differently from, that of Rojek discussed later (Rojek, 2001).

In light of this *hors d'oeuvre* for discussion there are three courses: the first considers design, the designer label and its antecedents; the second connects this with a now growing literature on celebrity and democracy; whilst the third attempts to pull things together in a case study of those oh-so-fashionable designer label donning celebrities *par excellence*, the Beckhams themselves.

Dissecting design: definitions and interpretations

Designer label fashion is in many ways a misnomer for something far more complex. Designer clothes, particularly those associated with large fashion houses such as Armani, Calvin Klein or Ralph Lauren, are neither necessarily designed by the designer in question nor constitutive of haute couture other than in cases of individual services offered to high profile clients and celebrities. Designer labels and designer label culture are, in essence, about branding. Brands in turn are themselves for the most part currencies in the market place for fashion – the currency for Versace is currently higher than that for Banana Republic for example. Smaller fashion houses however, for example Vivienne Westwood's unique and distinctive ranges of clothing and accessories, have a far stronger emphasis upon design itself and indeed the designer. Yet from another vantage point the current obsession with handbags and similar accessories has much to do with the logos and labels themselves – the Gucci Gs or the Chanel Cs – thus one needs to separate the various elements of the amorphous term "designer label" into: first, the role of the designer and the production methods in question; second, labels and logos that possibly signify a particular designer or more probably a wider fashion company; and third, the fashion brand itself and its currency in the market place for comparable commodities.

Despite its contemporary importance, designer label clothing is not without history or precedent. In particular, its development has much to do with the comparative and differing fortunes of haute couture and prêt-à-porter. Prior to the early twentieth century, the vast majority of clothing was handmade to order, whether through the "making up and making do" role of many women from lower or working classes or in relation to the employment of tailors and dressmakers by wealthier groups. The aristocracy and royalty extended this process through carefully selecting and accessing the finest materials and the greatest expertise in making clothes, accessories and other bodily adornments. As outlined in Chapter 1, dress has also had a near universal function as a signifier of status and rank. This accelerated greatly from the medieval period onwards and, most particularly, developed in importance with the rise of court society throughout the Renaissance. One only has to think of the extraordinary finery of the dress of Henry VIII or Elizabeth I, let alone the later excesses of Louis XIV, to realise that sumptuous dress, designed and made at great expense and used to signify elite status, has a long history.

The development of prêt-à-porter, or ready-to-wear and off-the-shelf clothing, however, has a far more recent history, and is a predominantly modern and western development. Its modernity has much to do with the dependence of the development of clothing *en masse* upon technologies that only arose during the industrial revolution and, in particular, the patenting of the sewing machine by Singer in 1851 (see Chapter 7). Then, and even now, the making of clothing and accessories remains difficult to mechanise, let alone automate, and is relatively labour intensive. Beading, for example, can usually only be done by hand. The development of the sewing machine, the mechanisation of some parts of the process of cloth making such as weaving and dyeing, and the rise of industrial capitalism *per se* in accelerating economies of scale all had their part to play in the eventual inception of prêt-à-porter clothing and accessories.

Thus in the early twentieth century fashion divided into the worlds of haute couture – an elite service for high status groups only – and the rise of ready-to-wear clothing for everyone else. As some commentators have noted, haute couture was effectively doomed from the outset – the costs of producing handmade garments for individuals were so extortionate as to always limit the potential of any expansion (English, 2007). Conversely, prêt-à-porter could only grow as more technologies became involved leading to greater economies of scale, falling costs and rising profits. Prêt-à-porter's only limit, and this remains significant, is its relative lack of status as neither as individual nor as elite in its execution or outcome as haute couture.

The solution to this conundrum of sorts came in the form of designer clothing which combines both the status and association of the couturier with the economies of scale offered by ready to wear. The contemporary worship of designers such as Giorgio Armani, Tom Ford or Ralph Lauren is not entirely dissimilar to the status of Parisian couturiers such as Dior, Poiret and Worth. Haute couture itself also continues in the rather different guise of pieces commissioned for high status individuals and celebrities often for a specific event only. The red carpet parade of film stars dressed in one-off or hired pieces at the Oscars is the prime example.

There are of course other factors that come into play in what otherwise tends to become an overly linear and technologically determinist story, or myth making even, in the world of fashion. These include the significance of design culture more widely, the rise of an overwhelmingly image and fashion conscious society, and the now global dominance of branding. The 1980s have often been seen as the "decade of design" (McRobbie, 1998). This is only partly due to the rise of designer fashion during this time – perhaps most powerfully the 1980s set up the reputation of Giorgio Armani – but the expansion of a culture of design more generally from a growing infatuation with architecture and increasingly image conscious shop, office and city spaces through to a concern with technology and gadgets – the mobile phone, the Sony Walkman, the Filofax were all key examples of an overall status consciousness visually displayed through "lifestyle" signifiers from perfumes to penthouses. The 1980s also opened up a culture of creativity more widely – media, advertising and image industries expanded at this time with the rise of Saatchi and Saatchi, PR events management for almost everything and lifestyle journalism that moved out of the confines of Sunday paper supplements and into the mainstream with titles such as *The Face* and *i-D*. Design started to seriously *matter*, whether it was for electronics, interiors or suits. As others have noted, it was also the decade that supposedly opened up design as a field of creative endeavour, linking it with entrepreneurial culture more widely, often with very mixed results for those involved as opportunities were opened up, yet often at high risk if not necessarily high cost (English, 2007; McRobbie, 1998; Nixon, 1996).

Underpinning all of this was an increasing emphasis on the visual. Television networks moved into a world of twenty-four-hour non-stop stimulation and simulation epitomised in the MTV channel; cinemas become entertainment multiplexes; high streets turned into shopping malls with themes, images and identities; entire commercial, retail and business sectors started demanding that their staff looked the part in ways that went beyond wearing a suit. This emphasis upon the visual has been explored most fully and perhaps most controversially by the French philosopher and critic, Jean Baudrillard (see also Chapter 2). Baudrillard's work is perhaps both best described and understood as an extension of semiotics, or the science of signs. Dress and fashion are seen by Baudrillard to form primary examples of the "commodity sign" which works as an axiom where the processes of commodification, or turning everyday objects into commodities with a primarily monetary rather than functional value, and signification, or the constant rise of visual and media driven cultures that rely on coded symbols to communicate, come together (Baudrillard, 1972, 1983). The interconnected worlds of fashion and design form key mechanisms in such processes. Perhaps one of the most famous examples of this is the Apple ipod which, despite being an mp3 digital music player much like any other, has a commercial and symbolic worth that far exceeds this, aided and abetted in turn by the power of advertising and the importance of design. Thus ipods now operate both largely as fashion accessories as well as, or even more than, small pieces of equipment with which to listen to music. The ipod's precedent and predecessor was of course the Sony Walkman – again no more than a travelling music player yet somehow an image, an identity and a lifestyle in a plastic case (Du Gay, 1997). Baudrillard's secondary argument that sign value has become more autonomous of the commodity value is also highlighted in the ludicrous costs of haute couture as well as the desire for "authenticity", the construction of "classics" and the increasing difficulty individual designers face in trying to differentiate their designs from their imitators. More importantly, this also ties up with wider societal processes of "reproduction" and "simulation" and their consequences of uncertainty and confusion concerning social values, whilst fashion and dress is seen as increasingly "out of control" and anarchic. The processes of reproduction and simulation refer, in particular, to the importance of the media and similar visual cultures in reproducing images of goods so effectively that the simulation, or visual representation of commodities, creates greater significance or status than the actual goods or services themselves. Of course the primary mechanism in this is advertising, particularly in glossy magazines, and this has been crucial in the maintenance and development of many fashion labels and their related empires. Moreover, for Baudrillard this is then seen to lead to increasing confusion and uncertainty concerning exactly what *is* still real or authentic, in turn rocking the foundations of more traditional social values; a vision which, in its most extreme form, is almost apocalyptic (Baudrillard, 1998).

Perhaps most importantly this set up what Chris Breward, drawing on Debord, calls a society of spectacle, where what is produced – and the currency of the marketplace – is precisely signs and meanings rather than things, something that in turn can drive the development of entire cities (Breward, 1995; Debord, 1992; Zukin, 1995). In turning attention to fashion this becomes the separation of the label from the clothing. Thus what one at least begins to buy is not a shirt or a jacket at all but the label in the back. This becomes in fact quite paradoxical as, for example, a Savile Row suit will not bear a label at all or it will be buried so far inside a pocket as to disappear, yet the suit remains completely emblematic of the design process – a one-off, haute couture even – and expressive of this through fabric, cut and detail and not through a label. Conversely the ubiquitous designer suit will be based on a mass-produced template with its design significance displayed through labels in linings, logos on hangers and the branding on the bag its buyer carries it out in. Of course branding also works internationally, even globally, as logos and labels become independent signifiers of meaning or what Breward calls a kind of Esperanto. The "designer label", then, is precisely the triumph of label over design.

From design to label: the designer label as brand

Into this swirling conglomeration of the visual and the commercial dropped the designer label. Perhaps above all else, designer label clothing and culture manage to combine the elements of art and business, design and commerce, consumption and status, more successfully than any other commodity form. Most importantly, clothing remains unique in its role as a communicator of status, rank and identity as it moves, quite literally, with its wearer and does not require a specific location. The quite extraordinary popularity of and significance of mobile phones also now plays into this as they become fashion conscious accessories akin to hairstyles or jewellery. And most fundamental in all of this is their connection with branding and more particularly the conflation of branding with design. Designer clothing *is*, quite precisely, about labels, logos and signifiers and all of this is in turn encapsulated, condensed and summarised by the power of the brand. Brands in themselves are essentially shorthand for a series of far more complex ideas, values and meanings. Thus, in buying a given brand one is not buying the brand, which is fundamentally nothing, but its *meaning*. To put it bluntly, people do not just buy BMW cars because of their engineering or because they are better than any other car in existence but because BMW the brand connotes success, status and aspiration better than most if not all of its competitors. However, with clothing this relationship does, perhaps, become more complex. Most major designer labels do have design elements – Armani deconstructs tailoring, softens it and mutes it down with malleable flowing fabrics in neutral colours, Versace does it loud with gold brocade and swirling patterns on expensive fabrics, Westwood takes elements of aristocratic couture and mixes them with street and punk styles, Paul Smith menswear endlessly does the modern with a twist, including strong colours and loud linings, whilst Gucci bares flesh, uses sensual materials and tends to repeatedly emphasise the "V" of any given silhouette – yet none of this equates to their meanings – Armani exudes elegance and style, effortless "Italianness" on a hanger, whilst Gucci connotes luxury and screams "SEX", to unpack but two.

What is often at stake here is a mixing of elements and, in particular, fashion's association with art at the level of design and its far more commercial significance at the point of advertising. The influence of French Romanticism as art, and art form, is immense in the later work of Vivienne Westwood, whilst the reinvention of Gucci under Tom Ford would have meant almost nothing if it were not for the sometimes grossly sexualised advertising campaigns that ran the gamut, from etching logos into women's pubic hair and near pornographic displays of male genitalia in tight trousers, to scenes of nudity and spanking. This is a trend that has continued with the crotch grabbing advertisements for Tom Ford menswear more recently.

Designer labels, then, offer a uniquely effective mechanism for combining these elements – the visual, the status conscious and the commercial – in a way strongly suited to late capitalist consumer society. For these reasons, they are unlikely to lose their significance until wider processes of change occur in society more deeply. Despite its often preposterous costs and precarious economics, it would take a major challenge to the entire foundations of consumption, the role of the visual, and the communication of status for the culture of the designer label to crumble.

For some, this emphasis upon fashion as branding, label and empire building amounts to something of a conspiracy:

> But the fashion conspiracy is not simply a conspiracy of expensive clothes being marked up around the world, it is a conspiracy of taste and compromise: the prerogative of the international fashion editors in determining how the world dresses, and how their objectivity can be undermined, the despotic vanity of the designers and the ruthlessness of the store buyers in distributing their immense "open to buy" budget.
>
> (Coleridge, 1988: 4)

Perhaps not surprisingly, the academic world of fashion often has little to say about designer labels, no real perspective or point of view. Consequently, whilst shelf-loads of texts exist to extol the virtues of this designer or that, most fashion historians and commentators remain more enraptured by the power of design than by the more commercial significance of the label *per se*. This is particularly unsurprising if one views designer fashion culture essentially as a conspiracy to make money, extort profit and create empires for its leading players. This perspective is put most forcefully in the travelogue-cum-documentary *The Fashion Conspiracy* (Coleridge, 1988). Although now rather dated, Coleridge documents and articulates the rise of designer culture with some perspicacity. Whilst lacking in any coherent theory, he highlights to varyingly explicit degrees the significance of several key factors in the rise of the designer fashion label. The first of these is to expose the fashion industry as far more than a simple process of selling goods at extortionate profit but as a network of players including designers, magazine editors, advertisers and store buyers that – combined – exert enormous power over what people, particularly the status conscious middle classes and wealthy elites, wear. What is important here is the sense in which these groups are seen to conspire together to further their own ends. Coleridge rather undermines the ways in which the interests of these groups may also conflict; yet through a series of 400 interviews with designers, buyers, editors and other fashion glitterati he also illustrates the *consistency* of their attempts to manipulate consumers and create profit. Second, he highlights the significance of licensing as one of the primary means through which fashion empires are made. The precedent of sorts for this development came from Pierre Cardin who diversified his product line so intensively it diluted any sense of design into nothing more than the curly lettered logo. The prime example here, though, is Calvin Klein who does not so much make money through the simplistic chic of his designer clothes but through his licensing of the Calvin Klein name and logo to a huge range of other products including sunglasses, underwear and, most famously, perfume. Fragrance now forms a mainstay of many fashion houses as the profit made is infinitely higher than that gained on clothing, which both costs more to produce and is far more precarious to sell. More importantly, however, the selling of perfume links, once again, to the power of advertising, particularly in magazines, and it is the role of magazine editors that forms the third element in his conspiracy theory. Whilst much sociological work has challenged the power of persuasion both in magazines and advertising more widely, the fundamental point remains that the media – and in particular the print media of magazines such as Vogue – remain the main means through which the masses become aware of the existence of much fashion. Most ordinary people do not attend fashion shows nor traipse the streets of a select few fashion capitals, but gain their awareness of fashion goods through the glossy pages of magazines or what Wernick has called the "promotional culture" of the media more widely (Wernick, 1991). Thus the ability of advertisers and editors to set agendas, if not dictate purchases, remains immense. If a fashion label is not advertised in such magazines then, in many senses, it ceases to exist. What this also starts to explain is the meteoric rise in importance of cultural intermediaries – advertisers, editors, photographers, buyers and other arbiters of taste – first understood in the work of Bourdieu and now diffused into something bordering on a research specialism of its own (Bourdieu, 1984).

The assault on fashion as branding is at its most blistering, however, in Naomi Klein's highly influential bestseller *No Logo* (Klein, 2000). Klein savages large global brands for their ruthless exploitation of resources and labour in developing societies, relentless extortion of profit in inflated pricing, and invocation of branding to get away with both. Her primary target is sportswear, particularly Nike, where the "swoosh" logo is used to validate the exploitation of workers and consumers alike. Her critique leads her to advocate direct action campaigns, boycotts, protests and the support of fair trade initiatives. However, her perspective is neither as new nor as inventive as it often appears. The US has a long history of critiquing its own corporate power, particularly in the legacy of veteran campaigner Ralph Nader and Vance Packard's influential critique of advertising in the 1950s (Packard, 1957), yet it hammers the point home harder and longer given Klein's flowing journalistic prose. Klein's 500-page-long polemic makes scant reference to much theory or empiricism – with the exception of much trawling of marketing journals – and is located in a long line of North American "blockbusters" that slither uneasily between academic investigation and journalistic sensationalism, whilst attempting to "chime in" with the times. A prime example here is the work of Susan Faludi who first attempted to document the so-called "backlash" against second wave feminism then turned it on its head a decade later in *Stiffed*, a book that made men out to be the ultimate victims of shifts in gender politics (Faludi, 1992, 2000).

Also of interest here is Klein's relentless targeting of fashion companies; Tommy Hilfiger in particular is a source of much ire, yet total neglect of fashion as a phenomenon of consumer culture *per se*. As I have argued previously, fashion in many ways acts as the epitome, or nadir depending on your point of view, of consumer culture more widely, in highlighting the dizzying contradictions of extravagance and exploitation, consumption to excess and production as sweatshop, and its power to do all of this through its connection with the fundamental nexus of the individual and the social in its appeal to primary human needs to both individuate and belong (Edwards, 2000). Connecting all of this is fashion's importance as a symbolic communicator, or signifier of status, rank and affiliation, and it is this factor that creates its strength of bond with branding, for brands are also primarily symbols, shorthand verbal and visual languages for wider values. This triangulation of fashion, signification and branding would appear to be sufficient in itself to sustain its economic and social, even political, significance – and clearly encapsulated in the world of the designer label – but one factor remains missing; celebrity. If the desire for fashion, whether "labelled" or not, is about anything it is about the relationship between the desiring human subject and the desired fashion object. The problem that perhaps then ensues is that the human subject may sooner or later begin to realise that, whatever desires s/he may place upon it s/he is engaging with an object only – there is, in short, a *lack* – and it is into this gap that celebrity walks in.

The cult of celebrity

The cult of celebrity would appear to be growing within contemporary westernised societies like a flower or a fungus depending upon your point of view. Chris Rojek has provided one of the most effective analyses of the contemporary obsession with celebrity (Rojek, 2001). As he points out there are essentially three elements to this development: first, the rise of the mass media in enabling communication between cultural intermediaries, such as editors or style experts and an increasingly wide and sometimes more unified audience; second, the fundamental importance of capitalism and processes of accumulation and commodification; and third, the cultural and political contradictions of contemporary democracy in uniting society along egalitarian lines of opportunity yet simultaneously dividing groups according to their levels of perceived success.

This in turn leads to three perspectives on celebrity. First, the economic and structuralist view that sees celebrity as another facet of the culture industry designed to maximise profit and accumulation, and minimise political resistance; second, the subjectivist view that sees celebrity culture simply as an expression or reflection of charismatic individuals and their unique qualities or talents; and third, a more cultural or poststructuralist view that stresses the significance and consumption of visual culture, surfaces and aesthetics. As Rojek also states there are fundamentally three means through which individuals or groups may gain celebrity status: first, ascription as in the case of

being born to high public status or rank, of which royalty would be the primary example; second, achievement where an individual may become famous
for being skilled or even "the best" in a particular area, and here sports stars
are a particular case in point; and third, attributed celebrity which is for the
most part status simply given to an individual or group possibly by the public
at large or more probably the media. The rise of so-called "reality" and talent
contest style television shows where groups or individuals are filmed and
displayed whilst engaging in tasks of some sort is significant here. He calls this
last group "celetoids", given their dependence upon the mass media for their
existence.

The most sociological background to subjectivism comes from classical
sociologist and founding father of much social scientific enquiry, Max Weber.
In his extensive work on authority, he identified three types of authority –
charismatic, traditional (or status and rank ascribed by society) and bureau-
cratic (seen as characteristic of modern western industrialised societies) – all of
which exert power through consent and compliance rather than force (more
characteristic of dictatorships). Clearly, charismatic authority is the most
relevant form to our investigation of celebrity culture here; yet Weber, writing
in the nineteenth century, was more concerned with the importance of single
figures in history such as Jesus Christ rather than the contemporary importance of multiple, highly visible, publically acclaimed individuals and groups.
A significant contrast here is with notoriety or what Rojek calls the gaining of
celebrity through transgression – excesses of drinking, drug use, sex or crim-
inality are often key here and exemplified in the "celebrification" of individuals
as diverse as Ted Bundy, the Kray twins and more recently Amy Winehouse.
What unites both fame and notoriety as forms of celebrity however is the
fundamental importance of the mass media.

It is also the mass media which informs many of the structuralist perspectives on celebrity culture which link it to the rise of the culture industries more
widely. The work of the Frankfurt School in developing both a strongly
structuralist and Marxist approach is important here. The work of Theodor
Adorno and Max Horkheimer in particular sought to expose the rise of the
mass media and many of the arts in the 1940s as a form of cultural *industry*
(Adorno and Horkheimer, 1973). Thus the production of radio shows was
essentially not dissimilar to the production of cars on an assembly line, with
the same tendencies to produce standardised products with only a "pseudo" or
superficial difference and false individuality. Such perspectives were influential
across the canon of social scientific inquiry into the arts and culture, of whatever
form, up to and including the 1970s, but have since come under significant
attack both for their elitist and patrician views towards popular culture (to put
it simply, they sounded snobbish) and for their construction of the consumer
as a passive dupe easily manipulated by the media industries.

A more contemporary example of such a perspective, as applied to the
rise of celebrity, is given by Marshall in his book *Celebrity and Power*

(Marshall, 1997). Marshall criticises accounts of celebrity that attempt to explain its significance merely in terms of individual leadership and stardom. He sees celebrity as a profoundly relational system that both constructs and legitimates a particular set of values and meanings:

> Moreover, the celebrity as public individual who participates openly as a marketable commodity serves as a powerful type of legitimation of the political economic model of exchange and value – the basis of capitalism – and extends that model to include the individual.
>
> (Marshall, 1997: x)

This operates on two levels: from the top down in the construction and management of the mass public into audience groups and from the bottom up in the attempts made by individuals and groups to rationalise their "affective identifications", or more emotional involvements, with celebrities. Despite Marshall's considered and level analysis of such processes, the part which remains missing, and all the more significant by its absence, is the real audience as opposed to the more imagined one he invokes. Critical in this is not the dependency of celebrity upon audience support, nor the tendency of fame and worship to turn into notoriety and pillory, but rather the sense in which many audiences are merely indifferent and do not play the game either way. The lack of more empirical work in many accounts of celebrity and its importance and construction is telling here.

One exception is the work of Gamson who in *Claims to Fame* attempts to conduct a more empirical analysis of the consumption of celebrity in the United States (Gamson, 1994). Similarly, Turner, Bonner and Marshall have provided an empirically driven analysis of the media in Australia and the ways in which it constructs, perpetuates and even "produces" celebrity, considering a range of angles including the role of agents and publicists as well as the coverage given in print and television media (Turner, Bonner and Marshall, 2000). This would seem to both extend and apply the work of Bourdieu on cultural intermediaries such as advertisers and buyers to the world of celebrity (Bourdieu, 1984).

Given the rise of globalised media companies headed by powerful figures such as Rupert Murdoch, Rojek is less critical of such structuralist accounts yet remains concerned with their connection to more subjective and psychological questions. Much of Rojek's work on celebrity explores the tensions around what he sees as the "veridical", or true and real, self and the wider split between public and private personas. This operates both in relation to celebrities and their public admirers, so celebrities themselves will frequently complain of a sense of split between their private and public selves, or even rage against a sense of misrepresentation, whilst their worshippers experience a strong sense of longing and admiration for the qualities or lifestyles of their chosen celebrities; often at odds with the reality of what is achievable or even possible within their own lives. In both cases, the result is a powerful tendency towards dissatisfaction at its mildest and destructive psychotic behaviours at its most severe, ranging from drug use to stalking.

Given this intense psychological and social engagement, or even involvement between celebrities and their worshippers, Rojek questions whether celebrity culture has become a more secular form of religion. Interestingly he notes many similarities in the observation of rites and rituals, sacrifices made, creations of altars and a profound sense of the importance of touching that exists in many religions and also in the behaviour patterns of many celebrities and their followers. Words such as "icon" and "worship" clearly have an obvious parallel meaning and significance in both cultures. In addition to this there are also parallels in the wider processes of ascent, immortality, descent, redemption, confession and prodigality in religious and celebrity cultures alike. However, Rojek rejects any simple equation between the two: "Celebrity culture is no substitute for religion. Rather, it is the milieu in which religious recognition and belonging are now enacted" (Rojek, 2001: 97). It is perhaps more a conjunction between fame and religion, rather than a secular take over, as the Catholic Pope develops celebrity status.

At this point it is worth considering what connections may exist between this analysis of celebrity culture and the world of fashion. At first glance this may appear little, but Rojek highlights two themes that are worth considering in more detail here – the first relates to the process of *aestheticisation* and the rise of visually orientated cultures and questions of taste, and the second concerns the rise of an increasingly abstract, disconnected and diffuse sense of *desire*. These are also in many ways the key elements of the third, more poststructural and consumption based perspective on celebrity. In relation to the former, Rojek highlights the eighteenth century as the crucial turning point in the development of more aesthetically oriented and visually driven cultures; key within this is fashion:

> In the eighteenth century, fashion became a more prominent marker of cultural capital. In becoming more prominent, it also became more differentiated, since individuals began to compete more intensively with one another to impress others with aesthetic impact and body culture.
>
> (Rojek, 2001: 107)

He also highlights the significance of photography and popular music as further to this development, more implicitly demonstrating the importance of performance in understanding celebrity. Celebrities are not only mediatised but embodied and adorned in particular ways to display and perform their celebrity status. These elements of music, or sounds, and image – both bodily and stylistically – are often strongly interlinked. One under-developed example in Rojek's analysis here is the film *American Gigolo* which combines both Richard Gere's body and sex appeal with strongly fetishised and branded clothing, particularly a signature collection of Armani suits, jackets and formal wear, in turn enhanced and distilled in the film's signature theme tune Blondie's *Call Me*, a synthesised disco paean to the sexuality of the designer lifestyle.

Although Rojek does not truly make the connection, this also links to his discussion of abstract desire in the last chapter. Here he discusses the "celebrification" of culture and politics more widely, asserting:

> I take "the celebrification process" to describe the general tendency to frame social encounters in mediagenic filters that both reflect and reinforce the compulsion of abstract desire.
>
> (Rojek, 2001: 186–7)

Abstract desire is fundamentally a construction of the capitalist economy designed to stimulate demand for more and more commodities and services, tending to displace and even dislocate sexual need. The added – and unspoken – coda here is that commodities become fetishised, given meanings and values they do not have, through the process of exchange in the market place as outlined by Adorno and Horkheimer many years earlier. However, celebrity culture has a more particular role to play here as it is seen to make this desire more personal and therefore more real and, implicitly, less easy to resist: "In a word, they *humanize* desire" (Rojek, 2001: 189).

Whilst Rojek pursues this argument in another, more political, direction I wish to highlight its connection to the world of fashion. Fashion goods, including clothes, accessories and bodily adornments of all sorts have historically acted as signifiers of status or rank almost as soon as they have been invented. As Simmel and others have noted this often then sets up a paper chase of emulation and separation (Simmel, 1904). At a simple level celebrity culture has an important part to play here in maintaining such processes. However, Rojek's notion of abstract desire, and its connection to wider patterns of commodification, has clear connections with the rise of designer label culture more particularly. Celebrity culture maintains, perpetuates and arguably escalates this abstracted desire for commodities and, in conjunction with this, the desire to emulate a particular person or group. The common lynchpin in all of this is fashion, so the desire is not only provoked for the commodity but for the person, which heightens the process further. Thus in essence celebrity fashion forms a "double whammy" of abstracted desire.

Similar arguments have been made and continue to be made concerning the rise of commodified "lifestyles" during the 1980s era of Thatcherism, Reaganomics and the general legitimation of greed and conspicuous consumption (Chaney, 1996). At their crudest, lifestyles – whether real or mediatised – are simply miscellanies of commodities. The yuppie of the 1980s needed not only the suit but the Filofax, the car, the loft conversion and the restaurant booking. Clearly it is great selling. Yet the more significant catch here is the psychology of desire invoked. Desiring a fast car is one thing, even if you've merely fallen for the advertising for it on TV, desiring it because you think a particular celebrity does too is a far more invasive state of affairs. This is the *diffuse* nature of abstract desire that Rojek discusses – its very lack of fixity on any given commodity, its illusory "now you have it now you don't" quality, the temporary façade that sets up the frantic longing. My point here is that fashion, as something that is already enmeshed within such patterns of desire and longing, is not only sold through this process but is precisely the vehicle through which individuals get sold themselves. Clothing and hair, jewellery and scent are second skins, intimate to us and to others, and the mechanism through which a far more intense set of emotions can be invoked. Consequently, it is hardly selling frocks that are at stake, but rather the very construction of ourselves. Moreover, this is precisely what takes our analysis in a far more political direction, but this time in relation to fashion.

Celebrity politics, power and fashion

One of the repeated arguments of many contemporary analyses of celebrity – or at least those that claim to be more sociological in their approach – is that celebrity is a form or mechanism of power and legitimation within capitalist society. In straddling two key dimensions of contemporary western society – democracy and capitalism – celebrity comes to form both a mechanism for capitalist accumulation and a form of legitimation of media, and more widely, political power. The increasing tendency to present politicians as media celebrities brings these two elements together most forcibly. To put it more simply, celebrity offers the population at large the possibility of wealth, emancipation and success whilst masking the structural reality of massive inequality in opportunity and outcome. Rather like the National Lottery, "it could be you" but the odds are seventeen million to one that it won't be. In short, celebrity is myth.

There is also a certain connection here with the world of fashion, particularly those aspects of fashion which are linked to aspiration. The 1980s saw the expansion of aspirational culture into an entire way of life – a conspicuous, consumerist and commodity obsessed set of principles and practices whereby everything from little black dresses and sharp suits through to sunglasses and cars became not so much status symbols as communicators of an entire value system that governed interaction from buy to sell and from boardroom to bedroom. At the nub of this was the sense of exclusivity – being part of some club by virtue of the cards in your wallet or the label in your jacket. Of profound significance within this aspirational process was the designer label. Arguably, what designer label fashion represents more than anything else is the attempt to assert success or at least the desire to aspire. It does this on several levels: first, designer fashion – like all clothing and adornment – is a visible indicator of status and rank and, unlike cars, houses and many other commodities, follows the individual wherever they go and is therefore a constant indicator of standing; second, it also juxtaposes an assertion of individuality through an allegiance to a brand or style, with a sense of collective belonging to an elite group that can afford it; and third, more politically, it underlines the democratic sense in which anyone with money can have the clothes or accessories, wear them and look the part. Importantly here, designer fashion becomes the microcosm of capitalist consumer culture more widely, or an emblem of the ideology of sovereignty – the open shop that offers the opportunity to anyone regardless of gender, race, class or status – you too can shop at Gucci; all you need is the money.

Interestingly, this also accounts for some its "naffness" – the overriding of cultural capital by economic capital – or, by way of example, the sports car driving, fake tan adopting, label wearing, bleached blonde is as much as a figure of pillory as prestige. The "true" aristocracy and upper classes don't care what they look like, they just *are*. This is also at the heart of the transformation of Burberry. Previously a not very fashionable but undeniably British clothing label strongly associated with the upper middle classes, rural elites and "county jet set", it became the emblem of the "Chav" wannabe when the company decided to up its advertising profile and apply its well-known chequered designs to a far wider variety of products from bags to fragrance. CHAV, understood by some at least to be an acronym for Council House And Violent, became a short-hand term to describe showy, working class and often rather aggressive groups of young(er) men and women who adopted the Burberry check in the form of baseball caps and miniskirts, rather than hunting jackets and riding gear. Whilst commercially successful, the original kudos associated with the label has now been almost entirely lost.

Of course this returns us to more Simmelian perspectives concerning the overall fashion cycle and the paper chase of imitation and differentiation. The additional factor here, however, is that contemporary processes of emulation are far more high speed and far more invasive. Thus wanting to look like Victoria Beckham is hardly just about the maintenance of the class system but a far more insidious situation of personality construction or entire identity formation from lifestyle consumer choices through to values, mores, personal relationships and life event decision making. The implications here can be very dark indeed – and most fully explored in fiction. Bret Easton Ellis's downright nasty depictions of an affluent American culture so consumed by its own material desire it renders the human inanimate, cutting up women like cutting up old credit cards; or Carol Topolski's tale of a yuppie couple so obsessed with aspiring to make everything, including themselves, totally "look the part" they lock up their baby daughter and leave her to die (Ellis, 1991; Topolski, 2008). Without wishing to invoke such nihilistic visions, the culture of celebrity and the designer label have their part to play in abstracting desire, in turning human needs such as wanting to be attractive, valued or loved into goods to be bought and sold as brands and, once commodified, then re-humanised as hologram personalities called celebrities. The mention of the Beckhams at this point is not coincidental, and it is to a case study of their particular brand of celebrity and fashion iconography to which we now turn.

Brand celebrity: the Beckham phenomenon

It should be said that there are two Beckham phenomena not one, David and Victoria, and – whilst different – both in turn unite the power of celebrity to the power of the designer label. David and Victoria both wear designer labels – Gucci and Dolce & Gabbana have been particular favourites over the years – and, moreover, advertise them. Most importantly here they have both become leading models for Armani underwear with, most famously, David's oiled and bulging body being hung quite literally multi-metres high across Times Square, New York in 2008. Perhaps more significantly, they have become brands themselves, endorsing a wide range of products from sportswear to shaving gel, and launching their own logo – "dVb" – to adorn their own fragrance lines. In short the word Beckham is as much a brand label as Gucci or Versace. However, here many of the similarities end and it has to be said that David – as symbol of the new über masculinity, metrosexuality – has gained far more academic attention. Much of this discussion of David Beckham has centred on his apparent reconstruction of masculinity or the notion that successful men can be caring, fashion conscious, family-centred, gay icons. It is Beckham's *combining* of these elements – sportsman, family man and fashion icon that marks him out as unique; yet what links these elements together is the culture of celebrity and it is also precisely this mechanism that potentially neutralises much of their more radical impact. The phenomenon that is "David Beckham" is therefore primarily made up of four elements: sport, the family, sexuality and fashion.

Of course, of foremost interest here is the factor of fashion. It is a common conception that the reason why David Beckham "gets away" with a level of vanity even the most famous of men would often be pilloried for – whether that be donning nail varnish, displaying ever sharper suits or having ever more changing hairstyles – is because he is in the otherwise securely "masculine" profession of sport, and the most internationally "laddish" of games at that, football. Apart from the ambivalences concerning quite how "masculine" football really is, this remains only part of the story. There are also several other reasons why Beckham has been not only able to go where no footballer has been before but to become a fashion icon and a symbol for consumerist metrosexual fashion-conscious masculinity. First of these is his body. Beckham is not just good looking but the kind of good looking that carries clothes well, photographs easily and adapts to a multitude of commodified personalities. He is unusually tall for a footballer, with long legs, a slender torso and good posture – or, in other words, the proportions of a would-be male model. In addition, his hair and skin tone easily adapt to many styles, colourings and lighting – he can go shorter or longer, rougher or smoother, lighter or darker – and all of this revolves around his face, which is both distinctive enough in its strong bone structure and bland enough to be a malleable *tabula rasa* to any number of personas. Second, and coupled with this, is his own self-proclaimed love of fashion, dressing up and overall fastidiousness with his appearance, notoriously endlessly tidying and filing his clothing in what is bordering on an obsessive compulsive disorder if some accounts are to be believed. It is hardly surprising, then, that he adorns billboards, magazine stands and TV screens worldwide. The commercial world would be hard pressed to find a better (role) model. Third, in addition to all of this, his media fashion importance gains potency from his personality, or rather the lack of it, his near Everyman status. Women love him not only for his looks but because he reveres his wife and adores his children. Men admire his sportsmanship and his ability to have it all somehow. And gays love him, given his ease with fashion, appearances and indeed with them. Only his stilted diction, flat accent and weak sounding voice let the show down but that barely matters in the two dimensional and primarily visual world of appearance that is fashion.

Consequently, we are returned to our discussion of contemporary fashion as a reflection of wider visual culture, and it is Beckham's role in this floating signifier of some new form of masculinity that remains significant. For Garry Whannel:

> His image has become the dominant icon of British sport representation, yet it is a strangely elusive and anchorless image – a floating signifier that can become attached to a range of discursive elements with equal plausibility.
>
> (Whannel, 2002: 202)

Whilst for Momin Rahman the question centres more on Beckham's capacity to "queer the pitch" of prevailing conceptions of heteronormative masculinity:

> The modes of meaning surrounding Beckham do indicate a shift in the possible effective constructions of masculinity, with the incorporation of a feminised interest in fashion (hairstyles, nail varnish, presentation in general) and the affirmation of gay icon/object of desire. It is in these constructions of dissonance that the de-essentialising of masculinity occurs, which may be the productive moment of disruption for those receiving the images and texts, and incorporating them into their own meaning systems around Beckham, footballers, masculinities, heteronormativities.
>
> (Rahman, 2006: 227)

Thus Beckham's "feminised" masculinity, strongly centred in turn upon his interest in fashion alongside his ease with gay sexuality marks a potential undermining of more dominant conceptions of masculinity, particularly those centred on traditional values such as work, thrift and bodily labour rather than bodily display. The problem here, to return to my earlier point, is that all of this is achieved on the basis of Beckham's celebrity and malleability as an icon of an array of identities, which not only potentially contradicts but rather has the tendency to cancel each other out. Thus Beckham's feminised con- sumption of fashion is crucially juxtaposed with his location in the production of working-class masculinities through sport, and his gay iconography is counteracted, or at least counterbalanced, by his love for his wife and his fatherhood of three young sons. And holding all of this together is his celebrity status which returns us to the role of celebrity itself once again as some- thing that creates a primarily fake sense of democracy. As Cashmore in his "socio-biography" of Beckham writes:

> Beckham is not just well suited to the requirements of a culture in which consumption is of paramount importance: he is perfect. Without knowing it, he conveys ideas that have become germane: that They, the celebs, are both different and yet the same as Us; that we could be more like them, at least theoretically – if only we had a little more talent and tad more industry; that this is a system that rewards and punishes according to just principle and that we all end up with what we deserve.
>
> (Cashmore, 2004: 220)

Thus the three key elements of fashion and visual iconography, fame and celebrity, and consumption and democracy, become united in one giant designer label brand called "David Beckham".

When considering his wife things do, and do not, become different. Victoria Beckham, formerly Victoria Adams, rose to fame as one member of the temporarily but hugely successful all girl band The Spice Girls in the 1990s. The group were famous for promoting "girl power" – a kind of have-it-all attitude towards gender politics that in practice often meant little more than dressing up, going out and asserting a degree of sexual independence (see Chapter 4). In fact, dressing up was perhaps the key element here as each of the five members donned differing personas as "sporty spice" (tracksuit, pony tail), "scary spice" (wild hair, leopard print, and er, darker skin ...), "baby spice" (blonde hair, smock style dresses, pastel colours), "ginger spice" (red hair and "firey") and "posh spice" (apparently classy, high heels, little black dresses). Victoria was "posh spice" and indeed her posh-ness had less to do with her background – the middle class daughter of an engineer, not a member of the aristocracy – and more to do with her appearance – skinny, rather model-esque poses, lots of makeup and designer frocks. Despite a more recent reunion tour, the band subsequently split up to pursue solo projects, and Victoria launched a singing career that after a few hit singles and one only moderately successful album effectively ended. Yet Victoria Beckham in many ways remains "posh spice" – an apparently appearance-obsessed fashion plate who is both used by and uses the world of celebrity and designer labels to forge a career beyond being an otherwise strongly family-centred mother of three and wife to David. An ill-judged attempt at breaking into reality TV in the United States notwithstanding, she has by and large become increasingly defined by her appearance and interest in fashion and, whether by choice or by force, little else. Indeed she has gained far more success through launching her own ranges of clothing and fragrance, making occasional catwalk appearances, promoting such brands as Dolce & Gabbana, and publishing two books, including an autobiography and her own guide to fashion and style entitled *That Extra Half an Inch* that became bestsellers (Beckham, 2002, 2007). Thus, in spite of the endless miles of press attention she gets this rarely extends further than how she looks and what she is wearing, or often wholly speculative rumours concerning her relationship with David, thus maintaining her position as the world's number one "WAG". However, as Germaine Greer (of all people) noted in commenting on her wearing of a shocking pink Roland Mouret near origami-style "moon" dress to attend her husband's premiere for LA Galaxy, Victoria is *awfully good* at it:

> Victoria Beckham may have seemed the least talented of the Spice Girls but her real talent lay elsewhere. She is an artist in the same genre as Damien Hirst: marketing. In an era of bare bellies, painted legs, visible underwear, junk jewellery and grisly computer generated prints, she is a lone champion of elegance for working girls.
>
> (Greer, 2008)

Wafer thin with bleach blonde bobbed hair, the obligatory goggle sized sunglasses and designer label handbag, all balanced on a pair of to-die-for Balenciaga five inch heels, Victoria "pulls off" the international cash ringing photo opportunity with considerable aplomb and at least some skill.

Thus, in considering the significance of Victoria rather than David Beckham certain factors become apparent. First, and perhaps foremost, her success as a "fashion designer" reveals just how sloppily the term designer is now used. Like many other celebrities, Victoria has no particular fashion or design expertise other than as a style conscious consumer, and in calling such people "designers" reveals just how conflated the term "design" has become with that of branding, marketing and indeed celebrity. Similar examples include Kylie Minogue's forays into underwear and interiors, or Kate Moss's association with TopShop. Perhaps what is more particularly concerning is that Victoria, unlike Minogue who has become one of the world's most successful female pop acts of all time or Moss who retains a stellar position as the world's top supermodel, Victoria Beckham is effectively *nothing but* fashion and celebrity. Indeed, Victoria Beckham *is* designer label celebrity *incarnate*. Victoria Beckham has thus in a sense become a hologram, the ultimate brand to sell a brand whether that be brand Beckham or Armani.

A second factor here, and this is key in our analysis of celebrity more generally, is that it has been Victoria and not David who has become defined in this way. Wider cultures of being famous for being famous are, for the most part, dominated by women, Paris Hilton and Katie Price aka Jordan being two of the strongest examples. On top of this, the magazine market upon which the world of celebrity culture depends for much of its promotion is primarily, if not exclusively, aimed at women. Thus titles such as *OK, Hello* or *Heat* alike not only trawl the world of celebrity gossip but present page upon page of how to dress like the stars, female stars that is. Thus the earlier point I raised concerning fashion's role alongside celebrity in constructing abstract desire is also a gendered one. Whilst many young men may admire, seek to aspire to be like, or buy razors endorsed by David Beckham, they are less likely to extend this into dressing like him, copying his endless haircuts, or reading magazines about how he dresses, and those who do are more likely to be doing so as part of his gay following. This in many ways reflects the limits of a more appearance conscious masculinity as I have noted previously (Edwards, 1997). It also highlights the significance of celebrity culture as a profoundly gendered construction.

This is, and is not perhaps, in need of explanation. As pointed out repeatedly in Chapters 3 and 4, fashion – at least within contemporary western cultures – is primarily, if not exclusively, a *feminine* phenomenon. Whilst consumerist and narcissistic forms of masculinity – interestingly epitomised by David Beckham as the ultimate metrosexual – have done much to challenge this, the "fact" (albeit a socially constructed one) remains. More significantly, femininity – particularly in the wake of the decline of more traditionally "anti-feminine" second wave feminist politics – is still, perhaps increasingly, constituted through appearance. Mulvey's original argument that men look and women are looked at – whilst battered by a barrage of critique as outlined in Chapter 4 – still stands, albeit with a few bullet holes through it, in the world of fashion (Mulvey, 1975). Thus, whilst David Beckham will always be known as an England footballer and not just as a metrosexual man about town, Victoria – even if she may well be the brains behind brand Beckham – will never be more than "*that* body in *that* dress".

Thus, to return to the point made earlier concerning designer label culture working through a particular relationship between the world of objects and human subjectivity, that connection is a particularly gendered one. If women have always been defined more through their appearance than men are, then that process is now developing in a new direction under late consumer capitalism, for it is female subjectivity that is being constituted more through consumerism than men's. Whilst men's use of cars, sports and technology – and indeed some clothing – has much to do with the construction of their masculinity it does not void them of subjectivity or agency in the way that the clamour for overpriced handbags does for women. In the world of high end commodity fashion women are voided, indeed emptied out, of individuality, of subjectivity, of meaning and then filled up literally like plastic dolls with surgery, makeup, clothing and accessories. Of course they may still enjoy, engage or resist the process; yet that does not deny the existence of the process. It is particularly easy here to step into what one might call "feminist conspiracy theories", where women are seen as victims of male power in their enslavement to fashion. As explained more fully in Chapter 4, the difficulty here is that this perspective in itself denies women an agency or subjectivity; the problem becomes one of trying to open up spaces within which it may form rather than close them down. The world of female celebrity, to be clear, does not help here in adopting and promoting an overly liberal notion of female emancipation through looks-obsessed celebrity. The former glamour model Katie Price aka Jordan is undoubtedly the primary example of this process. As a once topless model famed for her overly large breast implants and frequent uses of plastic surgery, she has become both famous and wealthy through what one might loosely call her "media career" as a reality TV star, and what some see as her flagrant courting of publicity through a series of high profile personal relationships. It is not my intention here to enter such disputes, but rather to raise the question of what such processes start to imply. Price, having now attained millionaire and star-like status, is now held by some to be a symbol of female emancipation, often topping polls of women that other women apparently aspire to be like. Despite the dubious validity of such surveys the fact remains that Price has attained her status through what one might call "traditionally feminine" pursuits – her looks and her personal relationships – rather than any particular skills or abilities, and thus the problem becomes one of the reinforcement of such definitions of successful femininity. What is at stake here is the *conjunction* of matters of style and appearance with the role of the media in forming idealised notions of gender, so rather than examining one or the other we need to do both and at the same time.

Conclusions: desiring subjects

The world of fashion is commonly assumed to be about desiring objects or, more specifically, particular clothes, looks or styles. Hence the common conception of having to have it – that jacket, that dress, that one cannot do without. The current rise of designer fashion – albeit something of a misnomer for branded fashion – does not contradict this, though clearly it may well escalate the process. What *does* at least start to add a twist here is the connecting of that process with matters of fame or, more importantly, the cult of celebrity. It is precisely the *combining* of the desire for a designer label with the desire – whether sexual or more diffuse – for another person that turns contemporary fashion not only into a process of desiring objects but one of desiring subjects. More problematically still it also becomes a process of desiring subjectivity *per se*. Not only is the fashion consumer a desiring subject who desires both objects and other subjects but a desirer of alternative forms of subjectivity. Once again the example of David and Victoria Beckham is relevant here – not only does one desire David's suit or Victoria's dress but one also desires them and, more fundamentally, to *be* them or to have their subjectivity rather than one's own. What is crucial to celebrity culture, to state the obvious, is the desire to be one – a desire pedalled through reality TV and magazine media in particular. Of course, not everyone wants this and those, most particularly, with otherwise well-formed senses of self or career are less exposed. It is perhaps not surprising then that it is the more ordinary, less educated or simply working classes that appear most desperate here. As I have also made clear this is a process that inscribes and invades female subjectivity far more than it interferes with that of males. It is young, not particularly skilled or educated *women* who are most at risk here. Once again this is not entirely surprising as despite the recent advances of feminism women are still granted far less agency in forming their own subjectivity than men – the image of the Stepford wife erased of her own self and filled with an alternative one is rather extreme yet remains germane. More academically, this is an argument that follows on from Marxism – commodity fetishism becomes subject or even personality re-appropriation, and it extends the arguments of Baudelaire, Benjamin, Deleuze and Guattari – to mention only some – on the near opiate effects of capitalism (Baudelaire, 1995; Buck-Morss, 1989; Deleuze and Guattari, 1984). It also develops alongside the more postmodern ideas of Baudrillard and the Krokers considered in Chapter 2 (Baudrillard, 1998; Kroker and Cook, 1988). However, what is more pertinent here than polemics on consumer capitalism are the peculiarities of fashion and dress. As stated in the previous chapter, clothing and style are the most personal of object worlds, involving levels of subjectivity and indeed sensuality that most other commodities do not; as a result, fashion becomes particularly vulnerable to these processes of desiring subjectivity and subjective desire. More problematically this has to some extent always been the case, yet the increasing inscription of fashion within the escalating powers of the media combined with celebrity give particular cause for concern. To return to where I started – if fashion began as a Pandora's Box opened with innocent curiosity then it now risks becoming a far more malevolent Medusa, through its godlike celebrities reducing its staring subjects to stone.

Conclusion

The fashion invasion

The key defining feature of the past century of fashion, in the west at least, has not been its globalisation, the apparent implosion of many gendered divisions, or the rise of both youthfulness and subcultures – although all of these factors are substantially in evidence – but its casualisation. The decline in formality, when practically every occasion – from eating out to working, from births to deaths to visiting friends – had previously demanded its marker in dress, even its own outfit, has been almost relentless. It is now not unusual for people to work in high status positions, visit expensive restaurants, or attend major events in the same jeans and sweater they wore to watch TV and generally "chill out" the night before. This has little to do with retailers or designers, although the banality of some North American fashion houses holds some responsibility, but the choices and appropriations of such designs by consumers. Almost all high street stores now offer a quite dazzling array of colours, styles and fashions but the average consumer emerges often having bought nothing more than another pair of jeans much like before, a regulation white shirt for work, or yet another little black something. Where more outlandish clothing is bought it is either in small amounts to be mingled in with more conservative clothing – the bright tie for example – or kept for a very few occasions such as a party, special event or night out. There is of course some variation here – most Mediterranean cultures demonstrate a continued love of colour and the French and Italians remain more elegant than most. Similarly, the youthful like to stand out at least some of the time and metropolitan elites can still assert status through style. Yet this is only partly a matter of style, or more frankly the fact that most people appear not to have, or perhaps want, much of it and is more largely about inhibition – that dressing up, making an effort is somehow showing off, demanding attention – which accounts for the herds of high heels and glitter that clutter the average English high street on a Friday night having had a few, or many, drinks. Of significance here are celebrities, the new aristocrats of style. Yet it remains the case that even they do not feel compelled to don hats unless they feel like it when their Hollywood forebears would not have been seen dead without. More importantly, formality still has much to do with status – the higher the rank the more preposterously impractical, uncomfortable or flashy outfits become – one only has to think of the ceremonial robes of kings and queens on state occasions to get the idea here – and this has led some to argue that increasing casualisation correlates with greater equality or even a classless society. Yet given the relentless construction of status if not class inequalities, this makes little sense. More pronounced is the significance of the informality of society itself – the abandoning of dress codes, rules and regulations.

Thus, in the early twenty-first century we are presented with something of a conundrum in understanding fashion. Whilst clothing has diversified and expanded into a myriad of forms, colours and styles – all increasingly accessible to more and wider sections of the population – fashion *per se* seems almost dead. Haute couture and bespoke tailoring are afforded by only the wealthy, and designers at all levels increasingly rely on star-studded celebrities, diffusion lines, and franchises to function at a profit at all. Similarly, any glance at what people are wearing on any given major high street in or in any world city displays both an extraordinary degree of homogeneity, an apparent lack of effort or frankly dullness. It is difficult to imagine how an individual as eccentric or unique as Quentin Crisp could arise a century or even 50 years later than he did when presented with a sea of jeans and tops or ill-fitting suits.

There are perhaps two dimensions to this situation: first, the rise of more casual clothing itself; and second, the enormity of the relaxation in dress codes and mores. The former is easily evidenced in the rise of jeans, sweaters and T-shirts, let alone sports clothing and what is sometimes now called "lounge wear", none of which existed in any *en masse* sense a century ago. This is in fact the most fundamental defining feature of all fashion over the past century – its expansion to the population as a whole, even the poor, a development for the most part explained through the rise of prêt-à-porter. Yet these two elements connect; for as dress codes relax the sense in which anyone can stand out at all is negated – the significance of detail is lost. Whilst merely the addition of an extra inch of lace on a sleeve could cause a storm of controversy in the nineteenth century, a hundred or so years later and outside of the workplace at least almost anything goes anywhere. The idea of having to dress one way for dinner, another for afternoon tea, and yet another on Sundays has next to disappeared. This lack of constraint – or even liberalism – can be no bad thing, yet paradoxically collapses into a sea of uniformity. It is the emphasis upon informality which is key here – the sense in which neither walking the streets nor dining with friends, a trip to the opera or even an important meeting at work necessarily requires any particular form of self-presentation at all. And all of this has happened remarkably quickly in the space of probably under 50 years; yet if the sense of formality has declined the emphasis upon uniformity has not – people increasingly look the same. As a hair stylist said to me recently, when referring to the legions of young women wanting poker straight hair, "here come the clones". Ghds – the salon hair straighteners – are indeed a new religion. Thus, despite the dizzying diversity on offer it all ends up looking remarkably samey.

To pursue this theme to its more apocalyptic conclusion implies – quite literally – the death of fashion. When everything is in, or at least not really out, then what is fashion? Thus one can sit on a city metro with a man in a pinstripe suit, another with dreadlocks, a woman in five inch heels and another in jeans and a sweater, and an obviously gay guy dressed in a lot of pink Lycra, and not turn a hair at any of it. Judgements may still be made here – "flash git", "slapper", "ponce", etc. – yet there is no real sense of outrage. Thus there is also some linkage here of casualisation with wider social tolerance, at least of overall patterns of dress; yet where does this leave fashion more specifically?

To paraphrase a point raised by Flügel in Chapter 2, fashion many end up as little more than a moment in history (Flügel, 1930). If anything goes then what goes is fashion, for if nothing is out then nothing is in either; yet perhaps the more accurate picture here is that that there are differing levels of fashion consciousness, and still a sense of chasing what's *most* in at least by some. Once again, key within this is celebrity and designer label culture. If fashion now only exists as a celebrity endorsement then this both highlights and strengthens the role of the fashion media and rather disempowers the fashion consumer. A more fundamental point here is that fashion is becoming less about clothes and more about images, magazines and media reports on what's hot or who wore what where. What the average consumer now purchases is not so much a particular colour, cloth or cut so much as a hologram fantasy of what it *means*, informed by advertisers, branding and celebrity. As I pointed out extensively in Chapter 8, this at least starts to construct a new kind of fashion subjectivity that is not so much a process of commodity fetishism, or giving things meanings they do not have, but of human appropriation – buying a bit of "Beckhamness" or branding so getting a Gucci dress is not so much an engagement with materiality as some gateway to sexual identity. Post-modernists would call this hyper-reality – the image is more "real" than the object – and this is undoubtedly the case that is now developing within fashion when Marks and Spencer, that British bastion of style-less dress, now sells "Twiggy-ness" to get its disillusioned lower middle class, middle aged women shopping again. Whilst concern is constantly raised in relation to consumer demand it is driven more by the fashion media, and once again it is primarily though not exclusively women who are on the front line here. Thus the real disorder is not eating but rather consuming more widely. The fashion world, whether popular or academic, has yet to truly get to grips with these wider questions of consuming fashion as bodies, images and subjectivities rather than clothes, and this is a situation not so much virtual as invasive. As women and many more fashion conscious men cease to buy things not just because they like the colour or the fit but because somehow in their heads it equates with something that somebody else has told them that they might want to *be* – this is indeed a fashion invasion.

Bibliography

Adorno, T. W. & Horkheimer, M. (1973) *Dialectic of Enlightenment*, London: Allen Lane.

Alford, H. (2009) "The Zoot Suit: Its History and Influence" in P. McNeil and V. Karaminas (eds.) *The Men's Fashion Reader*, Oxford: Berg.

Amies, H. (1994) *The Englishman's Suit: A Personal View of Its History, Its Place in The World Today, Its Future and the Accessories Which Support It*, London: Quartet.

Aries, P. (1962) *Centuries of Childhood*, London: Jonathan Cape.

Ash, J. & Wilson, E. (eds.) (1992) *Chic Thrills: A Fashion Reader*, London: Pandora.

Ash, J. & Wright, L. (eds.) (1988) *Components of Dress: Design, Manufacturing and Image-Making in the Fashion Industry*, London: Comedia.

Ash, J. (1989) "Tarting Up Men: Menswear And Gender Dynamics" in J. Attfield & P. Kirkham (eds.) *A View from the Interior: Feminism, Women and Design*, London: The Women's Press.

Ashenden, S. (2004) *Governing Child Sexual Abuse: Negotiating the Boundaries of Public and Private, Law and Science*, London: Routledge.

Barnard, M. (1996) *Fashion as Communication*, London: Routledge.

Barnes, R. & Eicher, J. B. (eds.) (1992) *Dress and Gender: Making and Meaning in Cultural Contexts*, Oxford: Berg.

Barrett, M. (1980) *Women's Oppression Today: Problems in Marxist Feminist Analysis*, London: Verso.

Barthel, D. (1992) "When Men Put On Appearances: Advertising and the Social Construction of Masculinity" in S. Craig (ed.) *Men, Masculinity and the Media*, London: Sage.

Barthes, R. (1985) *The Fashion System*, London: Jonathan Cape.

——(2006) *The Language of Fashion*, Oxford: Berg.

Baudelaire, C. (1995) *Les Fleurs du Mal*, London: Bristol Classical Press.

Baudrillard, J. (1972) *For a Critique of the Political Economy of the Sign*, St. Louis, NY: Telos Press.

——(1983) *Simulacra and Simulations*, New York: Semiotext(e).

——(1983) *Simulations*, New York: Semiotext(e).

——(1998) *The Consumer Society: Myths and Structures*, London: Sage (orig. pub. 1970).

Bauman, Z. (1990) *Thinking Sociologically*, Oxford: Blackwell.

Beckham, V. (2002) *Learning to Fly*, Harmondsworth: Penguin.

——(2007) *That Extra Half an Inch: Hair, Heels & Everything in Between*, Harmondsworth: Penguin.

Benwell, B. (ed.) (2003) *Masculinity and Men's Lifestyle Magazines*, Oxford: Blackwell.

Berger, M., Wallis, B. & Watson, S. (eds.) (1995) *Constructing Masculinity*, London: Routledge.

Bersani, L. (1988) "Is the Rectum a Grave?" in D. Crimp (ed.) *AIDS: Cultural Analysis, Cultural Activism*, London: MIT Press.

Bingham, D. (1994) *Acting Male: Masculinities in the Films of James Stewart, Jack Nicholson, and Clint Eastwood*, New Brunswick, NJ: Rutgers University Press.

Blachford, G. (1981) "Male Dominance and the Gay World", in K. Plummer (ed.) *The Making of the Modern Homosexual*, London: Hutchinson.

Blumer, H. (1969) "Fashion: From Class Differentiation to Collective Selection" in *The Sociological Quarterly*, 10, 3, pp. 275–91.

Bly, R. (1991) *Iron John: A Book About Men*, Shaftsbury: Element.

Bordo, S. (1993) *Unbearable Weight: Feminism, Western culture, and the Body*, Berkeley, CA: University of California Press.

——(1999) *The Male Body: A New Look at Men in Public and in Private*, New York: Farrar, Straus & Giroux.

Bourdieu, P. (1984) *Distinction: A Social Critique of the Judgement of Taste*, London: Routledge & Kegan Paul.

——(1993) *Sociology in Question*, London: Sage.

Bowlby, R. (1993) *Shopping with Freud*, London: Routledge.

Bray, A. (1982) *Homosexuality in Renaissance England*, London: Gay Men's Press.

Brenninkmeyer, I. (1962) *The Sociology of Fashion*, Winterthur: P. G. Keller.

Breward, C. (1995) *The Culture of Fashion: A New History of Fashionable Dress*, Manchester: Manchester University Press.

——(1999) *The Hidden Consumer: Masculinities, Fashion and City Life 1860 – 1914*, Manchester: Manchester University Press.

——(2006) "Fashioning Masculinity: Men's Footwear and Modernity" in G. Riello & P. McNeil (eds.) *Shoes: A History from Sandals to Sneakers*, Oxford: Berg.

Bristow, J. (1989) "Homophobia/Misogyny: Sexual Fears, Sexual Definitions" in S. Shepherd & M. Wallis (eds.) *Coming on Strong: Gay Politics and Culture*, London: Unwin Hyman.

Brownmiller, S. (1975) *Against Our Will: Men, Women and Rape*, New York: Simon & Schuster.

——(1984) *Femininity*, New York: Simon & Schuster.

Buchbinder, D. (1994) *Masculinities and Identities*, Melbourne: Melbourne University Press.

——(1998) *Performance Anxieties: Re-Producing Masculinity*, St Leonards, NSW: Allen & Unwin.

Buckingham, D. (2000) *After the Death of Childhood: Growing Up in the Age of Electronic Media*, Cambridge: Polity.

Buck-Morss, S. (1989) *The Dialectics of Seeing: Walter Benjamin and the Arcades Project*, Cambridge, MA: MIT Press.

Burman, B. & Leventon, M. (1987) "The Men's Dress Reform Party 1929–37" in *Costume*, 21, pp. 75–87.

Butler, J. (1990) *Gender Trouble: Feminism and the Subversion of Identity*, London: Routledge.

Byrde, P. (1979) *The Male Image: Men's Fashion in Britain 1300–1970*, London: Batsford.

Cahill, M. (1994) *The New Social Policy*, Oxford: Blackwell.

Cahill, S. (1989) "Fashioning Males and Females: Appearance Management and the Social Reproduction of Gender" in *Symbolic Interaction*, 12, 2, pp. 281–98.

Califia, P. (1994) *Public Sex: The Culture of Radical Sex*, San Francisco, CA: Cleiss Press.

Caplan, P. J. (1993) *The Myth of Women's Masochism*, Toronto: University of Toronto Press.

Carlyle, T. (1869) *Sartor Resartus: The Life and Opinions of Herr Teufelsdröckh in Three Books*, London: Chapman and Hall.

Carrigan, T., Connell, R. W. & Lee, J. (1985) "Toward A New Sociology of Masculinity" in *Theory and Society*, 14, pp. 551–604.

Carter, M. (2003) *Fashion Classics from Carlyle to Barthes*, Oxford: Berg.

Cashmore, E. (2004) (2nd. ed.) *Beckham*, Cambridge: Polity.

Chaney, D. (1996) *Lifestyles*, London: Routledge.

Chapman, J. (2000) *Licence to Thrill: A Cultural History of the James Bond Films*, New York: Columbia University Press.

Chapman, R. & Rutherford, J. (eds.) (1988) *Male Order: Unwrapping Masculinity*, London: Lawrence & Wishart.

Chapman, R. (1988a) "The Great Pretender: Variations on the New Man Theme" in R. Chapman and J. Rutherford (eds.) *Male Order: Unwrapping Masculinity*, London: Lawrence & Wishart.

Chenoune, F. (1993) *A History Of Men's Fashion*, Paris: Flammarion.

Chin, E. (2001) *Purchasing Power: Black Kids and American Consumer Culture*, Minneapolis, MN: University of Minnesota Press.

Chodorow, N. (1978) *The Reproduction of Mothering: Psychoanalysis and the Sociology of Gender*, Berkeley, CA: University of California Press.

Cohan, S. & Hark, I. A. (eds.) (1993) *Screening the Male: Exploring Masculinities In Hollywood Cinema*, London: Routledge.

Cohan, S. (1997) *Masked Men: Masculinity and the Movies in the Fifties*, Indianapolis, IN: Indiana University Press.

Cohen, S. (1972) *Folk Devils and Moral Panics: The Creation of Mods and Rockers*, London: Martin Robinson.

Cole, S. (2000) *Don We Now Our Gay Apparel: Gay Men's Dress in the Twentieth Century*, Oxford: Berg.

Coleridge, N. (1988) *The Fashion Conspiracy: A Remarkable Journey through the Empires of Fashion*, London: Heinemann.

Connell, R. W. (1987) *Gender and Power: Society, The Person and Sexual Politics*, Cambridge: Polity Press.

——(1995) *Masculinities*, Cambridge: Polity.

Cook, D. T. (2003) "Agency, Children's Consumer Culture and the Fetal Subject: Historical Trajectories, Contemporary Connections" in *Consumption, Markets and Culture*, 6, 2, pp. 115–132.

Cook, D. (2004) *The Commodification of Childhood: The Children's Clothing Industry and the Rise of the Child Consumer*, Durham, NC: Duke University Press.

Corrigan, P. (1993) "The Clothes-Horse Rodeo: or, How the Sociology of Clothing and Fashion Throws its (W)reiters" in *Theory, Culture and Society*, 10, pp. 143–55.

——(2008) *The Dressed Society: Clothing, The Body and Some Meanings of the World*, London: Sage.

Cosgrove, S. (2007) "The Zoot Suit and Style Warfare" in L. Welters & A. Lillethun (eds.) *The Fashion Reader*, Oxford: Berg.

Coveney, L., Jackson, M., Jeffreys, S., Kay, L. & Mahony, P. (1984) *The Sexuality Papers: Male Sexuality and the Social Control of Women*, London: Hutchinson.

Cox, C. (2004) *Stiletto*, London: Mitchell Beazley.

Craig, S. (ed.) (1992) *Men, Masculinity and the Media*, London: Sage.

Craik, J. (1994) *The Face of Fashion: Cultural Studies in Fashion*, London: Routledge.

——(2005) *Uniforms Exposed: From Conformity to Trangression*, Oxford: Berg.

Crane, D. (2000) *Fashion and Its Social Agendas: Class, Gender, and Identity in Clothing*, Chicago: University of Chicago Press.

Creed, B. (1993) "Dark Desires: Male Masochism in the Horror Film" in S. Cohan & I. R. Hark (eds.) *Screening The Male: Exploring Masculinities In Hollywood Cinema*, London: Routledge.

Crisp, Q. (1968) *The Naked Civil Servant*, Glasgow: Collins.

Cronin, A. M. (2004) *Advertising Myths: The Strange Half-Lives of Images and Commodities*, London: Routledge.

Daly, M. (1979) *Gyn/Ecology: The Metaethics of Radical Feminism*, London: The Women's Press.

Damhorst, M. L., Miller-Spillman, K. A. & Michelman, S.O. (2005) *The Meanings of Dress*, New York: Fairchild Publications.

David, D. S. & Brannon, R. (eds.) (1976) *The Forty Nine Percent Majority: The Male Sex Role*, Cambridge, MA: The Addison-Wesley Publishing Company.

Davis, F. (1992) *Fashion, Culture, and Identity*, Chicago: University Of Chicago Press.

Debord, G. (1992) *Society of the Spectacle*, London: Rebel Press.

Deleuze, G. and Sacher-Masoch, L. von (1989) *Masochism: Coldness and Cruelty/Venus in Furs*, New York: Zone Books.

Deleuze, G. & Guattari, F. (1984) *Anti-Oedipus: Capitalism and Schizophrenia*, London: Athlove.

Dinnerstein, M. & Weitz, R. (1994) "Jane Fonda, Barbara Bush and Other Aging Bodies: Femininity and the Limits of Resistance" in *Gender Issues*, New York: Springer, 14, 2, pp. 3–24.

Du Gay, P. (ed.) (1997) *Production of Culture/Cultures of Production*, London: Sage.

Dutton, K. R. (1995) *The Perfectible Body: The Western Ideal of Physical Development*, London: Cassell.

Dworkin, A. (1981) *Pornography: On Men Possessing Women*, London: Women's Press.

Dyer, R. (1985) "Male Sexuality in The Media" in A. Metcalf & M. Humphries (eds.) *The Sexuality Of Men*, London: Pluto.

——(1989) "Don't Look Now: The Instabilities Of The Male Pin-Up" in A. McRobbie (ed.) *Zoot Suits and Second-Hand Dresses: An Anthology of Fashion and Music*, London: Macmillan.

Easthope, A. (1986) *What a Man's Gotta Do: The Masculine Myth in Popular Culture*, London: Paladin.

Ebong, I. (ed.) (2001) *Black Hair: Art, Style and Culture*, New York: Universe Publishing.

Edwards, T. (1990) "Beyond Sex and Gender: Masculinity, Homosexuality and Social Theory" in J. Hearn and D. Morgan (eds.) *Men, Masculinities and Social Theory*, London: Unwin Hyman.

——(1994) *Erotic & Politics: Gay Male Sexuality, Masculinity And Feminism*, London: Routledge.

——(1997) *Men in The Mirror: Men's Fashion, Masculinity and Consumer Society*, London: Cassell.

——(2000) *Contradictions of Consumption: Concepts, Practices and Politics in Consumer Society*, Buckingham: Open University Press.

——(2003) "Sex, Booze and Fags: Masculinity, Style and Men's Magazines" in B. Benwell (ed.) *Masculinity and Men's Lifestyle Magazines*, Oxford: Blackwell.

——(2006) *Cultures of Masculinity*, London: Routledge.

Eglinton, J. Z. (1971) *Greek Love*, London: Neville Spearman.

Eicher, J. B. (ed.) (1995) *Dress and Ethnicity: Change Across Space and Time*, Oxford: Berg.

Eisenstein, H. (1984) *Contemporary Feminist Thought*, London: Unwin.

Elliot, R. & Leonard, C. (2004) "Peer Pressure and Poverty: Exploring Fashion Brands and Consumption Symbolism among Children of the 'British Poor'" in *Journal of Consumer Behaviour*, 3, 4, pp. 347–59.

Ellis, B. E. (1991) *American Psycho*, London: Picador.

English, B. (2007) *A Cultural History of Fashion in the Twentieth Century: From the Catwalk to the Sidewalk*, Oxford: Berg.

Entwistle, J. (2000) *The Fashioned Body: Fashion, Dress and Modern Social Theory*, Cambridge: Polity.

Evans, C. & Thornton, M. (1989) *Women and Fashion: A New Look*, London: Quartet.

Faludi, S. (1992) *Backlash: The Undeclared War Against Women*, London: Vintage.

——(2000) *Stiffed: The Betrayal of Modern Man*, London: Vintage.

Farrell, W. (1974) *The Liberated Man Beyond Masculinity: Freeing Men and Their Relationships With Women*, New York: Random House.

Faurschou, G. (1988) "Fashion and the Cultural Logic of Postmodernity" in A. Kroker and M. Kroker (eds.) *Body Invaders: Sexuality and the Postmodern Condition*, London: Macmillan.

Featherstone, M. (1991) *Consumer Culture and Postmodernism*, London: Sage.

Fejes, F. J. (1992) "Masculinity As Fact: A Review Of Empirical Mass Communication Research on Masculinity" in S. Craig (ed.) *Men, Masculinity and the Media*, London: Sage.

Fine, B. & Leopold, E. (1993) *The World of Consumption*, London: Routledge.

Finkelstein, J. (1991) *The Fashioned Self*, London: Polity.

——(1996) *After a Fashion*, Melbourne: Melbourne University Press.

Fiske, J. (1987) *Television Culture*, London: Methuen.

Flügel, J. C. (1930) *The Psychology of Clothes*, London: Hogarth Press.

Flusser, A. (2002) *Dressing the Man: Mastering the Art of Permanent Fashion*, New York: Harper Collins.

Foucault, M. (1978) *The History of Sexuality – Volume One: An Introduction*, Harmondsworth: Penguin.

Freud, S. (1977) *On Sexuality: Three Essays on the Theory of Sexuality and Other Works*, London: Penguin (orig. pub. 1905).

Gaines, J. (1986) "White Privilege and Looking Relations: Race and Gender in Feminist Film Theory" in *Cultural Critique*, Fall, pp. 59–79.

Gamman, L. & Makinen, M. (1994) *Female Fetishism: A New Look*, London: Lawrence & Wishart.

Gamson, J. (1994) *Claims to Fame: Celebrity in Contemporary America*, Berkeley, CA: University of California Press.

Gay, P. (ed.) (1995) *The Freud Reader*, London: Vintage.

Gibbings, S. (1990) *The Tie: Trends and Traditions*, London: Studio Editions.

Goldstein, L. (ed.) (1994) *The Male Body: Features, Destinies, Exposures*, Ann Arbor: University of Michigan Press.

Gough, J. (1989) "Theories of Sexual Identity and the Masculinization of the Gay Man" in S. Shepherd & M. Wallis (eds.) *Coming on Strong: Gay Politics and Culture*, London: Unwin Hyman.

Grant, I. J. & Stephen, G. R. (2005) "Communicating Culture: An Examination of the Buying Behaviour of 'Tweenage' Girls and the Key Societal Communicating Factors Influencing the Buying Process of Fashion Clothing" in *Journal of Targeting, Measurement and Analysis for Marketing*, 14, 2, pp. 101–14.

Green, I. (1984) *Male Function: A Contribution to the Debate on Masculinity in the Cinema* in *Screen*, 25, 4–5, pp. 36–48.

Greer, G. (1971) *The Female Eunuch*, London: Paladin.

——(2000) *The Whole Woman*, London: Anchor.

——(2008) "Who Cares if She Can't Sing and Can't Dance? Posh Spice is the Damien Hirst of Dress-Wearing", see http://www.guardian.co.uk/lifeandstyle/2008/may/19/fashion1 (accessed on 7 July 2010).

Gross, L. (1989) "Out of the Mainstream: Sexual Minorities and the Mass Media" in E. Seiter (et al.) (eds.) *Remote Control: Television, Audiences and Cultural Power*, London: Routledge.

Hall, S. & Jefferson, T. (1976) *Resistance Through Rituals: Youth Subcultures in Post-war Britain*, London: Unwin Hyman.

Hall, S. (ed.) (1997) *Representation: Cultural Representation and Signifying Practices*, London: Sage.

Hanke, R. (1992) "Redesigning Men: Hegemonic Masculinity In Transition" in S. Craig (ed.) *Men, Masculinity and the Media*, London: Sage.

Harper, S.J.A., Dewar, P-J & Diack, B. A. (2003) "The Purchase of Children's Clothing – Who Has The Upper Hand?" in *Journal of Fashion Marketing and Management*, 7, 2, pp. 196–206.

Hearn, J. & Morgan, D. (eds.) (1990) *Men, Masculinities and Social Theory*, London: Unwin Hyman.

Hebdige, D. (1979) *Subculture: The Meaning Of Style*, London: Routledge.

——(1987) *Cut'n'Mix: Culture, Identity and Caribbean Music*, London: Comedia.

Hoch, P. (1979) *White Hero, Black Beast: Racism, Sexism and the Mask of Masculinity*, London: Pluto.

Hogg, M. K., Bruce, M. & Hill, A. J. (1998) *Fashion Brand Preferences among Young Consumers* in *International Journal of Retail & Distribution Management*, 26, 8, pp. 293–300.

Hollander, A. (1988) *Seeing Through Clothes*, New York: Knopf.

——(1994) *Sex and Suits*, New York: Knopf.

Hood-Williams, J. (1990) "Patriarchy for Children: On the Stability of Power Relations in Children's Lives" in Chisholm, L. (et al.) (eds.) *Childhood, Youth and Social Change*, London: Falmer.

Jackson, P., Stevenson, N. & Brooks, K. 2001) *Making Sense of Men's Magazines*, Cambridge: Polity.

Jackson, S. & Scott, S. (eds.) (1996) *Feminism and Sexuality: A Reader*, Edinburgh: Edinburgh University Press.

Jackson, T. & Shaw, D. (eds.) (2006) *The Fashion Handbook*, London: Routledge.

James, A., Jenks, C. & Prout, A. (1998) *Theorising Childhood*, Cambridge: Polity Press.

Jameson, F. (1984) "Postmodernism, or the Cultural Logic of Late Capitalism" in *New Left Review*, 146, pp. 53–93.

——(1988) "Postmodernism and Consumer Society" in E. A. Kaplan (ed.) *Postmodernism and Its Discontents: Theories, Practices*, London: Verso.

Jeffords, S. (1994) *Hard Bodies: Hollywood Masculinity in the Reagan Era*, New Brunswick, NJ: Rutgers University Press.

Jeffreys, S. (1990) *Anticlimax: Feminist Perspectives on the Sexual Revolution*, London: The Women's Press.

Johnson, D. C. and Foster, H. B. (eds.) (2007) *Dress Sense: Emotional and Sensory Experiences of the Body and Clothes*, New York: Berg.

Johnson, R. (1986) *The Story So Far: and for the Transformations* in Punter, D. (ed.) Introduction to Contemporary Cultural Studies, London: Longman.

Kaiser, S. B. (1997) *The Social Psychology of Clothing: Symbolic Appearances in Context*, New York: Fairchild Publications.

Kaiser, S. B., Nagasawa, R. H & Hutton, S. S. (1995) *Construction of an SI Theory of Fashion: Part 1. Ambivalence and Change* in *Clothing and Textiles Research Journal*, 13, 3, pp. 172–83.

Kean, R. C. (1997) "The Role of the Fashion System in Fashion Change: A Response to the Kaiser, Nagasawa and Hutton Model" in *Clothing and Textiles Research Journal*, 15, 3, pp. 172–77.

Keenan, W. J. F. (ed.) (2001) *Dressed to Impress: Looking the Part*, Oxford: Berg.

Kimmel, M. S. (1987) "The Contemporary 'Crisis' of Masculinity in Historical Perspective" in H. Brod (ed.) *The Making of Masculinities: The New Men's Studies*, London: Hutchinson.

Kirkham, P. & Thumin, J. (eds.) (1993) *You Tarzan: Masculinity, Movies and Men*, London: Lawrence & Wishart.

Kitses, J. & Rickman, G. (eds.) (1998) *The Western Reader*, New York: Limelight Editions.

Klein, N. (2000) *No Logo: No Space, No Choice, No Jobs, Taking Aim at the Brand Bullies*, London: Flamingo.

Kline, S. (1995) *Out of the Garden: Toys, TV and Children's Culture in the Age of Marketing*, London: Verso.

Krafft-Ebing, R. (1965) *Psychopathia Sexualis: A Medico-Forensic Study*, New York: G. P. Putnam's Sons [orig. pub. 1886].

Kroker, A. & Cook, D. (1988) *The Postmodern Scene: Excremental Culture and Hyper-Aesthetics*, London: Macmillan.

Kroker, A. & Kroker, M. (1988) *Body Invaders: Sexuality and the Postmodern Condition*, London: Macmillan.

Kunzle, D. (1982) *Fashion and Fetishism: A Social History of the Corset, Tight-Lacing and Other Forms of Body Sculpture in the West*, Totowa, NJ: Rowman & Littlefield.

Lasch, C. (1979) *The Culture of Narcissism: American Life in an Age of Diminishing Expectations*, London: Norton.

Laver, J. (1945) *Taste and Fashion: From the French Revolution to the Present Day*, London: George C. Harrap & Co. Ltd.

——(1950) *Dress: How and Why Fashions in Men's and Women's Clothes Have Changed During the Past Two Hundred Years*, London: John Murray.

——(1968) *Dandies*, London: Weidenfeld and Nicolson.

——(1982) *Costume and Fashion: A Concise History*, London: Thames and Hudson.

Laver, J. C. & Laver, R. H. (1981) *Fashion Power: The Meaning of Fashion in American Society*, Englewood Cliffs, NJ: Prentice-Hall.

Lee, J. A. (1978) *Getting Sex: A New Approach – More Fun, Less Guilt*, Ontario: Mission Book Company.

Lehman, P. (ed.) (2001) *Masculinity: Bodies, Movies, Culture*, London: Routledge.

Levi-Strauss, C. (1964) *Le Cru et le Cuit*, Paris: Plon.

Lurie, A. (1981) *The Language of Clothes*, London: Heinemann.

Lury, C. (1996) *Consumer Culture*, Cambridge: Polity.

Lyotard, J. F. (1984) *The Postmodern Condition*, Manchester: Manchester University Press.

Mackinnon, C. A. (1987) *Feminism Unmodified: Discourses on Life and Law*, Cambridge, MA: Harvard University Press.

Mackinnon, K. (1997) *Uneasy Pleasures: The Male as Erotic Object*, London: Cynus Arts.

Maffesoli, M. (1991) "The Ethic of Aesthetics" in *Theory, Culture and Society*, 8, pp. 7–20.

——(1996) *The Time of the Tribes: The Decline of Individualism in Mass Society*, London: Sage.

Mains, G. (1984) *Urban Aboriginals: A Celebration of Leathersexuality*, San Francisco, CA: Sunshine Press.

Marshall, P. D. (1997) *Celebrity and Power: Fame in Contemporary Culture*, Minneapolis, MN: University of Minnesota Press.

Marshall, P. D. (ed.) (2006) *The Celebrity Culture Reader*, London: Routledge.

Martin, R. & Koda, H. (1989) *Jocks and Nerds: Men's Style in the Twentieth Century*, New York: Rizzoli.

McCracken, G. (1985) "The Trickle-Down Theory Rehabilitated" in M. Solomon (ed.) *The Psychology of Fashion*, Lexington, MA: Lexington Books.

Martin, R. and Koda, H. (1989) *Jocks and Nerds: Men's Style in the Twentieth Century*, New York: Rizzoli.

Marx, K. (1975) *Early Writings*, Harmondsworth: Penguin.

McCracken, G. (1988) *Culture and Consumption: New Approaches to the Symbolic Character of Consumer Goods and Activities*, Indiana, IN: Indiana University Press.

McDowell, L. (1997) *Capital Culture: Gender at Work in the City*, Oxford: Blackwell.

McKendrick, N., Brewer, J. & Plumb, J. H.(1982) *The Birth of a Consumer Society*, London: Europa.

McNeal, J. (1992) *Kids as Consumers: A Handbook of Marketing and Children*, New York: Lexington.

McNeil, P. & Karaminas, V. (eds.) (2009) *The Men's Fashion Reader*, Oxford: Berg.

McRobbie, A. (ed.) (1989) *Zoot Suits and Second-hand Dresses: an Anthology of Fashion and Music*, Basingstoke: Macmillan.

McRobbie, A. (1991) *Feminism and Youth Culture: From 'Jackie' to 'Just Seventeen'*, Basingstoke: Macmillan.

——(1998) *British Fashion Design: Rag Trade or Image Industry?*, London: Routledge.

McRobbie, A. & Nava, M. (eds.) (1984) *Gender and Generation*, London: Macmillan.

Mead, M. (1977) *Sex And Temperament In Three Primitive Societies*, London: Routledge & Kegan Paul.

Mercer, K. & Julien, I. (1988) Race, "Sexual Politics and Black Masculinity: A Dossier" in R. Chapman and J. Rutherford (eds.) *Male Order: Unwrapping Masculinity*, London: Lawrence & Wishart.

Mercer, K. (1999) *Black Hair/Style Politics* in, K. Owuso (ed.) *Black British Culture and Society: A Text Reader*, London: Routledge.

Miller, D. *et al.* (1998) *Shopping, Place and Identity*, London: Routledge.

Miller, D., Jackson, P., Thrift, N., Holbrook, B. & Rowlands, M. (1987) *Material Culture and Mass Consumption*, Oxford: Blackwell.

Millett, K. (1971) *Sexual Politics*, London: Sphere.

Mintel (2008) *Childrenswear Retailing, Retail Intelligence*, January, London: Mintel Group Ltd.

Mitchell, J. (1974) *Psychoanalysis and Feminism*, New York: Pantheon Books.

Molloy, J. T. (1985) *Dress for Success*, New York.

——(1988) *New Dress for Success*, New York: Grand Central Publishing.

——(1996) *New Women's Dress for Success*, New York: Grand Central Publishing.

Moore, S. (1988) "Getting a Bit of the Other – The Pimps of Postmodernism" in R. Chapman and J. Rutherford (eds.) *Male Order: Unwrapping Masculinity*, London: Lawrence & Wishart.

Mort, F. (1986) "Image/Change: High Street Style and the New Man" in *New Socialist*, November, pp. 6–8.

——(1988) "Boy's Own? Masculinity, Style and Popular Culture" in R. Chapman and J. Rutherford (eds.) *Male Order: Unwrapping Masculinity*, London: Lawrence & Wishart.

——(1996) *Cultures of Consumption: Masculinities and Social Space in Late Twentieth-Century Britain*, London: Routledge.

——(1997) "Paths to Mass Consumption: Britain and the USA Since 1945" in M.

Muggleton, D. & Weinzierl, R. (eds.) (2003) *The Post-subcultures Reader*, Oxford: Berg.

Muggleton, D. (2000) *Inside Subculture: The Post-modern Meaning of Style*, Oxford: Berg.

Mulvey, L. (1975) *Visual Pleasure and Narrative Cinema* in *Screen*, 16, 3, pp. 6–18.

Nagasawa, R. H., Kaiser, S. B. & Hutton, S. S. (1995) "Construction of an SI Theory of Fashion: Part 2. From Discovery to Formalization" in *Clothing and Textiles Research Journal*, 13, 4, pp. 234–44.

——(1996) "Construction of an SI Theory of Fashion: Part 3. Context of Explanation" in *Clothing and Textiles Research Journal*, 14, 1, pp. 54–62.

Nava, M. (1992) *Changing Cultures: Feminism, Youth and Consumerism*, London: Sage.

Nava, M., Blake, A., MacRury, I. & Richards, B. (eds.) (1997) *Buy This Book: Studies in Advertising and Consumption*, London: Routledge.

Neale, S. (1982) *Images of Men* in *Screen*, 23, 3–4, pp. 47–53.

——(1983) "Masculinity as Spectacle: Reflections on Men and Mainstream Cinema" in *Screen*, 24, 6, pp. 2–16.

Nelson, J. A. (1989) "Individual Consumption within the Household: A Study of Expenditures on Clothing" in *The Journal of Consumer Affairs*, 23, 1, pp. 21–44.

Nixon, S. (1992) "Have You Got The Look? Masculinities And Shopping Spectacle" in R. Shields (ed.) *Lifestyle Shopping: The Subject of Consumption*, London: Routledge.

——(1996) *Hard Looks: Masculinities, Spectatorship and Contemporary Consumption*, London: UCL Press.

O'Keefe, L. (1996) *Shoes: A Celebration of Pumps, Sandals, Slippers and More*, New York: Workman Publishing.

Osgerby, B. (2001) *Playboys in Paradise: Masculinity, Youth and Leisure-Style In Modern America*, Oxford: Berg.

Packard, V. (1957) *The Hidden Persuaders*, London: Longmans, Green & Co.

Palahnuik, C. (1996) *Fight Club*, New York: Hyperion Books.

Pannabecker, R. K. (1997) "Fashioning Theory: A Critical Discussion of the Symbolic Interactionist Theory of Fashion" in *Clothing and Textiles Research Journal*, 15, 3, pp. 178–83.

Phizacklea, A. (1990) *Unpacking the Fashion Industry*, London: Routledge.

Piore, M. (1997) "The Economics of the Sweatshop" in A. Ross (ed.) *No Sweat: Fashion, Free Trade, and the Rights of Garment Workers*, London: Verso.

Plummer, K. (ed.) (1981) *The Making of the Modern Homosexual*, London: Hutchinson.

Polhemus, T. (1994) *Street Style: From Sidewalk to Catwalk*, London: Thames & Hudson Press.

Radner, H. (1995) *Shopping Around: Feminine Culture and the Pursuit of Pleasure*, London: Routledge.

Rahman, M. (2006) "Is Straight the New Queer? David Beckham and the Dialectics of Celebrity" in P. D. Marshall (ed.) *The Celebrity Culture Reader*, London: Routledge

Rechy, J. (1977) *The Sexual Outlaw: A Documentary*, London: W. H. Allen.

Reynaud, E. (1983) *Holy Virility: The Social Construction of Masculinity*, London: Pluto Press.

Rich, A. (1984) "Compulsory Heterosexuality and Lesbian Existence" in A. B. Snitow *et al* (eds.) *Desire: The Politics of Sexuality*, London: Virago.

Riello, G. & McNeil, P. (eds.) (2006) *Shoes: A History from Sandals to Sneakers*, Oxford: Berg.

Ritzer, G. (1995) *Expressing America: A Critique of the Global Credit Card Society*, Thousand Oaks, CA: Sage.

Roach, M.E. and Eicher, J. (1973) *The Visible Self*, Englewood Cliffs, NJ: Prentice-Hall.

Rodowick, D. (1982) "The Difficulty of Difference" in *Wide Angle*, 5, 1, pp. 4–15.

Rojek, C. (2001) *Celebrity*, London: Reaktion Books.

Ross, A. (ed.) (1997) *No Sweat: Fashion, Free Trade, and the Rights of Garment Workers*, London: Verso.

Rubin, G. (1984) "Thinking Sex: Notes for a Radical Theory of the Politics of Sexuality" in C. S. Vance (ed.) *Pleasure And Danger: Exploring Female Sexuality*, London: Routledge & Kegan Paul.

Rubinstein, R. P. (1995) *Dress Codes: Meanings and Messages in American Culture*, Oxford: Westview Press.

Russo, V. (1987) *The Celluloid Closet: Homosexuality in the Movies*, New York: Harper & Row.

Rutherford, J. (1988) "Who's That Man?" in R. Chapman and J. Rutherford (eds.) *Male Order: Unwrapping Masculinity*, London: Lawrence & Wishart.

Rutherford, J. (ed.) (1990) *Identity: Community, Culture, Difference*, London: Lawrence & Wishart.

Rysst, M. (2010) "'I Am Only Ten Years Old': Femininities, Clothing-Fashion Codes and the Intergenerational Gap of Interpretation of Young Girls" in *Clothes in Childhood*, 17, 1, pp. 76–93.

Sapir, E. (1931) "Fashion" in *Encyclopaedia of the Social Sciences*, 6, pp. 199–144.

Savage, J. (1996) "What's so New about the New Man? Three Decades of Advertising to Men" in D. Jones (ed.) *Sex, Power and Travel: Ten Years of Arena*, London: Virgin.

Savran, D. (1998) *Taking It Like a Man: White Masculinity, Masochism, and Contemporary American Culture*, Princeton, NJ: Princeton University Press.

Scheuring, D. (1988) "Heavy Duty Denim: 'Quality Never Dates'" in A. McRobbie (ed.) *Zoot Suits and Second Hand Dresses: An Anthology Of Fashion And Music*, London: Macmillan.

Schickel, R. (2000) *Intimate Strangers: The Culture of Celebrity in America*, Chicago: Ivan R. Dee.

Schwichtenberg, C. (ed.) (1993) *The Madonna Connection: Representational Politics, Subcultural Identities and Cultural Theory*, Oxford: Westview Press.

Scott, S. & Morgan, D. (eds.) (1993) *Body Matters: Essays on the Sociology of the Body*, London: Falmer Press.

——(1993) *Body Matters: Essays on the Sociology of the Body*, London: The Falmer Press.

Screen (ed.) (1992) *The Sexual Subject: A Screen Reader in Sexuality*, London: Routledge.

Seiter, E., Borchers, H., Kreutzner, G. & Eva-Maria Warth, E-M. (1989) *Remote Control: Television, Audiences, And Cultural Power*, London: Routledge.

Semmelhack, E. (2006) "A Delicate Balance: Women, Power and High Heels" in G. Riello. & P. McNeil (eds.) *Shoes: A History from Sandals to Sneakers*, Oxford: Berg.

Shilling, C. (1993) *The Body and Social Theory*, London: Sage.

Silverman, K. (1992) *Male Subjectivity at the Margins*, London: Routledge.

Simmel, G. (1904) *Fashion* in *International Quarterly*, **10**(1), October, pp. 130–155.

Simpson, M. (1994) *Male Impersonators: Men Performing Masculinity*, New York: Routledge.

——(1996) *It's a Queer World*, London: Vintage.

Slade, T. (2009) "The Japanese Suit and Modernity" in P. McNeil & V. Karaminas (eds.) *The Men's Fashion Reader*, Oxford: Berg.

Slater, D. (1997) *Consumer Culture and Modernity*, Cambridge: Polity.

Smith, P. (1997) "Tommy Hilfiger in the Age of Mass Customization" in A. Ross (ed.) *No Sweat: Fashion, Free Trade, and the Rights of Garment Workers*, London: Verso.

Spencer, N. (1994) "Menswear in the 1980s: Revolt into Conformity" in J. Ash and E. Wilson (eds.) *Chic Thrills: A Fashion Reader*, London: Pandora.

Sproles, G. B. & Burns, L. D. (1994) *Changing Appearances: Understanding Dress in Contemporary Society*, New York: Fairchild Publications.

Sproles, G. B. (1981) "Analyzing Fashion Life Cycles – Principles and Perspectives" in *Journal of Marketing*, 45, Fall, pp. 116–24.

Steele, V. (1996) *Fetish: Fashion, Sex & Power*, Oxford: Oxford University Press.

Sternheimer, K. (2003) *It's Not the Media: The Truth About Pop Culture's Influence on Children*, Boulder, CO: Westview Press.

Stockbridge, S. (1990) "Rock Video: Pleasure and Resistance" in M. E. Brown (ed.) *Television and Women's Culture: The Politics of the Popular*, London: Sage.

Swain, J. (2002) "The 'Right Stuff': Fashioning Identity through Clothing in a Junior School" in *Gender and Education*, 14, 1, pp. 53–69.

Swann, J. (1982) *Shoes*, London: Batsford.

Swinyard, W. R. & Sim, C. Peng (1987) "Perception of Children's Influence on Family Decision Process" in *The Journal of Consumer Marketing*, 4, 1, pp. 25–38.

Tapinç, H. (1992) "Masculinity, Femininity, and Turkish Male Homosexuality" in K. Plummer (ed.) *Modern Homosexualities: Fragments of Lesbian and Gay Experience*, London: Routledge.

Tasker, Y. (1993a) "Dumb Movies for Dumb People: Masculinity, The Body, and The Voice in Contemporary Action Cinema" in S. Cohan & I. R. Hark (eds.) *Screening the Male: Exploring Masculinities In Hollywood Cinema*, London: Routledge.

——(1993b) *Spectacular Bodies: Gender, Genre and the Action Cinema*, London: Routledge.

Thompson, B. (1994) *Sadomasochism: Painful Perversion or Pleasurable Play*, London: Cassell.

Tolson, A. (1977) *The Limits of Masculinity*, London: Tavistock.

Topolski, C. (2008) *Monster Love*, London: Penguin.

Tseëlon, E. (ed.) (2001) *Masquerade and Identities: Essays on Gender, Sexuality and Marginality*, London: Routledge.

Tulloch, C. (2004) *Black Style*, London: V&A Publications.

Turner, G., Bonner, F. & Marshall, P. D. (2000) *Fame Game: The Production of Celebrity in Australia*, Cambridge: University of Cambridge Press.

Vance, C. S. (ed.) (1984) *Pleasure And Danger: Exploring Female Sexuality*, London: Routledge & Kegan Paul.

Veblen, T. (1934) *The Theory of the Leisure Class: An Economic Study of Institutions*, New York: The Modern Library (orig. pub. 1899).

Vianello, A. (2006) "Courtly Lady or Courtesan? The Venetian Chopine in the Renaissance" in G. Riello & P. McNeil (eds.) *Shoes: A History from Sandals to Sneakers*, Oxford: Berg.

Vinken, B. (2005) *Fashion Zeitgeist: Trends and Cycles in the Fashion System*, Oxford: Berg.

Wark, M. (1997) "Fashion as a Culture Industry" in A. Ross (ed.) *No Sweat: Fashion, Free Trade, and the Rights of Garment Workers*, London: Verso.

Watney, S. (1987) *Policing Desire: Pornography, AIDS and the Media*, London: Comedia.

Weeks, J. (1977) *Coming Out: Homosexual Politics in Britian from the Nineteenth Century to the Present*, London: Quartet.

——(1985) *Sexuality and its Discontents: Meanings, Myths and Modern Sexualities*, London: Routledge and Kegan Paul.

Weisberger, L. (2003) *The Devil Wears Prada*, London: Harper.

Wernick, A. (1991) *Promotional Culture: Advertising, Ideology and Symbolic Expression*, London: Sage.

——(1994) "From Voyeur To Narcissist: Imaging Men in Contemporary Advertising" in M. Kaufman (ed.) *Beyond Patriarchy: Essays By Men on Pleasure, Power, and Change*, Toronto: Oxford University Press.

Whannel, G. (2002) *Media Sports Stars: Masculinities and Moralities*, London: Routledge.

Whelehan, I. (2000) *Overloaded: Popular Culture and the Future of Feminism*, London: The Women's Press.

Willemen, P. (1981) *Anthony Mann: Looking at the Male* in *Framework*, Summer 1981, pp. 16–20.

——(1994) *Looks and Frictions: Essays in Cultural Studies and Film Theory*, London: BFI Publishing/Bloomington, IN: Indiana University Press.

Willis, P. (1977) *Learning to Labour: How Working Class Kids Get Working Class Jobs*, Farnborough: Saxon House.

Wilson, E. (1985) *Adorned in Dreams: Fashion and Modernity*, London: Virago.

Winship, J. (1987) *Inside Women's Magazines*, London: Pandora Press.

Wolf, N. (1991) *The Beauty Myth: How Images of Beauty are Used Against Women*, London: Vintage.

Wright, L. (1996) "The Suit: Common Bond or Defeated Purpose?" in P. Kirkham (ed.) *The Gendered Object*, Manchester: Manchester University Press.

Wyness, M. (2000 *Contesting Childhood*, London: Falmer.

York, P. (1995) "Nineties, What Nineties?" in *Arena*, December, pp. 20–22.

Zakim, M. (2009) "The Reinvention of Tailoring" in P. McNeil and V. Karaminas (eds.) *The Men's Fashion Reader*, Oxford: Berg.

Zamperini, P. (2006) "A Dream of Butterflies: Shoes in Chinese Culture" in G. Riello. & P. McNeil (eds.) *Shoes: A History from Sandals to Sneakers*, Oxford: Berg.

Zukin, S. (1995) *The Cultures of Cities*, Oxford: Blackwell.

Index

adornment 3
Adorno, T 13, 146, 149
aestheticisation 9
American Gigolo 148
American Psycho 61
Arcadia Group 131
Armani, Giorgio 48, 54, 62, 138, 139, 142, 149
Asda 131, 132

Banana Republic 138
Barnard, M 13, 28–29
Barthes, R 26–27, 29
Bartle, Bogle & Hegarty 48
Baudrillard, J 29, 36–37, 140–41
Beckham, David 9, 51, 138, 152–54, 156
Beckham, Victoria 9, 152, 153–55
Blahnik, Manolo 83
blazer 56, 117
Blondie 149
Blumer, H 29–31
BMW 3, 36, 142
Bond, James 57, 64
Boss, Hugo 63
Bourdieu, P 2, 7, 17–18, 87
branding 94, 141–45
Brando, Marlon 57–58
Breward, C 79, 141
bricolage 111
Brownmiller, S 68–69
Burberry 151
Burton, Montague 58
Bush, Kate 80

Campbell, Naomi 111
Carlyle, T 13
Cashmore, E 154
casualisation 160–61

celebrity theory of 145–50; politics 150–52
Chapman, R 48
Chanel 138
"CHAV" 151
Chenoune, F 43
childhood 89–90
children's fashion 91–97
Chippendales, the 48
chopine 80–81
circuit of culture 88
clone culture 106
Cole, S 107–8
Coleridge, N 143–44
commodification 9, 36
Concorde 81
constructionism 9
consumption 87, 89; and gender, 104
Cook, D 90, 100
costume history 4–5, 11
Cox, C 81–82
Craik, J 41, 42, 59, 116
credit 127–28
Crisp, Q 107
cultural capital 9
cultural intermediaries 9, 19

dandies 64
designer fashion 6, 137–45
Devil Wears Prada, The 83
Dior – new look 81, 139
discourse 9
Dolce & Gabbana 152, 155
drag 107
dress 3, 88–89, 105; at work 114–18; legality of 118
Durkheim, E 10
Dynasty 82

Eicher, J 116
Elizabeth I 139
Ellis, Bret Easton 151
Entwistle, J 34
ESRC 87
essentialism 9, 24
ethnicity 10
Eurythmics 37
executive dress 61–63

Face, the 140
Faludi, S 144
fashion: aging and 98–99; the body and
    121–22; definitions of 2–4; display 21;
    language and 24–28; parenting and 93,
    97–98; protection 121; psychology 20–21;
    sexualisation of 98–99; sociology and
    1–2, 5; status 13, 16; unconscious and
    24–25, 38; *see also* men's fashion
fashion industry 123–25
fashion theory 7, 11–28
fast fashion 95–96, 13–3
feminism, first wave 15
feminism, second wave 11–12, 47, 50,
    67–73
femininity, *see* gender
fetishism 75–78
FHM 48, 50
Filofax 140, 149
Fine, B 124, 128–29
Finkelstein, J 27–28
Flügel, J 20, 29, 41, 42, 52, 79, 161
Flusser, A 43
Footballers' wives 93
Ford, Tom 64, 125, 139
Foucault, M 35
Frankfurt School 13
Freud 21, 76
functionalism 10, 17, 21

Gaultier, Jean-Paul 45, 54
Gammon, L 77–78
Gamson, J 147
Gap, the 91
gay liberation 47
gay sexuality 10, 106–8, 153–54
gender 10, 129; masculinity 41–43, 50;
    femininity 68–73
"girl power" 71–72
globalisation 160
golden lotus, the 80
GQ 48

Grant, Cary 57
Greer, G 72, 82, 155
Gucci 78, 138, 142, 151, 152, 161

Hamnett, Katherine 18
haute couture 12, 138–39
Hayes, Chanelle 138
Hebdige, D 109–10, 112, 113
heels 80–84
Henry VIII 139
Hilfiger, Tommy 144
Hilton, Paris 156
hippies 104–6
Hoch, P 51–52
Hollander, A 33, 58–59, 61
Horkheimer, M 13, 146, 149
Hudson, Rock 57

i-D 140
identity politics 103–8
ipod 14–1

Jameson, F 37
J C Penney 132
John, Elton 81
Julien, I 11

Kaiser, S 30–32
Keenan, W 14
Khan, Chaka 67
Klein, Calvin 37, 47, 138
Klein, Naomi 5, 126, 144
Kroker, A and M 36, 158
Kunzle, D 77

Lauren, Ralph 47, 54, 139
Laver, J 22–24
"Laver's Law" 23
Leopold, E 124, 128–29
Levi's jeans 36, 48, 129
Loaded 50, 72
Lurie, A 24–25, 26
Loren, Sophia 81
Louis XIV 45, 55, 139

Makinen, M 77–78
Mapplethorpe, R 111
Marks & Spencer 131, 161
Marshall, P 146–47
Marxism 13, 125–26, 137
masculinity, see gender
McCracken, G 18

McDonalds 115
McDowell, L 61
McRobbie, A 110, 130
men's dress 12, 16, 38
men's dress reform party 61
men's fashion 42–48; marginalization of
    42–47; and status 46, 60
Mercer, K 111
Merleau-Ponty 35
methodology 4–8
metrosexual 51, 156
Minogue, Kylie 96
Modernity 12–20, 32–38
mods 60–61
Molloy, J T 6
Monroe, Marilyn 81, 83
Moore, S 72
Mort, F 49
MTV 140
Mulvey, L 73–74

National Lottery 150
Next 91
new lad 49–50, 71, 72
new man 18, 48–52, 43, 48–52, 71

Pandora's Box 1, 115, 158
pantaloons 54
Phizacklea, A 71, 126–27
Poiret, Paul 139
Polhemus, T 112–13
ponchos 96
post-industrialism 35, 130
post-modernism 3, 35–37, 112–14, 161
post-structural theory 69
Prada, Miuccia 54
prêt-à-porter 138–39
Price, Antony 61
Primark 130–33
production definitions of 119–25,
    exploitation in 125–30
psychoanalytic theory 69, 75–77
Price, Katie 156, 157
punk 25, 110, 112
puritanism 45–46, 104

Quant, Mary 109

racial difference 10, 103, 111–12, 114
Rahman, M 153
Rastafarianism 110, 114
Reaganomics 117, 149

Red Shoes, The 80
Reformation, the 104
Rhodes, Zandra 18, 109
Roach, M 116
Rojek, C 145, 147–49
Ross, A 127
Rowell, S 48
Rutherford, J 48

Sacher-masoch, L von 82
Sapir, E 26
Saturday Night Fever 61
Saussure, F de 115
Savile Row 122, 141
Sears Group 132
Second World War 35, 47, 50,
    81, 131
Semmelhack, E 84
Sex 83
sexual objectification 73–75
Shilling, C 34
shoes 78–80
Simmel, G 1, 17, 21, 26, 29, 149
Simpson, M 51
Singer, sewing machine 124, 139
Single White Female 82
skinhead 110
Smith, P 127–28
Smith, Paul 18–19, 48, 54
Sony Walkman 140
Spencer, N 62
Spice Girls 154
stiletto 67, 69, 78–84
style 3–4, 112–14
sumptuary laws 104
subcultural style 109–14
subjectivity 156–58
suit 18, 42–43, 44, 110, 115; history of
    52–58; masculinity and 58–63, 149;
    zoot 61, 110
Swann, J 79
symbolic interactionism 29–32, 38

teddy boys 109–10
textiles 122, see also production
Thatcher, Margaret 6, 117, 149
tie 56
Topolski, C 151
Travolta, John 61
trickle down theory 129; see also
    Simmel, McCracken
Trinny and Susannah 7

tweenager 89, 93
uniforms 115–16
United States 6, 15–16, 47, 80, 91, 117, 160

V&A, museum 22, 112
VAT 103
Veblen, T 1, 15–17
Versace, G 138, 142
Vogue 144
vogue movement 107–8

walmart effect/value fashion 92, 131, 132
Wernick, A 144
Westwood, Vivienne 18, 45, 109, 125,
  138, 142

Whannel, G 153
Whelehan, I 72
Willemen, P 74–75
Wilson, E 15, 25, 32–33, 34
Wintour, Anna 83
Wolf, N 69
wool 57; *see also* production,
  textiles
Worth, Charles 139
Wright, L 59

yuppie 61, 149

Zakim, M 45
Zamperini, P 80

The Fashion History Reader
Global Perspectives

Edited by Giorgio Riello and Peter McNeil

The Fashion History Reader is an innovative work that provides a broad introduction to the complex literature in the fields of fashion studies, and dress and fashion history.

A comprehensive resource for those who wish to further their engagement with fashion as a contemporary phenomenon, the book connects a diverse range of approaches and incorporates non-Western literature within better-known studies from Europe and North America.

It identifies the history of fashion as a meeting point between the long-standing historical investigation of 'dress' and 'costume' and the more recent development of those sociological and anthropological-inspired studies that have come to be called 'fashion theory'.

Twenty-three chapters and over forty shorter 'Snapshot' texts cover a wide range of topics and approaches within the history of fashion, ranging from object-based studies to theory-driven analyses. The book is divided into six parts, surveying some of the key themes in the history of fashion. Themes also move in and across time, providing a chronology to enable student learning:

- parts 1–3 cover the fifteenth to the eighteenth-century
- parts 4 and 5 cover the nineteenth-century to the contemporary (with particular attention given to non-European countries)
- part 6 provides a survey of the global setting and current globalised nature of fashion.

A comprehensive introduction by the editors will contextualise debates for students, synthesising past history and bringing them up-to-date through a discussion of globalisation. Each section also includes a short, accessible introduction by the editors, placing each chapter within the wider, thematic treatment of fashion and its history, and an Annotated Guide to Further Reading encourages students to enhance their learning independently.

ISBN 13: 978-0-415-49323-9 (hbk)
ISBN 13: 978-0-415-49324-6 (pbk)

The Fashion Handbook

Tim Jackson and David Shaw

Series: MEDIA PRACTICE

Series editor: James Curran

The Fashion Handbook is the indispensable guide to the fashion industry. It explores the varied and diverse aspects of the business, bringing together critical concepts with practical information about the industry's structure and core skills, as well as offering advice on real working practices and providing information about careers and training.

The Fashion Handbook traces the development of the fashion industry and looks at how fashion can be understood from social, cultural and commercial perspectives. Each chapter contributes to the knowledge of a particular academic or vocational area either through building on existing research or through the dissemination of new research undertaken into specialist vocational disciplines.

The Fashion Handbook uses case studies, interviews and profiles and includes chapters written by recognised academics and fashion industry experts. Specialist topics include fashion culture, luxury brands, fashion journalism, fashion buying, design and manufacturing, retailing, PR and styling.

The Fashion Handbook includes:

- a unique and wide overview of the fashion industry
- chapters on specialist topics
- contributions from recognised experts in both academia and the fashion industry
- expert advice on careers in fashion retailing.

ISBN 13: 978-0-415-25579-0 (hbk)
ISBN 13: 978-0-415-25580-6 (pbk)
ISBN 13: 978-0-203-32117-1 (ebk)

Related titles from Routledge

The Fabric of Cultures
Fashion, Identity, and Globalization
Edited by Eugenia Paulicelli and Hazel Clark

Fashion is both public and private, material and symbolic, always caught within the lived experience and providing an incredible tool to study culture and history.

The Fabric of Cultures examines the impact of fashion as a manufacturing industry and as a culture industry that shapes the identities of nations and cities in a cross-cultural perspective, within a global framework. The collected essays investigate local and global economies, cultures and identities and the book offers, for the first time, a wide spectrum of case studies which focus on a diversity of geographical spaces and places, from global capitals of fashion such as New York, to countries less known or identifiable for fashion such as contemporary Greece and Soviet Russia.

Contributors include: Valéria Brandini, Hazel Clark, Olga Gurova, Karen Tranberg Hansen, Ann Marie Leshkowich, Christina H. Moon, Rachel Morris, Eugenia Paulicelli, Helena Cunha Ribeiro, Michiel Scheffer, Jane Schneider and Michael Skafidas.

Highly illustrated and including essays from all over the world, *The Fabric of Cultures* provides a comprehensive survey of the latest interdisciplinary scholarship on fashion, identity and globalisation.

ISBN 13: 978-0-415-77542-7 (hbk)
ISBN 13: 978-0-415-77543-4 (pbk)
ISBN13: 978-0-203-86902-4 (ebk)

Available at all good bookshops
For ordering and further information please visit:
www.routledge.com

Related titles from Routledge

Fashion Theory
A Reader

Edited by Malcolm Barnard

Series: ROUTLEDGE STUDENT READERS

What is fashion theory? Do we need it? Can we avoid it?

From its beginnings in the fifteenth century, intensified interest in fashion and the study of fashion over the last thirty years has led to a vast and varied literature on the subject. There is now barely a discipline in the humanities or social sciences that does not take a position on what fashion is, what it does and how it works.

This collection of essays surveys and contextualises the ways in which a wide range of disciplines (including sociology, cultural studies, anthropology, fashion history, gender studies and cultural history) have used different theoretical approaches to explain, and sometimes to explain away, the astonishing variety, complexity and beauty of fashion. Themes covered include individual, social and gender identity, clothes and the body, the erotic, consumption and communication.

Each extract is introduced, placed in its historical and theoretical context and its significance for fashion theory is explained.

By collecting together some of the most influential and important writers on fashion and exposing the ideas and theories behind what they say, this unique collection of extracts and essays brings to light the presuppositions involved in the things we think and say about fashion.

Fashion Theory: A Reader is a timeless and invaluable resource for undergraduate students across a range of disciplines including sociology, cultural studies and fashion.

ISBN 13: 978-0-415-41339-8 (hbk)
ISBN 13: 978-0-415-41340-4 (pbk)

Available at all good bookshops
For ordering and further information please visit:
www.routledge.com